A Corporal's War

The World War II Adventures of a Royal Engineer

Pauline Hayton

A Corporal's War

The World War II Adventures of a Royal Engineer

Copyright © 2003 by Pauline Hayton

Second edition 2013
All rights reserved
ISBN: 1492181862
ISBN: 9781492181866

No part of this book may be reproduced or transmitted in any form or by any means, graphic, electronic, or mechanical, including photocopying, recording, taping, or by any information storage retrieval system, without the written consent of the publisher.

For information address:
Pauline Hayton
3446 13th Ave S.W.
Naples, FL 34117 USA

This book is to honour my father Norman Wickman and ordinary people everywhere, who, when called upon in extraordinary times, make extraordinary sacrifices.

Books by Pauline Hayton

A Corporal's War
Naga Queen
Myanmar: In my Father's Footsteps
Chasing Brenda
If You Love Me, Kill Me

Contents

Glossary	v
PROLOGUE	1
JULY 1939–APRIL 1940	3
How it all Began	3
In the Army Now	8
APRIL 26th–JUNE 1st 1940	25
Baptism in France	25
Dunkirk	47
JUNE 1940–APRIL 1942	65
Dunkirk Leave	65
Defending the Realm	69
Ilfracombe	75
Practice Makes Perfect	84
APRIL 1942–DECEMBER 1942	90
The Cape Town Castle	90
Welcome to Durban	95
Destination India	103
Deolali	107
Transport Detail	119
Camp Moves	126
Shanta Kumar Morajee	130
Christmas in Deolali	144

1943	148
Madras	148
Assam	153
Encounter with a Goddess	161
Pastimes in the Valley	166
Flying the Hump	169
Fearsome Jungle, Fearsome People	174
News from Assam, October 1943	180
Disgruntled Yanks	184
Depot Raiding	187
The Gurkhas	194
Surprises at the Airfield	200
1944	207
The Ledo Road	207
Battleground	211
Lord Louis Mountbatten	213
Patrol	216
Bombay Explosion	220
Return to Assam	228
Foray into Burma	231
Safe and Sound	249
River Rescues	253
Goodbye to Assam	259
1945	263
25th Stores and Port Section R.E	263
Teknaf	265
Cox's Bazar	272
The Homecoming	277
EPILOGUE	288
Glossary for poems	290
Poems by men of 62 Company RE	291

List of Maps:
    Retreat to Dunkirk 38
    Norman's Travels in India and Burma 149
    North Burma 231

Acknowledgements

This is my father's story as told to me over many months. The accuracy of his memory astounded me, particularly his account of events at Dunkirk, which was so clear and precise it could have happened only weeks before instead of half a century ago. To fill gaps in his knowledge of background situations that affected his army service, I researched the archives at the Imperial War Museum and the Public Records, London.

The staff of the central library in Naples, Florida amazed me with their ability to find the most obscure titles, which enabled me to do as much research as possible in my hometown. When I made international calls to the reference library in Middlesbrough, I always received a prompt helpful response. Brigadier Bullock, curator of the Gurkha Museum in Winchester, England, helped by clarifying army terminology and possible dates of events. Photographs of the Bombay explosion are used with the permission of the National Archives and Records Administration in Maryland, USA. Photographs from the Imperial War Museum are reproduced with the permission of the Trustees of the Imperial War Museum, and my father supplied some of his personal photographs.

Many thanks to family members: Richard and Chris Hayton, my husband Peter for his advice and patient listening, and also my writing friends, "The Scribblers of Naples" for their support, encouragement, and editing assistance.

Glossary

Anna	sixteen equal one rupee
Baksheesh	a gratuity or tip
Banzai	Japanese battle cry
Barfi	fudge-like rectangles
Blast-furnace	a smelting furnace that produces intense heat
Blighty	the home country
Brasserie	a bar serving simple meals as well as beverages
Cadre	the permanent skeleton of a military unit, the commissioned officers and non-commissioned officers etc., around whom the rank and file may be quickly grouped
Cha	tea
Charpoy	Indian bedstead made of wood and rope
Chaung	Burmese word for a creek or stream
Cheroot	small cigar not pointed at either end
Chindits	British infantry long range penetration units in Burma
Chippy	slang for fish and chip shop
Coolie	a labourer (hired for a pittance)
Co-op	short for cooperative society or store
Dhobi-wallah	washerman
Gone for a Burton	dead or lost in action from RAF in WWII (Burtons was a beer from that period)
Half-a-crown	eight equalled one pound

Jammy	fortunate, lucky
Kukri	short curved sword/knife used by Gurkha soldiers
Laager	defensive ring of ox-wagons, an encampment
Mahout	the keeper and driver of an elephant
Manky	disgusting (English slang)
NAAFI	Navy, Army and Air Force institute(s)
Natter	to chat, talk
Nowt	slang for nothing
Panga	a large knife or machete
Pani-wallah	dishwasher
PX	Post Exchange, American canteen
R.A.M.C.	Royal Army Medical Corp
Ramsammy	Indian Army slang for a party
Rota	rotation of duties
Sapper	a private in the Royal Engineers
Scarper	(British slang) to go, make off in a hurry
Squaddies	soldiers
Tiffin	lunch, a light meal
Tommy	a British soldier
Wadi	a dry river bed
Walla/wallah	a man, a servant
Wangle	to obtain by scheming

PROLOGUE

The force of the bullet snapped my head back and knocked me from the motorcycle. I crashed to the ground with an agonizing thud.

Only minutes before, I'd been riding through the verdant French countryside, as yet unspoiled by the ugliness of war. Rushing to deliver dispatches, I had slowed, allowing myself a moment's pleasure. With the wind on my face and the warmth of the morning sun on my back, I almost forgot the dire circumstances requiring this ride.

I was also unaware I was being tracked in the rifle-sight of a German sniper hiding in the shadows of the Forêt de Nieppe. Crack! The high velocity bullet gouged a deep furrow across my forehead, narrowly missing my eye before striking my shoulder. There was a savage stinging in my eyebrow. Lying dazed and shaken, blood trickled from my left temple into the hairline. My sense of invincibility in tatters, I was incredulous then indignant. *Oh God, I've been shot! They got me! They bloody well GOT me!* I didn't seem to be in much pain, thought it must be shock. I prayed to make it back to camp. I didn't want to die there on that road.

I lay motionless while my mind raced. *What did they instil in us in training? The sniper could still be watching, waiting to finish you off. If you move, you're dead. If you move, you're dead. You'd be *proud if you could see me, Sarge; I'm not moving, just like you taught me.*

When I set out with the dispatches, I hadn't planned to play dead for thirty minutes in the middle of a French country lane. I closed my eyes against the bright sunshine. Brief, violent outburst over, I could hear one of the motorcycle wheels spinning close by, clicking with each rotation as if something was catching the spokes. Beyond the motorcycle, I listened to birds singing, insects droning, life in the country going on as if nothing had happened.

How the hell did I get into this mess?

My mind wandered to that fateful day, less than a year earlier, when I decided to enlist in the army.

JULY 1939—APRIL 1940

How it all Began

With a shriek of tortured metal, the heavy, cast iron doors of the coke oven opened, releasing a monstrous cloud of superheated, fume-filled smoke. It mingled with discharges, spewing from neighbouring steelworks, chemical plants, and domestic chimneys to create the lingering pall of pollution, which covered the lower Tees river basin, besmirching every home and inhabitant in the area.

White-hot walls of coke surged from the oven's innards, cascading into the batteries below. As the coke cooled, I set to work moving railway wagons along the track. I used a long bar and sheer muscle power to lever the wheels, forcing the wagons along, until they were in position beneath the chutes leading from each battery. A hard tug on a heel bar released the coke, which tumbled into the containers with a dusty, deafening roar. Then the wagons moved on, carrying the piled-high coke away for use in the steel foundry.

The day was exceptionally hot and sticky for June. I was ready for a rest when break-time arrived, and I joined the other men on the shift.

"Hiya, Ernie." I greeted Ernie Miller, a solid, fatherly figure I'd taken a liking to.

"'ello, son. Come and sit wi' me," said Ernie in his strong, Yorkshire accent.

Sitting next to Ernie, I wolfed down beef sandwiches and quenched my thirst with tea from a chipped enamel mug, all the while listening as the men discussed the economic situation. The world was slowly coming out of the Great Depression of the 1930's. In Britain, industry was starting to re-employ some of the country's millions of desperate, unemployed men, many of whom had been out of work and struggling to survive for years. I felt fortunate at having secured a job at the coke ovens even though the work was dirty and tiring. Nevertheless, my ears pricked up as Ernie told the group about his son Stan, who, like me, was twenty years old and married with a wife and young child to support.

"As soon as the government came out wi' military conscription a few months ago, our Stan decided to join the army," Ernie told the group.

"Conscription? Isn't that when men are called up at twenty-one years of age to go and do six months military service?" I'd asked.

"Aye, that's right. Our Stan went down to the army recruiting office as soon as 'e found out that 'im and 'is missus would be a bit better off living on Stan's army pay than on the thirty-five shillings a week 'e was getting in the steelworks."

George, who had fought in the First World War, tutted in disgust.

"Silly bugger! Doesn't 'e know we'll be at war soon?"

"Nay, that can't be right. The Prime Minister signed a peace treaty wi' them Germans," Sid interrupted.

"You mark my words," George persisted. "That 'itler's got too big for 'is boots. 'e's going to cause us a lot of trouble, just you wait and see."

"Well, I can't see us being at war anytime soon," said Ernie. He got to his feet to return to work. "But if it does come to that, then all our young lads are going to be called up, and there's nowt we can do about it."

Walking back to the coke ovens, I pumped Ernie for more information. The more I learned, the more I liked the idea of following in Stan's footsteps. During the rest of the shift, I worked on automatic pilot, my mind preoccupied with the idea of enlisting in the army. I argued with myself. *If I go in the army, the extra money will come in useful. It's not much more, but every bit helps. I'll be twenty-one when I get out, and my wages will be higher then. But that means leaving Ivy on her own for six months, looking after Joan. That's not much of a life for her. She'll be lonely. Yes, but sooner or later I'll have to go anyway, and her mother and sisters live just round the corner, so she won't be all by herself. How can I tell Ivy that I want to go in the army now? What will she say? I've just got to pluck up the courage somehow if I'm going to do it.*

I was filled with dread as I turned the corner into Thorrold Terrace. It was a grand sounding name for the row of tiny, terraced cottages. The boomtown of Middlesbrough consisted of hundreds of similar houses thrown together to accommodate the influx of people seeking work in the heavy industries that mushroomed after the discovery of iron ore in the nearby Cleveland Hills. I walked past the weathered brick walls stained black from years of attack by polluted air. No gardens or flowers here. My living room window looked out onto a cobbled road. On the far side, a mere twenty-five feet away, was an eight-foot-high fence of corrugated metal sheeting topped with barbed wire, all that separated the residents of Thorrold Terrace from Cleveland Bridge Engineering works. My humble home was far from perfect, but it was our first home, mine and Ivy's, and I loved it. Usually, I was eager to step through the front door to be with my wife and daughter. But that day, there was a reluctance. I had made a decision, and I worried about Ivy's reaction to it.

That evening, with daughter Joan tucked in bed, Ivy and I sat in our small, sparsely furnished living room, listening to the wireless. I was tense, flexing my fingers and tapping my knees. While I fidgeted, I studied Ivy's dark, wavy hair pulled back and fastened at the nape of her neck. With head bent low, her fingers deftly worked the needle and yarn as she darned my socks. Thinking of her shy, sweet nature and her Mona Lisa smile, I gazed at her, my heart filled with love.

Hard to believe I had ever been attracted to Marjorie. From across the room at the church hall dance in Brambles

Farm, Marjorie's vivaciousness had caught my attention. At sixteen years of age, I was an adventurous daredevil, growing into a handsome young man, at least, that's what my mother said. My good looks and charm had the desired effect, and it was not long before Marjorie became my girl.

Quiet and reserved Ivy was Marjorie's friend. She belonged to the same social circle, but I was so smitten by Marjorie's zest for life, I scarcely noticed Ivy. Then fate stepped in.

I formed a cycling club with some friends. Marjorie had no desire to participate in the club's activities. Cycling was not her cup of tea, but Ivy came along. The club's outings took us onto the nearby North Yorkshire Moors where many a pleasant day was spent exploring small moorland villages. We marvelled at the beauty of the surrounding hillsides, carpeted with purple heather, which reached out to meet the distant horizon—a sharp contrast to the greyness of industrialized Middlesbrough. We picnicked beside peaceful streams surrounded by grazing sheep. We stretched out on grassy banks propped up on elbows, heads tilted back, eyes squinting against the day's brightness, to watch swallows and house martins diving and swooping. In such settings, I came to know and appreciate the depth and beauty of Ivy's character hiding beneath her timidity. As Ivy came to know me, she became more at ease, allowing me to catch glimpses of an adventurous spirit and a playful sense of humour every bit as lively as I could wish for. Marjorie was soon forgotten.

◆　　◆　　◆

My heart swelled with love as I watched Ivy darning. She lifted her head and caught me looking at her.

"You're staring at me."

I mustered the courage to speak.

"I've been thinking."

She studied at me with her baby-blue eyes.

"You sound serious. What's the matter?"

"You know, it'll be six months before I'm twenty-one and able to earn a full wage. Right now, we're struggling on what I'm bringing home in my wage packet." I paused then rushed

JULY 1939—APRIL 1940

on before my nerve failed me. "I thought I'd enlist in the army now instead of waiting until I'm conscripted. That way we'll all be better off. Army pay will mean more money coming in, and my Military Service will be out of the way, over and done with. I'll be twenty-one when I come out, then I'll be entitled to earn a full wage instead of the junior's wage I'm earning at present."

Ivy bent her head and examined her fingers, studiously picking at her cuticles while mulling over this idea and what it would mean for us.

Since leaving school, I'd been out of work more than I'd been in it. The best pay I ever earned was after the country was placed on a war alert, and the labour exchange sent me on a temporary job building sandbag barricades round the town hall to protect it from possible air raids. I had a job now, but for how long?

By the time Ivy raised her eyes to meet my anxious gaze, she had decided I was right. Life had been a difficult hand-to-mouth existence in the two years since we married.

◆ ◆ ◆

After my interview at the army recruiting office followed by a medical, life continued as usual while we waited for the army's letter to arrive. Coming home from work two weeks later, I opened the door.

"Hello, sweetheart, I'm home."

Wiping her hands on her apron, Ivy came from the kitchen to receive her usual hug and kiss. She smiled as our toddler daughter Joan squeezed past to fling herself into my arms. I swung her high into the air. Joan squealed with delight. Then I put her down and ruffled her hair.

"Hello, pet. Glad to see your dad?"

Joan, looked up at me with her wide, blue eyes, crinkled her nose and chuckled, repeating the only word she was old enough to say clearly, "Daddy, Daddy."

"Go and wash," said Ivy. "I've a casserole in the oven when you're ready."

At the kitchen sink, I lathered the yellow bar of coal tar soap, carelessly splashing water and soapsuds around as I swilled my face, arms, and upper body, dirty and sticky with sweat after a hard shift at the coke ovens. Ivy placed Joan in her high chair to keep her safe and out of reach of the sizzling hot steak and kidney pie now on the table. While Ivy served the food, I towelled myself dry then pulled up my chair. Ivy removed a buff-coloured envelope from her apron pocket and handed it to me.

"This came this morning. I promised myself I'd wait until this evening to give it to you, but I can't wait a minute longer."

My eyes held hers for a moment as I took the official looking letter from her. After tearing open the envelope, I eagerly scanned the page until I found the information I needed. My heart fell, and I handed the letter to Ivy.

She read it once and then once again.

"Oh no, Norman! July 17th? They can't mean it!" she cried, as its meaning sank in.

"Sorry, Ivy, I didn't plan this."

"It's like a bad joke. You're going off to the army on our wedding anniversary! Couldn't you get them to change the date?"

"Not really, pet. I'm sorry. It's not a good present, is it?"

Ivy shook her head, her eyes brimming with tears. Seeing her distress, I stood up, pushing back the chair. It scraped on the linoleum-covered floor. Moving quickly round the table, I wrapped my arms round her.

"Don't cry, love. It's only for six months. I'll soon be home again."

In The Army Now

I was posted to Hadrian's Camp, Carlisle, for basic training in 23 Searchlight Regiment 106 Battery. The train chugged and puffed over the Pennines towards the town. It was crammed with young men compelled by military conscription, instituted

JULY 1939—APRIL 1940

only a few months before, to spend the next six months serving in his Majesty's forces.

My compartment was full. We were strangers when we entered the carriage. By the time we stepped onto the platform at Carlisle railway station, lasting friendships were already being forged.

Being a friendly, extroverted chap, I soon broke the ice.

"Hello, I'm Norman Wickman. I'm going to Hadrian's Camp. Is that where you're going?" I asked a fair-haired man with a serious expression on his face and a frown creasing his brow. When he smiled at my greeting, it was as if the sun had come out from behind a dark cloud so bright and dazzling was his smile. But, as suddenly as it appeared, the smile vanished, and his face promptly settled back into its stern countenance.

"How d'you do, Norman. I'm Andy Wilson, and yes, I was called up too."

"Oh, I wasn't called up. I enlisted."

"What! You volunteered to join the army when you didn't have to?" another young man interjected. "I'm Darky, Darky Watkins," he introduced himself. Sweeping back his unruly black hair, which kept falling over his forehead despite a liberal application of Brylcream, Darky continued. "I'll tell you straight, I'm really fed up with this army lark. I've just finished my apprenticeship as a painter and decorator. Now I'm twenty-one, all I want is to get on with finding a job and earning some decent money after five years on an apprentice's wage, and what am I going to be doing? Marching up and bloody down, that's what!"

"That's rotten luck, but it's different for me. I'm better off coming into the army now and getting my military service out of the way before I'm twenty-one," I said.

"Well, the army's the last place I want to be," said Andy. "I don't fancy it at all."

Another passenger spoke. "I'm Bob Henderson," he introduced himself in his soft, lilting northern accent, "and I'm not complaining. There isn't much work where I'm from in County Durham. I'm happy to be here. Maybe I'll learn something useful in the army. Who knows, I might stay in longer than six months, if I like it."

Tommy Sharrow, who had travelled from Middlesbrough with me, introduced himself, saying, "I'm looking forward to my army service too. My cousin's been in The Green Howards for five years. He thinks army life is great."

"Let's see how you like it after you've been put through the mill for a few weeks. I bet you change your tune," said Andy.

Only one man in the carriage had not volunteered any information about himself. He was tall, almost folded into his seat. Mousy-brown hair, plastered down above his long thin face, matched his pale brown eyes. Initial conversations over, our interest turned to him.

"Are you going to Hadrian's Camp as well?" I asked.

The man coughed, clearing his throat.

"Yes, that's right. Don't mind me. I'm not always this quiet. I overindulged at my farewell party last night, and now my head's killing me. Oh, I'm Mac, and if you don't mind, I'll just nurse my head for a while."

The journey took several hours, during which we laughed, joked and complained about our predicament. We were all from the northeast of England and found that we got along just fine. It seemed no time at all before the train arrived at Carlisle. Outside the station, the army was waiting to gather us up.

"Making sure we don't get cold feet and scarper," said Darky, knowingly.

"Let's stick together if we can," I said, wanting to be with my new-found friends for the next six weeks.

We were ushered into waiting trucks and whisked away to a whole new life; no mothers to cook and iron, no wives to offer comfort, only a sergeant-major to satisfy and orders to obey.

Arriving at the camp, we were quick-marched to rows of bell tents erected in virgin pastureland.

"Looks like our accommodation is going to be as basic as our army training," I told Darky.

He agreed. "No expense spared for our comfort, that's for sure."

The tents, each housing twelve men, were to be our homes

JULY 1939—APRIL 1940

for the next six weeks. All the men who had travelled with me in the train scrambled to move into the same tent.

The sergeant-major was an ogre. Yelling and barking orders, he put us through our paces. He had us marching, crawling under barbed wire obstacles, running, jumping, climbing ten-foot high walls and racing through assault courses. We were all lean and fit, and the physical training was easy, a piece of cake, we boasted, staggering into our tent at the end of the day. The hardest part was the effort involved in trying to keep things clean. We learned how to use spit and polish to clean our boots until we could see our faces in them—a difficult business, living as we did, splodging around in a sea of oozing clay. Being a typical British summer, the abundant rainfall made for a muddy existence.

Lined up on parade, my eyes twinkled as I did my best to suppress a smile, knowing the sergeant-major would soon be shouting out his favourite overworked expression.

"What do you think this is, you 'orrible lot? An 'oliday camp?"

This was usually followed by, "That man there, wipe that smile off your face!" to any soldier he saw grinning.

We were soon pummelled into shape. No more stumbling and fumbling. By the time basic training ended, we were drilling and marching in unison, with pride and a sense of accomplishment. Our reward was a home on leave.

◆ ◆ ◆

With a mischievous grin, I posed and postured in front of Ivy, wearing riding breeches and puttees, my uniform being a remnant from World War 1.

"What do you think of your handsome young warrior now?" I asked.

Smiling, she shook her head at my teasing. I could tell she was pleased to have me home.

As we undressed for bed that night, she let me know exactly what she thought when I stripped off my uniform to reveal what it had hidden so well.

Norman with Ivy and daughter, Joan

She gasped, pointed at my legs.

"Norman, what are you wearing?"

I looked down at my underwear and then at Ivy in astonishment as she started to giggle.

"They're long johns. It's what all the best soldiers are wearing," I told her, feigning wounded pride.

"I thought only old men wore long johns," she said. "They aren't very flattering, Norman. They really emphasize your bandy legs."

Her giggles snowballed until she was roaring with laughter and tears rolled down her cheeks. I kept looking at Ivy, then down at my underwear, pretending not to understand what was causing such merriment. Forcing herself to take deep breaths, Ivy managed to curb her screeching just

JULY 1939—APRIL 1940

long enough to tell me, "Some handsome young warrior you are."

◆ ◆ ◆

A few days after I returned to Carlisle, Ivy was crossing North Ormesby market place when the air raid sirens sounded. She hurried to her mother's house. Nobody knew what the warning was for. Nothing seemed to be happening. Later that night, she listened to the news on the wireless. "This is London," a voice announced. "We will now hear a statement by the Prime Minister." Neville Chamberlain's voice was heard next:

> I am speaking to you from the cabinet room at 10 Downing Street. This morning the British Ambassador in Berlin handed the German government a final note stating that unless they were prepared to give his Majesty's government in the United Kingdom satisfactory assurance that the German government had suspended all aggressive action against Poland . . . . .No such undertaking was received by the time stipulated and consequently this country is at war with Germany.

The date was September 3rd, 1939.

I heard the same broadcast in the canteen with the lads. We all knew what that meant. We wouldn't be done and dusted with the army when December arrived.

◆ ◆ ◆

Shortly afterwards, while our company was on parade, a short, portly colonel walked up and down the rows of soldiers, swagger stick in hand. He looked each man up and down, studiously chewing on his ginger moustache with his lower lip. He stared intently into men's faces and selected sixty of us, me included, by tapping us on our chests with his swagger stick.

"You, you, you, and you. You are all now Royal Engineers. Pack up your gear. You're going to Salisbury."

Fortunately, all my pals were chosen as well. We hurriedly packed our kit bags.

"I think they've a cheek," said Darky. "I've just got used to being in the Royal Artillery. I don't want to be a Royal Engineer."

"Don't fret," said Bob. "The good thing is it looks as if we'll still be together, no matter whether we're in the Royal Artillery or not."

"Come on you lot. Get moving," shouted the sergeant, sticking his head through the entrance to the tent. "You 'aven't got all day."

Pleased at still being together, our happy band piled into the trucks waiting to ferry us 290 miles south to Porton, poison gas headquarters, just outside Salisbury. After settling in, I was told I would be a driver and was taught to drive all sizes of trucks, motorcycles, every type of vehicle except tanks. It was not all plain sailing. With a pained expression on his face and eyes lifted to the heavens as I once again ground and crunched my way through the gears, the driving instructor informed me time and time again, "You'll never make a driver, private, never!"

But, make a driver I did. It took two full weeks of driving tests round Winchester, before I finally obtained my licence. I was posted to 62 (Chemical Warfare) Company, HQ section, as a driver. Darky, Bob, Mac, Andy and Tommy were posted with me. Andy, also a driver, became Major Robinson's runabout. We referred to ourselves as "The Comical Wayfarers." Most of the men in 62 (CW) Company were from the northeast of England. As well as myself, there were seven other men from Middlesbrough. There were also men from the mining villages

JULY 1939—APRIL 1940

of County Durham and villages on the outskirts of Newcastle. We were proud to be a group of northern lads preparing to fight for our country. Thrown together from all walks of life, we developed friendships and a camaraderie, which sustained and supported us in our life away from home. Sergeant Wellington was the man we answered to. Patient and unshakeable, firm but fair, we held him in high regard.

It was the custom for each man in the forces to be given a nickname.

"I've already got my nickname," said Darky.

"Yes, we know. How come you're called Darky?" I wanted to know.

"I'm the odd one out in my family. All my brothers have blonde hair and blue eyes. I'm the only one with black hair and hazel eyes. I've been Darky since the day I was born. They kid my mother the coal man fathered me."

We all laughed.

"What shall we call you, Norman? What's your middle name?" Andy asked.

"Gasçon."

"Gasçon! Blimey, Norman, we can't call you Gas in a chemical warfare unit, it'd be too confusing," said Darky, laughing. "How about if we called you Gus?"

Darky Watkins

"That'll do. Gus is fine by me. What shall we call Andy?"

15

"With those golden curls it's got to be Blondie, even though the army does keep them under control with a short back and sides."

And so Blondie it was. Last but not least, Bob Henderson was called Hinny—a Geordie term of endearment in the Newcastle area where he lived.

Sergeant Wellington told us what we would be doing.

"You're here to learn about poison gases. We'll be using kits left over from The Great War. There're no manuals available, so it's going to be a case of trial and error to discover how the kits work. You are not to reveal to anyone that you are training with chemical weapons. That's an order. When it's time for company training, orders will be posted on the bulletin board. It will say that your section is 'out playing cricket'. Drivers, when transporting equipment and gases, you must keep everything well covered. We don't want anyone to get wind of what's in those trucks."

Blondie

We practised with Livens projectors capable of firing bombs containing thirty pounds of phosgene. Sappers set the steel tube projectors in the ground, in batteries of twenty, at an angle of 45°. At the push of an electric button, the projectors simultaneously fired the gas bombs. Sappers measured how far the gas bombs travelled and experimented to find out what kind of gases could be used. When training, we fired blank bombs so that when they exploded they produced only metal fragments, no gases were released. Only after much practising and numerous demonstrations were the deadly poisonous cargoes introduced.

I was relieved that as a driver, I had to retire well away from the practice area. The path of the projectiles was often erratic, and it was difficult to predict where they would finally

JULY 1939—APRIL 1940

land. Any sudden change of wind direction could bring the choking, burning cloud back onto the men deploying the weapon. Watched by officers assessing the effectiveness of these weapons, the company trained on Salisbury Plain and Porton Down using mustard and phosgene gases.

◆ ◆ ◆

The company was going to move camp from Porton to Lynton in the West Country. I was sent with an advance party of twenty men to prepare the new camp. With everything completed, the companies moved in. Hinny Henderson and I were promoted to lance-corporals, which, of course, called for a celebration. We sauntered down to the village and entered the Black Bull public house. Under the low-beamed ceiling stained yellow with nicotine, we stood at the bar, scrutinizing the selection of beers.

"I don't fancy any of those," said Hinny.

"Southern beer's as weak as gnat's piss," cursed Mac, under his breath.

"I've heard scrumpy's supposed to have a bit of kick," said Tommy.

"What's scrumpy?" I asked.

"I think it's a strong alcoholic cider," offered Darky.

"Okay," I said, "let's try the scrumpy. Four pints of scrumpy, please."

"Scrumpy packs a powerful punch, lads. You need to go steady with it," the corpulent barman warned us in his West Country burr.

We laughed off the warning.

"Where we come from, we brew the strongest beer in the country," Mac boasted. "We know how to take our ale."

"He's making a big fuss about this scrumpy, isn't he? It can't be too strong. It's only made from apples, isn't it?" I said.

The locals exchanged knowing glances as if to say, here's our night's entertainment, watching these fools. They looked on in dour amusement to see who would collapse first. We had no idea how potent the beverage was. We each bought a round of drinks. Each man drank five pints. With each successive pint of scrumpy, our voices grew louder, the laughter more raucous and at the end of the evening, we staggered from the pub.

"Ooh, I can't believe it. I think I'm drunk," said Mac, struggling to talk clearly.

The fresh air felled me. I collapsed in a heap on the road.

"Come on, Gus. Get up," Hinny encouraged.

"Can't. Too drunk to walk," I replied, slurring my words.

Swaying and staggering to stay upright, Darky told me, "Gus, if you don't get up, you're going to have to crawl back to camp. We're too drunk to carry you."

At the pub doorway, the locals gathered to watch as I crawled along the white line in the middle of the road. My companions lurched and reeled alongside me, occasionally toppling into the hedgerows on either side of the road. In this fashion, we managed to stumble back to camp. No mean feat for men in our condition.

◆ ◆ ◆

We started training exercises on Exmoor. Our company, along with 58, 60, and 61 Companies, was involved in exercises to defend Barnstaple from possible invaders. We used mustard gas and demolished bridges to hinder the invaders' advance. At one village, a bridge was prepared for demolition. As the lieutenant prepared to give the order to blow up the bridge, Sergeant Wellington approached him.

"Excuse me, Lieutenant."

"Yes, Sergeant."

"The way the explosives have been laid on the bridge will cause some problems, sir."

"Like what, Sergeant?" asked an irritated Lieutenant.

"Well sir, if you blow the bridge as it is, all the windows in the village will break."

Hearing his words, I saw the sappers pause in their work. Nudging each other, they watched the exchange between the lieutenant and the sergeant with interest. Sergeant Wellington was a good man, admired by the men under him. We felt he must have lived at least six lifetimes in this one. He'd been everywhere, done everything, traversed the Sahara Desert as part of a surveying team, and travelled round the world. Try as we might, we were unable to catch him in any lies or exaggerations. Those of us who knew him well knew he would be on the mark about the bridge. Hastily, bets were laid as to whether or not Sergeant Wellington would be proven right.

Dismissed with a scornful, "Thank you, Sergeant," Sergeant Wellington stepped back to watch; his well-lived-in face deadpan.

Without further ado, the lieutenant ordered the bridge demolished. Behind the crashing roars of the bridge's demise, he listened, red-faced, to the tinkling of falling glass. It seemed to go on forever as the shock waves reverberated throughout the streets. Even before the last sounds of crashing glass ended, Sergeant Wellington, quickly wiped the self-satisfied expression off his face and set the men to work. There was much clearing up to do before the company returned to barracks. We chuckled at the lieutenant's embarrassment.

"Did you see how red in the face he got?" someone sniggered.

"Was that from embarrassment, or did he have apoplexy?"

Muffled laughter spread on seeing the lieutenant besieged by angry villagers.

"He may think he's having a hard time dealing with that lot, just wait till the colonel gets his hands on him," I said to another driver.

"Serves him right for not listening to the Sarge," he muttered.

We broke into gleeful guffaws.

◆ ◆ ◆

Whenever we had a free evening, we usually headed for our home away from home—the Seven Stars public house—that was until we heard there was going to be a special dance in town on Saturday night. Our frustrated group sat grumbling in the NAAFI.

"Sounds like it's going to be a good dance," said Tommy.

"Yes it does, but we can't get there. There're no buses or trains," said Hinny. "We'll just have to forget about it or we'll go crazy."

"Don't worry," I promised, "we'll get to that dance come hell or high water."

"How do you figure we'll do that?" scoffed Hinny.

"I've got an idea. Just leave it to me."

"What've you got in mind, Gus?" "What are you going to do?" my friends clamoured.

"You'll find out soon enough, but you're definitely going to the dance."

I saw Darky looking hard at me, wondering what the hell I was up to.

Saturday night arrived. We all had passes to leave camp, but no one was enthusiastic about yet another night at the village pub when what they really wanted to do was chat up the girls in town and twirl them round the dance floor.

"Just leave the camp and walk down the road a quarter mile. I'll pick you up in a few minutes," I told them. "Darky, you come with me."

"Gus, you're never going to borrow a truck again?"

"Nooo. I wouldn't dream of it."

"That's a relief. We don't want you losing your stripe."

I led Darky to the officers' quarters.

"Keep an eye open. Whistle if you see anyone," I said, then disappeared round the corner.

Two minutes later, I was back, perched behind the steering wheel of Colonel MacLaren's Humber.

"Darky, quick! Get in!"

"Gus! This is the Colonel's car!"

"I know. I'm borrowing it. Get in."

"You'll be put on a charge."

"Only if I don't get it back before he notices it's gone. But even if he does, it'll be worth it."

Slipping out through the camp gate was not a problem. The guard accepted my story that I was going to pick up Colonel MacLaren. Outside the camp, Darky moved from his hiding place on the floor to the comfort of the back seat.

Chuckling with glee, we picked up four flabbergasted friends from the roadside before motoring to town in style.

It was a great night out. The lads flirted and fraternized with the young ladies. Judging by the profusion of fluttering eyelashes and blushing smiles, they obviously found the men in uniform of interest. I even enjoyed a few dances myself. The reckoning came next day, when I was ordered to Major Robinson's office. I stood ramrod straight at attention.

"Corporal Wickman, I received a message from Colonel MacLaren this morning. He told me you stole his car. Do you have an explanation for this?"

"I didn't steal his car, sir. I borrowed it. I did bring it back, sir."

"You *borrowed* Colonel MacLaren's car?" His face almost touching mine, Major Robinson's voice became an angry bellow. "You borrowed the Colonel's car? Why did you borrow the car, Corporal?"

Spittle flew from his lips, spraying my nose and cheeks.

"I went into town, sir."

A tight knot formed in the pit of my stomach as I observed Major Robinson's cheeks redden and his moustache bristle.

"You went into town? You took the Colonel's car so you could go into town? Damn it, Corporal, when are you going to learn that the army's transport is not for your own personal use. Remove that stripe. You're demoted."

My friends were waiting for me in the barracks.

"What happened? What did he say?"

"Demotion. Robo doesn't like me taking the truck for my own use, but he really blew a gasket about the Colonel's car."

I started to remove the stripe from my uniform.

"Lost your stripe again?"

"First it's on then it's off. At this rate, Gus, you'll be able to get a job as a tailor when you get out of the army."

We all laughed.

"How long this time, Gus?"

I grinned. "If it's anything like the other times, it won't be for long."

And it wasn't. A week later, Major Robinson called me to his office. The major didn't have much choice. The army was short of men who were NCO material, and even though I was a scoundrel, I wasn't a serious troublemaker.

"Corporal Wickman, you're getting your stripe back. I have a job for you." He handed me my orders. "Take a truck and transport two prisoners to Aldershot. Make sure all your papers are signed and in order when you hand the prisoners over at the detention barracks."

"Yes, sir. Thank you, sir."

I collected the prisoners and set off for the glass-house at Aldershot. Four hours later, I was ringing the bell to the detention barracks. I brought the men from the back of the truck to the gate and tried to hand my papers over to the guard.

"No good handing those to me, chum. You've got to sign them over to the officer of the day at reception. The sergeant will take you over."

"Attention!" barked the sergeant. "At the double!"

We all started running. First we went to one office, then another. *What the hell is this? When am I going to get my papers signed and get out of this madhouse?* Jogging our way to the third and, hopefully, the last office in the detention barracks, I called over to the sergeant, "Hey, Sergeant, I'm not a prisoner. What the hell am I running for?"

"Neither am I," said the sergeant, "but we do everything at the double in here, Corporal. Your feet won't touch the ground till you're outside those gates."

I finally obtained the signatures I needed. I couldn't get out of the place fast enough. With the gates clanging shut behind me, I heaved a sigh of relief. *Thank goodness that's over. It looks like those two are in for a rough time. I wouldn't like to be in their shoes, not for anything.*

◆　◆　◆

Soldiers were training, training, training to be ready to join the field overseas even though, since war had been declared, no soldier had yet been called upon to fight. The period from

JULY 1939—APRIL 1940

September 3rd, 1939 until May 1940 was called the 'Phoney War'. There were no air raids, no bombings, no sudden emergencies, in fact, no noticeable difference between the state of war and the state of emergency, which preceded it. War was just a word, something far away, so people simply kept on with their preparations. Air raid precautions were organized. Posters urged people to carry your gas-mask at all times". At first, everyone followed this injunction, carrying gas masks in cardboard boxes attached to shoulder straps, as they went about their daily lives. But, when nothing happened in the weeks after war was declared, complacency set in. A spot check, in November 1939, revealed that one third of gas mask boxes were being used to carry such things as packed lunches instead of gas masks.

A total blackout was ordered with wardens employed to enforce the regulations. No one was allowed to show a chink of light. Travelling at night without headlights or streetlights to guide them was difficult for drivers and deadly for pedestrians. Accident rates doubled with the coming of the long, dark winter nights.

Ivy went to work in Price's. It was called a tailoring factory, but to Ivy, it felt more like a sweatshop. In a room, where the racket of forty clackety-clacking, overheated sewing machines continuously assaulted her ears, she worked all day producing white camouflage suits for use by the British Army in Norway and khaki battle-dress uniforms for the large numbers of men being called up to do their duty.

In April 1940, the government called for scrap metals for the production of weapons. People cut down and donated metal railings, found old shell casings, souvenirs from an earlier war, and handed in their old aluminium pots and pans. Released from growing food, by the newly organized Women's Land Army, farm workers went into the forces. Food rationing was introduced. Bacon, butter, sugar, and later, meat, were all only available in limited amounts and only with coupons from ration books.

All these preparations and more were made, yet when the time came for action, the country was ill-equipped and ill-prepared.

APRIL 26th–JUNE 1st 1940

Baptism in France

11:00 a.m., April 26th, truckload after truckload of Royal Engineers filed out of the camp gates. Travelling along narrow lanes, we passed fertile green fields and blossoming hedgerows characteristic of the English countryside. The warm sun of late spring shone down on the dull army trucks. Inside, the men shouted to make themselves heard over the deafening roar of the engines. Bantering and joking, we journeyed to the south coast, relaxed and at ease with the job we had to do in France. Not one soldier thought he might end up fighting Germans. After all, hadn't the British Expeditionary Force been in France since September of 1939, with not one shot fired against the enemy? Nobody was the least bit concerned. Indeed, many expected it would be a pleasant change from the training and drilling we'd been put through since war was declared.

    At Southampton, it took several days to load soldiers and equipment aboard the transport ships waiting to take us across The English Channel to Le Havre.

    "France is only a few hours away" I reassured Tommy, who was worried about being seasick. "We won't be on the boat for long."

    Overhearing the conversation, Mac told Tommy, "Don't sit near me. I don't want you throwing up all over my boots."

Hinny threw in his halfpennyworth about how terrible seasickness is, which no one wanted to hear.

Darky, hoping he would be spared the embarrassment of becoming seasick himself, tried to put Tommy's mind at ease. "Don't worry. Sergeant Wellington said it was going to be a calm crossing."

And fortunately, for those prone to seasickness, it was.

Disembarking on April 30th, the motor transport party proceeded to its billet. I drove the 200-gallon water truck. Initially based at Yvetot, the unit soon moved to St. Pol, west of Arras.

Dotted about the French countryside were many small airfields. The Royal Air Force had flown all British planes from these airfields back to England, where it was thought they would soon be desperately needed. Set to work, the Royal Engineer companies' task was to clean up the airfields. Any equipment left behind was loaded into trucks and taken to the French ports to be returned to England. We worked industriously, moving from airfield to airfield, gradually making our way across France towards the Maginot Line, but we never got that far.

On May 10th, Germany invaded Holland, Belgium, and Luxembourg. With the onset of the German offensive, the British Expeditionary Force, together with the French armies, rushed into Belgium to counter the invasion. Unaware at first that this was exactly what the German High Command expected them to do, our forces played straight into the enemy's hands. With the best fighting units diverted to the north, the way was open for the German Army to flank the Maginot Line. Built by the French after the First World War to protect their eastern border between Montmédy and Belfort, the Maginot Line was an extensive chain of sophisticated fortifications. Believing it was impossible for any army to invade France by coming through the densely forested, hilly Ardennes region, the French did not extend the Maginot Line to that part of the frontier.

The German Army, however, achieved the impossible. Almost two thousand tanks made their way through the

APRIL 26th—JUNE 1st 1940

Ardennes. At dawn on the 13th, Rommel's 7th Panzer Division was assembling on the banks of the Meuse River opposite the town of Sedan. Using terrifying blitzkrieg tactics with Panzer divisions backed by the Luftwaffe, the German Army moved to conquer France. German planes repeatedly flew over Sedan, relentlessly dropping bombs, which fell like deadly, screeching raindrops, to obliterate the French defences. The explosions were devastating. Mercilessly, the planes kept dropping bombs, screaming bombs fitted with whistles. The French soldiers below crouched in trenches listening to the howling bombs, knowing that each screaming monster was bringing death. Then came the shelling to pound away at the town. Everything blended together, bombing, shelling, shelling, bombing. The troops in Sedan were not experienced fighting soldiers. It would have been a miracle if they had managed to repel such a savage attack. With shattered nerves and resistance gone, they escaped or surrendered to watch in horrified awe as great numbers of German Panzers and armoured cars, with the Luftwaffe overhead, swarmed into France. Turning northwest, the invading army headed toward Boulogne, the Channel ports, and the sea.

We were ordered to Arras to join regiments assembling to oppose the advancing German forces. Enemy planes dropped leaflets, warning that any soldier found with poison gas would immediately be shot, as would all Royal Engineers. We read the leaflets and burst into howls of laughter.

"I knew we should have stayed in the Royal Artillery," joked Blondie

I was angry, telling anyone who'd listen that we'd sort the buggers out if they came after us.

Despite the ominous warnings they carried, the leaflets were a welcome addition to our supplies. Owing to the shortage of toilet paper, they were promptly put to good use.

British officers, concerned about German threats to their men and the deadly outcome should the poisonous gases be hit by German shells or bombs, ordered the disposal of the lethal chemicals. Heading towards the small village of Lattre St. Quentin, 62 Company officers decided to see if this would be a suitable place. The main body of the company waited on the outskirts of Lattre St. Quentin ready for action, while dispatch riders on motorcycles and soldiers in small trucks cautiously entered the village. The noise of the engines disturbed the silent streets, unnaturally empty and deserted. Shops were closed and barred, houses locked up. The fleeing residents of Lattre St. Quentin had abandoned their homes, cats, dogs and chickens to the advancing armies.

Assured that no German troops were in the village, I was ordered to take a detail into the village and find a suitable place to dispose of the gases. With sixteen men in my truck, I roared into the village, scattering the cats and chickens roaming the streets.

"You four, break down those house doors," I ordered the men leaping from the truck. "You four, over there. You four, try the farmhouse. The rest of you come with me. We'll try the *brasserie.*"

We smashed our way into the houses and buildings that made up the village. My group struck it lucky at the *brasserie*.

"This looks good, Gus."

"It's champion," I said, looking over the cavernous wine cellar perfect for burying the mustard gas, phosgene and other deadly concoctions we carried. "Let's see what the others have found."

All the houses had large cellars, but when I checked them out, none of them was as suitable as the one in the *brasserie*. I reported to Sergeant Wellington.

"There's a suitable place in the *brasserie*, Sarge."

"Well done, Corporal." He scrutinized my left arm protectively holding three bottles of brandy. "What have you got there?"

"Got where, Sarge?"

Sergeant Wellington lifted his eyes to the sky and shook his head. "Never mind. Go on, get out."

Making my way to the truck, it was my bad luck to bump into Major Robinson.

"Corporal Wickman, did you find a suitable site in the village?"

APRIL 26th—JUNE 1st 1940

"Yes sir. There's a huge cellar beneath the *brasserie*, sir."

"Good work, Corporal. Now, where did you get that brandy?"

"I found it lying about, sir. Thought you might enjoy it, sir."

"How thoughtful of you, Corporal," said the major, his voice dripping in sarcasm. He pointed behind him to Blondie. "You can hand them over to my driver. He'll take care of them."

As Major Robinson walked off, I handed my loot over to Blondie. "Of all the rotten luck! That's tonight's shindig gone for a Burton."

"Never mind, Gus, it was a nice try. Maybe we can rustle up some more later."

It was hard work for the sappers. With long sleeves down and wearing gloves, they toiled for three days in the muggy heat, shirts dark and wet, faces streaked with sweat and blackened by dirt. Feverishly, they dug up the cellar floor, and carried the poison gas bombs down to the cellars before covering them with earth. Explosives were laid so that when detonated, the cellars imploded, safely sealing in the gases.

Despite the hard work, there was to be no respite for us. General Guderian's Panzers were rapidly rolling west. On May 20th, his army travelled forty miles in fourteen hours, taking Amiens and reaching Abbeville, effectively cutting the our forces in two. The British Expeditionary Force, two French armies and the Belgians, nearly one million men, were now trapped in Flanders. In Belgium, weary troops of the British Expeditionary Force, along with those French and Belgian units still holding together, were retreating towards the French border. Pulverized by the aggressive German advance, our units were crumbling. Days were spent fighting; nights they fell back behind some river or canal, readying themselves to fight once again when daylight arrived.

Before reaching Arras, we were suddenly ordered to Béthune. We had not yet come into contact with the enemy, nor been involved in any fighting, but this didn't stop me from finding a pot of paint and decorating the water truck. 'Berlin or

Bust' I advertised to the world with all the bravado and confidence of an invincible, young soldier not yet baptized in battle.

Our job was to ready for demolition the many bridges in the Bethune area.

"Get there as fast as you can," we were ordered. "Run the refugees off the road if you have to."

Of course, we couldn't bring ourselves to do that. It would have been too cruel.

We struggled along congested roads. Thousands of fleeing civilians were on the move. Pushing bicycles and wheelbarrows filled with their worldly goods, crowded into overloaded cars and farm carts, they clogged up the roads, hindering our passage. Travel to Béthune was slow and difficult, but eventually, we reached the town.

As our forces came under pressure from the German assault to the south, Lord Gort, Commander-in-Chief of the British Expeditionary Force, ordered a counter attack, which took place south of Arras on the afternoon of May 21st. The British offensive against Rommel's Panzers and superior German forces was ferocious, but nine hours later, the counterattack came to a standstill. There would be no breakthrough of the long, over-extended German columns. The battle continued for two and a half days, but on the night of May 23rd, British units were forced to withdraw. However, the effort expended by the British Army at the battle of Arras had not been in vain. This action delayed the German advance, allowing four British divisions and a large part of the French First Army to withdraw toward the Channel coast.

This extra time also helped us in the Bethune area as we worked to delay the German advance by frantically preparing for demolition the many bridges that spanned the La Bassée Canal.

I was the company waterman, making sure that units had the water they needed. Driving the water tanker could be hazardous. I was a frequent target for German Stuka pilots, who dived as low as car top height to strafe my vehicle, probably thinking I was carrying fuel. With my tin hat on, and

APRIL 26th—JUNE 1st 1940

sitting low in my seat, I drove along jeering and laughing if the planes came at me from behind.

"Go on, waste your bullets. You can't hurt me," I taunted them.

The bullets bounced harmlessly off the steel tanker, and I felt perfectly safe. Sometimes, however, a pilot was seemingly affronted at having so little impact. Seeing the water tanker continuing stubbornly on its way unaffected by his efforts, the pilot would return to approach the vehicle from the front, determined to make it explode. This was an entirely different matter. Such tactics had me ingloriously diving to safety into the roadside ditches, cursing the pilot with all my might.

While the sappers laid explosives on the bridges, I was given the job of dispatch rider, carrying messages between the various army divisions as commanders attempted to collaborate and organize a collective withdrawal of troops before the bridges were blown. Such an occupation was no less hazardous than driving the water tanker. As the distance between the opposing forces narrowed, and the battlefront became more fluid, we faced a new danger.

Briefing the dispatch riders, Sergeant Wellington warned us he'd received reports that German snipers were having fun playing hide and seek behind our lines. "They're crack shots with a rifle, and they'll be busy picking off any soldier who happens to pass their way," he told us. "Dispatch riders are one of their favourite targets because of the difficulty and confusion it causes to the lines of communication if dispatches don't get through. If you come across a sniper and you can't get through, return to base and report it immediately. We need to know where they're operating. That's all, men. Good luck"

◆ ◆ ◆

Good luck had not been with me when I set off that morning. Unsuccessful in delivering my dispatches thanks to a sniper's ambush, I found myself lying bruised and battered in the middle of a French country road not knowing how badly I was wounded. A fly buzzed about my eyebrow feasting on fluids seeping from my wound. The buzzing sound, interspersed with moments of silence, while the fly dined on some tasty morsel gradually pierced my consciousness. I blinked my eyes in the bright morning sunshine.

Bugger off fly! Leave me alone! Well, I didn't get through, Sarge. Let's see if I can get back. I could wiggle my fingers, a good sign. My shoulder didn't seem to be smashed. I was able to wiggle my toes; legs didn't seem to be broken. My head was killing me, and my parched mouth tasted like a sewer. It was time to test the water. I rolled onto my stomach. No bullets fired my way. Time to make a run for it.

Fast as a whippet, my body charged with adrenaline, I raced to the motorcycle, righted it and clambered on. Furiously, I tried to kick-start it. The engine refused to start. By the fourth kick, I was in a frenzy, expecting at any minute to be shot again.

"Come on, come on," I muttered between clenched teeth. Then the Norton roared into life. Relief flooded my body. "Get me out of here!"

Skidding and careening wildly in my haste to get away, I lay low over the tank and rushed back to camp at breakneck speed. Dismounting from the motorcycle, my legs turned to water. It was an unsteady corporal who reported to Sergeant Wellington. The sergeant looked up as I entered the tent.

"You look a bit rough, Corporal. What happened?"

"I couldn't deliver my dispatches. I was hit by a sniper on the Hazebrouck road, Sarge."

The sergeant looked me over, told me to calm down, that I'd had a lucky escape, that I could have had my brains blown out, that I needed to go and have a cigarette because I looked a bit shaky, and that I should get that wound seen to. I left him arranging to send out a patrol and muttering they'd find the bugger.

Finding a quiet corner, I examined my injuries. Gingerly, I dabbed at the sore, swollen spot above my eye. The sniper's bullet had done nothing more than crease the eyebrow. Missing my shoulder by a hair's breadth, it had ripped my epaulette to shreds, yet had left no other physical marks of my close encounter with death. With shaking hands, I lit a cigarette, inhaled and held the smoke deep inside. Slowly releasing the white haze, my thoughts turned to Ivy. *Gosh, Ivy, that was a narrow escape. You almost became a widow today.*

◆ ◆ ◆

By May 24th, the enemy had taken Boulogne. Calais was cut off. German advance units had reached the Aa Canal, a mere twelve miles west of Dunkirk. Our northern forces, comprising the British Expeditionary Force, French and Belgian troops, had managed to withdraw from Belgium to the French frontier. To the east, west, and south, there were German divisions. Only one way was open for withdrawal —north, to Dunkirk, the sole port remaining in Allied hands. In a situation becoming desperate, we were placed on half rations.

By holding back the enemy at Arras, our army had given us time to prepare twenty-two bridges for demolition in the area of Béthune. Hordes of refugees trying to cross the bridges made the work difficult. Seeing the problems they caused, and fearing fifth columnists could be travelling in the midst of the refugees, using them as cover, officers ordered soldiers guarding the bridges to stop the refugees from crossing.

"Shoot them if you have to."

Turned away from one bridge, the civilians hurried north to another and another until they found one they could use to cross to the safety of the east bank of the canal—a forlorn hope. The corridor of safety between the German front line in the west and the front line in the east was a mere fifteen miles. Squeezing this small pocket of safety, the German forces surrounded our trapped divisions, who by now were fighting for their lives with their backs to the sea.

◆ ◆ ◆

Driving the water truck, I had to wait to be last in line of our retreating soldiers falling back after dynamiting the bridges. Under orders not to blow up the bridges until the enemy was in sight, it was a race to stop them from coming over the rivers and canals. Once the way forward was blocked to the Germans, we fell back to the next bridge.

"We don't seem to be slowing them down," I said to the soldier beside me. We were guarding the road leading up to one of the bridges, listening to the rumble of guns in the distance. "How the hell can they move so fast? Only two weeks ago, we were pottering about on the airfields. What the hell happened?"

"Listen!" said the soldier.

Hearing the growl of German tanks moving up, I shouted to soldiers behind me. "Have they finished laying the charges yet? There're tanks coming for crying out loud!"

"Fall back, men. We're just about ready for them."

We ran back across the bridge. It was close. The sappers barely had time to prepare the detonator and hide round a corner before German Panzers and troops started crossing. Hastily, the explosives were detonated. I closed my mind and ears to the screams of German soldiers ripped apart by sizzling hot shrapnel. Tens of thousands of British soldiers' lives were at stake. We had to do whatever it took to hold back the enemy advance.

At one section of the Béthune Canal, there was a large number of barges full of army supplies—aviation fuel, leather jerkins, boots. An agitated captain strode up and down the banks of the canal looking at the barges, which were so thick in places they formed a bridge across the canal.

"We'll have to float them away, Sergeant. Set the men to it. I have to go to Watten to destroy two bridges there. I'm taking eight drivers, trucks and explosives, and I'm leaving you in charge. Get this canal cleared."

"Yes, sir."

The captain moved off, and we set to work.

An hour later, a soldier ran up to tell us Gerry was in sight."

"Damn it!" cursed the sergeant. "It's taking too long to float them away. Set them ablaze, men."

The barges erupted in a dazzling pyrotechnic display. We shielded our faces to watch a huge wall of flames soar sky-high.

APRIL 26th—JUNE 1st 1940

There were crashes like thunder as fuel exploded, and bits of steel, wood, and boots flew high into the air before clattering to the ground. Hotter than Hades the barges blazed, leaving charred wrecks useless to serve as a route across the canal.

At the next bridge, we found an advance unit of German troops had arrived ahead of us. Hurtling from our trucks, we hid in doorways and behind corners. All we had were rifles, machine guns, and a desperate determination to drive back the enemy. A fierce exchange of rifle fire started. At the rear of the convoy, I'd grabbed my rifle and was moving forward when Mac rode up on a motorcycle.

"Gerry got to the bridge before us. They've got us pinned down for now. Watch the rear in case there's more trying to surround us."

I manned the defences, thinking it was going to be touch and go whether we'd make it to the far bank. The sound of firing at the bridge petered out. In the rear, we exchanged tense, questioning looks, not knowing who'd won the fight at the bridge until Mac returned.

"Get moving. They'll be blowing this'un in a hurry," he shouted.

Trucks roared across, while sappers hastily set the charges. We held the recaptured bridge just long enough to lay the explosives and allow us to cross before blowing it to smithereens.

The enemy was hot-on-the-heels of our retreating army. At one bridge, our trucks raced across while under heavy fire from enemy rifles, machine guns and rapidly approaching tanks. Last in line with the water tanker, I'd barely left the bridge before one heroic soldier, driving a lorry load of explosives, shot past me onto the bridge. I pulled hard on the steering wheel to avoid a collision. Despite scraping his front end against the tanker, the driver didn't falter. I caught a glimpse of his determined face as he hurtled past. With lips set in a tight line, eyes narrowed in concentration, the driver rushed onto the bridge. I realized he was desperately attempting something important and stopped my vehicle to watch him through the mirrors. Halfway across, he brought the truck to a screeching stop, scrambled out of the cab and dashed for my water truck. I hastily reversed towards him. The open passenger door was swinging wildly.

I was frantic. "Come on! Get in! Get in!"

The soldier needed no encouragement. Under a hail of enemy bullets and with one brave man hanging onto the front passenger seat for dear life, his legs dangling outside the cab, I whisked him away to safety, while the company provided what cover they could. Enemy armoured cars immediately tried to rush the bridge before it was destroyed. Too late! With a tremendous roar, the truck exploded, demolishing the bridge and flinging metal debris far and wide only to fall moments later with a splash into the river, or crash noisily into the nearby streets.

◆ ◆ ◆

The Royal Engineer companies were to withdraw to Dunkirk, first blowing bridges at Merville, Merris, and then Méteren. The roads were awash with the flotsam and jetsam of war in full swing. French troops, bitter and disillusioned by the lack of leadership from their officers, straggled along the roads heading north, but not really knowing where they were going. What they did know was that the enemy was to the south, using tactics so terrifying, it was impossible to defeat them. The soldiers' faces dazed with fatigue, the hopelessness in their eyes, all bore witness to the horror of unrelenting Luftwaffe attacks.

Panic gripped French villagers when they saw defeated soldiers trudging through. Fearing they would soon be overrun by German troops, farmers, doctors, and shopkeepers abandoned homes and livelihoods at a moment's notice. Heaving crowds blocked the roads. In this mêlée, desperately needed British units were held up for hours as they struggled to reach the east bank of the Aa Canal, where they were to form a front line along the western edge of the corridor.

At Lille, the French First Army blocked the enemy's advance, holding them at bay for three days—three days, during which they tied down seven German divisions, while

APRIL 26th—JUNE 1st 1940

150,000 trapped British soldiers swarmed to Dunkirk, where the evacuation was making a slow start.

The enemy's advance was threatening the southern flank of the fleeing British Expeditionary Force. Royal Engineers, along with other specialist units, were formed into one of several special detachments. My unit was called 'Pol' Force. The other detachments were 'Mac' Force and 'Petre' Force.

◆ ◆ ◆

Company trucks thrust their way through the crowded roads. I followed in my tanker; there were still many canals, rivers and bridges to deal with. My heart went out to exhausted mothers struggling to carry their children. I was filled with sad admiration for one skinny old man determinedly pushing his plump wife along in a wheelbarrow, when they should have been at home in the comfort of their living room, not out in this mad free-for-all. Refugees surged north along the narrow corridor, all that was left of freedom. Dead women and children, a few horses, some men and abandoned vehicles lay by the roadside, testimony to some Stuka pilot's foray along the road.

On the morning of May 27th, we learned we'd been directed towards the Belgian border to hold back the Germans and protect the flank of the withdrawal.

"They want to make up their minds. I thought we were supposed to be withdrawing to Dunkirk," said Blondie.

"It looks like one big mess to me," said Hinny.

"Bloody chaos more like. We're scrambling round like lunatics and not getting anywhere," I said in disgust.

My company and other Royal Engineer units, formed into special detachments totalling three hundred and sixty men, were ordered to a place called Monts des Cats—a 518-foot hill, with a road winding its way to the Trappist monastery perched on the summit. Fighting their way north had been a blood bath for the West Kents caught in a valley by deadly mortar fire. They had suffered heavy casualties and needed ourtrucks to transport the wounded to Dunkirk. Left without vehicles, when the time came for us to withdraw, we would

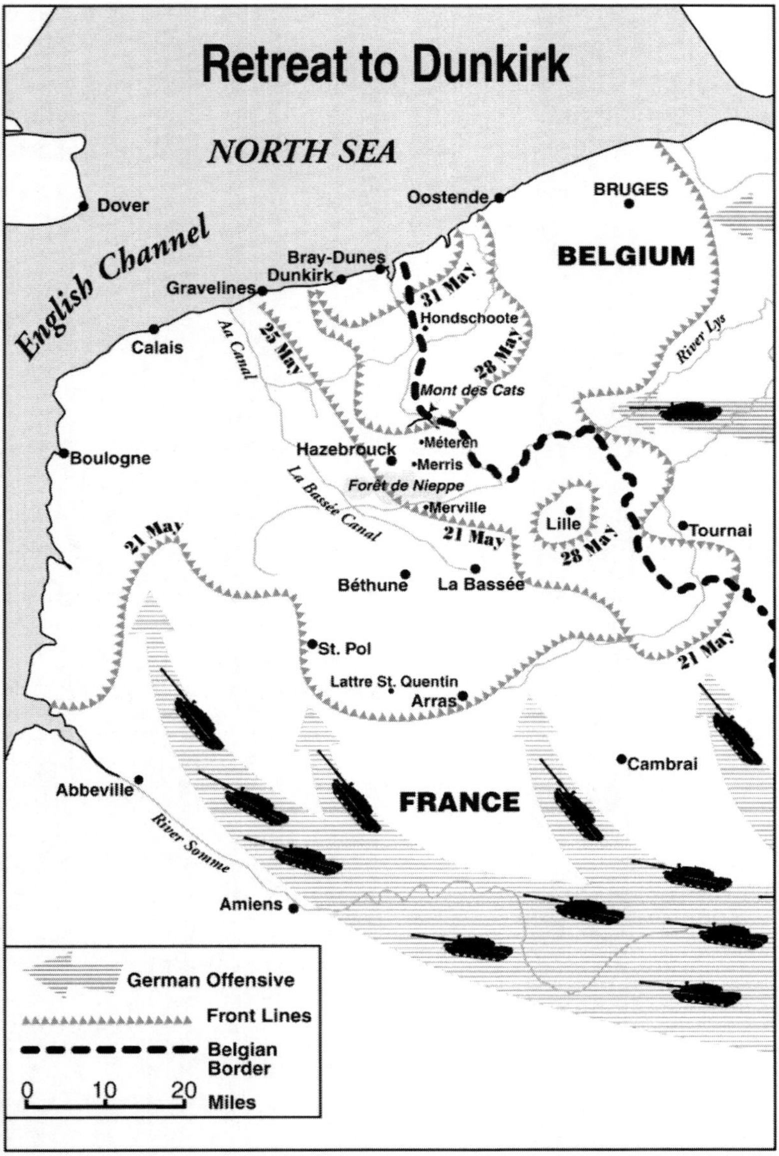
Retreat to Dunkirk
NORTH SEA
Dover
Oostende
BRUGES
English Channel
Bray-Dunes
Dunkirk
Gravelines
BELGIUM
31 May
Hondschoote
Calais
Aa Canal
25 May
28 May
River Lys
Mont des Cats
Hazebrouck
•Méteren
•Merris
Boulogne
La Bassée Canal
Forêt de Nieppe
•Merville
Lille
Tournai
21 May
21 May
28 May
Béthune
La Bassée
St. Pol
21 May
Lattre St. Quentin
Arras
Cambrai
Abbeville
FRANCE
River Somme
Amiens
German Offensive
Front Lines
Belgian Border
0 10 20 Miles

have to cover the twenty-two miles to Dunkirk on foot. We looked on grimly as mutilated, ashen-faced soldiers, eyes glazed in shock, uniforms saturated with blood, were helped into the trucks.

APRIL 26th—JUNE 1st 1940

"Looks like they've been through hell," said Hinny, taking in the maimed, heavily bandaged forms.

They were in a sorry state all right. *What on earth did Gerry throw at them?* I wondered.

A feeling of impending doom washed over me as I watched the trucks disappear down the road.

"Stone the crows! If they can do this to a fine fighting unit like the West Kents, what will they do to us?" someone piped up.

An uncomfortable awareness gnawed at my mind.

"Do they think we're not going to need those trucks because we're not going to make it through whatever Gerry's got for us?" I said to Darky.

"Nah, they reckon we'll still be fit enough to run to Dunkirk after we've sorted Gerry out."

I chuckled grimly at his show of bravado.

Hiking towards Mont des Cats, we walked straight into a mortar attack. Dead and wounded men started falling all around. I gagged in horror at seeing Major Thomas' knee blown off. Through the shelling, captains and lieutenants urged us forward. Soldiers and medics scrambled to drag and carry the wounded towards the hill, where they were taken to the monastery for medical attention. We were still shaking as we climbed almost to the top of the hill and settled ourselves into hollows by the roadside. Darky and I stayed close together. 'Pol' Force had to hold the enemy approach from the east at bay while, on the other side of the hill, wounded and exhausted remnants of infantry divisions, coming from the south, could withdraw. It was a bad do altogether.

Puffing on his pipe, a young lieutenant walked among us. We had seen little fighting so far. In a calming voice, he reassured us.

"Don't worry about the Germans when they come along. We'll just have to take them on. That's what we're here for. We have to hold this position for forty-eight hours to allow as many of our men as possible to get back to Dunkirk. They're depending on you. I know you won't let them down. In the meantime, just settle down and have a rest and a smoke."

I pulled out my Woodbines and offered Darky a cigarette.

"I'd say we're up to our eyes in it," said Darky. "You haven't got a tot of rum in your pocket have you, Gus? I could do with a drink."

"No, not today. Tell you what. When we get back, I'll buy you a pint. Will that cheer you up?"

"Best offer I've had all day."

Only eighty men covered our area of the hill. All we had were rifles and machine guns, and the advantages Mont des Cats provided—dominating height and a clear view of the German approach across the featureless plain of Flanders. With eyes transfixed, we watched the German Army's arrival. On the plain below, row upon row of Panzers lined up. There, before us, was the enemy, flagrantly displaying its superior fighting power. All was brought to bear on 'Pol' Force. That first afternoon, German artillery pinned us down in our hiding places but without gaining any advantage. With the coming of night, the guns fell silent. We snatched what little sleep we could in the few hours of darkness.

May 28th started with a dawn attack by the Luftwaffe. Through the early morning mist, we heard the drone of approaching Heinkels. Suddenly, the planes were roaring overhead, at first dropping bombs, then coming back to strafe our positions. Time and time again they left only to return for more menacing sorties. Whistling bombs rained down. The explosions were deafening. Earth and gravel spattered over us, but the planes' inaccuracies resulted in few casualties to our men, who were keeping their heads well down inside their hiding places.

Morale remained high. Derisive laughter spread contagiously from hollow to hollow.

"Get your eyes tested Gerry." "Can't you get your sights sorted out?" relieved soldiers yelled.

Throughout the remainder of the morning, a tremendous concentration of firepower was brought to bear on our positions.

"The German commanders have no idea how many brigades are entrenched on Mont des Cats, blocking their

APRIL 26th—JUNE 1st 1940

advance into the escape corridor," the Lieutenant advised us. "They're trying to flush us out to assess our strength. Stay calm men. So far you've come through it all very well. They're not inflicting any real damage upon us."

Seeing Panzers moving towards the hill, we prepared petrol bombs, until we could hear the rumble of approaching tanks. As the tanks neared, we became more and more jittery, glancing at one another with wide, fearful eyes. Rumbling turned into loud roars. Intense firing of the Panzers' guns had shells crashing and exploding around our positions, fortunately with little effect. When we could hear the tanks' tracks rattling and squeaking almost beside us, we started throwing petrol bombs. One man, dashing from his hiding place to hurl the bombs, slipped and died screaming, crushed beneath the massive bulk of one of the tanks. We lobbed burning bomb after burning bomb at the tanks, some men sobbing in fear and despair as we frantically attacked the Panzers. Suddenly, with voracious flames licking at tracks and turrets, the tanks turned and bolted back down the hill.

Stunned and shaken, I muttered to Darky, "So these are the cardboard tanks the government said Gerry had?"

Darky sniggered nervously.

"Those cardboard tanks certainly put the wind up me."

Late afternoon, German infantry appeared. Countenances became serious as we watched enemy soldiers creeping up the hill using whatever sparse cover they could find. They moved closer; we opened fire. A rapid exchange of rifle fire ensued. In the confusion, it was hard to say whether one of the German soldiers was a marksman having a bit of fun, or if it was only a freak shot, but the lieutenant's pipe was shattered by a German bullet. The stem fell from the shocked officer's mouth, leaving him spluttering, "What the . . . ? My God, they've shot the pipe out of my mouth!"

Loss of composure quickly turned to a roar of rage. "Bugger that! Fix bayonets! Up and at them men! Scatter them!"

In this fashion, I was introduced to my first experience of hand-to-hand combat. Scared stiff, mouth parched, stomach acids burning the back of my throat, my comrades and I charged down the hill, yelling blood-curdling screams like ancient Celts. The fiendish roars gave us courage as we ran down to meet the enemy soldiers. We must have looked like we meant business because the Germans started to fall back. Running towards one of the soldiers still recklessly charging up the hill, I lifted my rifle and shot him in the head. Surprise adorned the soldier's face as he toppled face down onto the hard earth. Swallowing down the sudden taste of bile, I moved past the fallen man, relieved not to have to see the face of the first soldier I had personally killed.

It was a brief skirmish. After only a few minutes, the scared German soldiers turned tail and ran. We stopped the charge and stood for a satisfying moment to watch the enemy fleeing down the hill.

"We showed 'em, lads. Didn't we show them?" we congratulated ourselves before returning to our positions.

The German troops were at a disadvantage, believing there were hundreds of Allied soldiers waiting to kill them, when, in fact, in my part of the hill there were only the remnants of the original eighty, relieved and jubilant after our triumphant spat with the enemy.

Despite everything the enemy had thrown at us, hardly a man was lost. During the night, German troops withdrew from our area of the hill. Seizing the opportunity, officers ordered 'Pol' Force to withdraw. It was two hours after midnight when I heard the whistles signalling our withdrawal.

"Right, men, you are now relieved. It's every man for himself. Make for Dunkirk as fast as you can. Don't stop for anything. Good luck."

We had held our position for two days and nights, allowing our retreating army to flee safely northwards to the coast. Now it was our turn—if we could make it.

We moved out. The birds' joyful dawn chorus fell on deaf ears while I strained all of my senses for signs of danger as we left the hill. Crossing the dew-damp fields to reach the road, we ran into a German reception committee using box formation mortar fire. Mortar shells whooshed past us at chest height.

APRIL 26th—JUNE 1st 1940

We started running. Men were falling all around me. From the corner of my eye, I saw the pay corporal's head blown off. With a scream of agony, Captain Chamier went down minus a leg. Unbidden, a tortured cry escaped from my throat. And I ran, rucksack bouncing crazily, tin helmet askew. I ran as if my shirt-tail was on fire. I ran for six miles before halting at the side of the road, gasping for breath, one of only eighty-seven men out of the three hundred and sixty defenders of Mont des Cats to survive.

In shock from the bloody butchery I'd so recently escaped, I slumped, wild-eyed, on the damp grass. Shudders racked my body as I struggled to regain control. I'd come through unscathed. Relief at being unharmed eased my distress. My breathing was almost back to normal, when seven more 'Pol' Force survivors arrived.

"Tommy, you got through!" I shouted, jumping up to greet my friend.

I peered down the road past Tommy and the other soldiers, searching for Darky, but there was no sign of him.

"Did you see Darky, Hinny, Blondie, Mac?" I asked.

"No. When they opened up with the mortars, we scattered. There's no telling where they'll be."

In silence, we sat and smoked, trying to determine our bearings. No one spoke a word about the horror of the mortar fire. The occasional refugee trundled past giving us a cursory glance then stoically went on with the business of trying to find a safe haven in a chaotic world.

I stood up.

"Come on, we'd better get going."

We moved on, soon coming to a road teaming with civilians. Most soldiers of the British Expeditionary Force and the French armies were already safely within the perimeter of the Dunkirk bridgehead.

"Anyone know the way to Dunkirk?" I asked my companions, but like me, nobody knew for sure which direction to go.

"Okay, we'd best join these people. At least we know they're moving away from trouble. Sooner or later, we're bound to come to the coast. Maybe we'll find a signpost for Dunkirk on the way."

Joining the flow northwards, we trudged along, mingling with exhausted refugees. Horses pulled carts piled high with suitcases and passengers. People had fastened mattresses onto their car roofs to protect them from the machine gunfire of the Luftwaffe—and were they needed. Time after time, out of the morning sun, German planes attacked, strafing civilians and soldiers alike. Stukas flew up and down the road in an orgy of death and destruction, while people dived for cover in ditches, or under carts. One sadistic pilot was intent on winning a medal for inventiveness. Not for him the routine strafing of people by flying along the road at car top height. No, he had more sport flying to and fro across the road. These unpredictable manoeuvres gave the travellers less warning in which to find cover. As a result, that pilot's death toll was high. His forays littered the road with death—old men, women, and children's bodies were scattered higgledy-piggledy among the chaos. In the stunned silence after each attack, survivors wept over their dead, horses snorted and reared in panic, then the crunch of wheels on gravel, feet shuffling, bicycle wheels squeaking as the movement northward started once again.

After three hours, the men were ready when I suggested we stop for a rest and a bite to eat. In the shadows of a farmhouse wall, we spread blankets before tucking into bully beef and hard tack. Some of the men dozed. From overhead, a German Stuka pilot spotted our group lying about like sitting ducks. The Stuka screamed steeply down from the sky as if to snatch a mouse hiding in the grass. Pulling out of the dive at the last minute, the pilot fired at us as he passed only feet above our heads. My eyes bulged in disbelief as a row of bullet holes appeared in my blanket barely twelve inches from my body. Looking to my left, I saw that two of the sappers had been killed as they slept. No one else was hurt. One soldier leapt to his feet, defiantly raising his fist to the sky.

"You bastard, Gerry! You bastard!" he yelled after the plane.

APRIL 26th—JUNE 1st 1940

We covered the dead with blankets and, numb with shock, hurried on our way. An hour later, we came upon three heavily bandaged, British soldiers leaning against a bullet-riddled ambulance by the side of the road.

"Will you look at this? What are you doing here?" asked Tommy.

"We decided we weren't going to sit around to be taken prisoner, so we stole the ambulance to make for Dunkirk, but it's all shot up by bloody Stukas. We can't get it to go. We've had it, mates. We just haven't the strength to go on on foot."

I walked to the front of the ambulance. "Lift the bonnet. Let's see if we can get it going."

We took turns to tinker with the engine, while the others ate and rested or passed out chocolate to tired, hungry children dragging their sore feet along the road, this small kindness bringing a weary smile to their mothers' strained faces. When it was my turn under the bonnet, I tried everything I could think of. I'd almost given up when the engine burst into life with a shaky roar.

"Quick, get in!" I shouted, slamming the bonnet shut.

The men piled inside.

"This is great. It's giving my aching feet a rest," said Tommy, with a delighted chortle.

Chugging along the crowded road as best we could, we developed a sense of optimism. It wasn't all bad. The weather was beautiful and sunny. Best of all, the Stukas were taking a break—but not for long. We'd travelled only four miles when Stukas swarmed overhead.

"Stukas!" I shouted, banging loudly on the partition behind the driver's seat. "In the ditch! Get in the ditch!"

Then I leapt and rolled to safety.

It didn't matter to the German pilots that the vehicle they were attacking clearly displayed a red cross. Down they came, strafing the vehicle without mercy, killing the three wounded and two more besides, who were unable to reach the safety of the ditches in time. Hit by more bullets, the ambulance spluttered and died. We who were spared gently placed our dead comrades inside the ambulance and shut the doors.

"They're shooting at ambulances now for God's sake! What kind of war is this?" cried a soldier, leaning his head against the vehicle.

"One we've got to live through," I said firmly. I patted the man's shoulder. "Come on. It's time to get going."

Wearily, we continued trekking towards the coast, passing through once picturesque French villages, the buildings now damaged by gunfire, walls scarred with bullet holes, streets deserted and desolate except for wary cats and barking dogs left to fend for themselves. Whenever we found an abandoned Allied rifle, we removed the bolt, rendering the weapon useless to the enemy. We collected so many bolts they weighed us down. Each time we came to a canal or river, we gratefully emptied our pockets, pitching the heavy bolts into the water, only to replace them with more bolts as we journeyed along the road. By late afternoon, we were walking along roads where destroyed and abandoned British Army trucks littered the roadside. In the fields outside the town of Hondschoote lay the smouldering, deliberately destroyed remains of the British Expeditionary Force's equipment; thousands of lorries, vans, trucks, motorcycles, Bren gun carriers, piles of new uniforms, and blankets lay charred and burned. It was a depressing sight.

"We must be close to Dunkirk now," said Tommy.

"Look! Over there. Looks like a roadblock on that bridge. Be careful. We're not sure if they're ours," I warned.

Using the hedgerows as cover, we cautiously approached the bridge until close enough to recognize the soldiers as British.

At the bridgehead along the Bergues-Furnes Canal, soldiers directed us to Bray-Dunes. To the northwest, I could see columns of black smoke rising high into the sky.

"What's going on over there?"

"That's Dunkirk. It's a shambles thanks to the German bombs, nothing but a burning wreck. The docks are destroyed, and the water supply's gone. You'll be better off at Bray-Dunes."

APRIL 26th—JUNE 1ˢᵗ 1940

Dunkirk

We stepped onto the beach at Bray-Dunes, dog-tired and heavy-eyed. In the twilight, I could see tens of thousands of troops congregated on the golden sands, slumped down and listless, not a spark of fight left in them. Other men, quiet desperation in their faces, formed long lines out to sea. Some stood chest-deep in water, oily and slick from the shipwrecks.

Puzzled, I surveyed the beach and tried to make sense of the scenario before me. Slowly, understanding dawned. I couldn't accept it. Horror, then anger, welled up, followed by intense shame. My eyes filled with tears. Until that moment, I'd believed we were an army in retreat. Now, I realized, I belonged to a defeated army. Pride fought against accepting this fact. I still had plenty of fight left yet. But looking round again at the thousands of dejected, defeated men, I could see these troops had had it. Days without sleep during the retreat, lack of food, nerves shattered by the relentless screaming of falling bombs, strafing Stukas, the loss of comrades in arms, battalions wiped out, I could see that most men had already surrendered. I was overcome with confusion and despair.

At Bray-Dunes beach Allied soldiers form lines out to sea as they wait to be rescued. (Imperial War Museum)

The four of us settled in the sand dunes, ate some hard tack and smoked cigarettes. And we waited, for God knows what. No one was giving any direction. We'd reached the coast. Now what? We soon found out. German spotter planes disturbed the night, flying overhead and dropping illuminated parachutes to light up the beach areas to make them easy targets for German gunners. Mercifully, with the sand absorbing the shock of the explosions, the shelling caused little damage, apart from making it impossible to sleep. I nestled low in the dunes, wondering, *How on earth did we get into this pickle?*

I tried to sleep, unaware that the day was ending with ten German divisions pressing on the Dunkirk perimeter, now a mere twenty miles long and six miles wide at its deepest point. It's just as well I didn't know how bad a pickle it was.

◆ ◆ ◆

May 17th: Winston Churchill, the new Prime Minister since Neville Chamberlain's resignation on May 10th, began to consider the possibility of evacuating the British Expeditionary Force from France. He did not believe it would come to this, but every contingency had to be faced. Although nobody realized it, some groundwork had already begun. A May 14th radio broadcast called on all small boat owners to send their particulars to the Admiralty. Boat yards were busy building wooden minesweepers because of the magnetic mine threat. Consequently, the Small Vessels Pool, unable to obtain the boats it needed, intended to requisition private yachts and motorboats.

May 19th, The War Office felt no sense of urgency regarding plans for the evacuation of the British Expeditionary Force. It was assured there was ample time to organize for such an unlikely event. The Admiralty put Vice-Admiral Ramsey in charge of the evacuation plans, code name 'Operation Dynamo'.

The astonishing speed of the German advance through France to the Channel ports of Boulogne and Calais took everyone by surprise. The evacuation of the British Expeditionary Force quickly moved from the bottom of the agenda to top priority. The original thirty-six vessels allocated to the Admiralty would not be enough. What Ramsey needed was every seaworthy craft in the nation. The Ministry of Shipping searched for vessels able to bring the men home—passenger ferries, barges, drifters, trawlers, coasters, dredgers, fishing boats, lifeboats, tugs, anything. Not knowing what to expect, many crews readily volunteered to go across The Channel to Dunkirk 'where there was trouble'.

Morning of May 26th: 4,000 German bombs rained on Dunkirk and the thousands of troops pouring into the area. The British Government finally realized they were on the brink of a disaster of catastrophic proportions. That evening, Admiral Ramsey was ordered to commence 'Operation Dynamo'. He had one hundred and twenty-nine vessels with which to evacuate hundreds of thousands of troops. The Admiralty's expectations were to save only 45,000 of them in the next two days. Even this modest calculation fell short as rescue vessels encountered dangers from mines, German guns, torpedo attacks by S-boats, and enemy planes. Damaged ships turned back or sank, sometimes with their load of evacuated troops. By midnight on May 27th, only 37,965 men had been saved.

As he received reports about the increasing numbers of men waiting on the beaches, Ramsey desperately called for destroyers, minesweepers, everything he could get his hands on. His one goal was to save as many men as possible.

◆ ◆ ◆

Senior Naval Officer Captain William G. Tennant was ordered to Dunkirk to organize the loading of the rescue fleet. With him went a naval shore party of eight officers and one hundred and sixty men. Arriving in Dunkirk at 5:30 p.m. on May 27th, he explored evacuation possibilities.

"Evacuation from Dunkirk harbour is not feasible. It's being bombed day and night, and Luftwaffe attacks have left it a blazing ruin. The beaches to the east seem to be our best bet," Tennant advised his commanders.

A CORPORAL'S WAR

He conferred with army officers, who told him, "We estimate the Royal Navy has twenty-four to thirty-six hours before Dunkirk is overrun."

Tennant sent a message to Dover.

"Send all available craft to the beaches east of Dunkirk."

He ordered the naval parties to round up the troops and send them to the beaches. Receiving reports that leaderless soldiers were becoming unruly, Tennant went to speak to them.

"I know you're jittery and scared that you might become prisoners of war. I assure you plenty of ships are coming to take you back to England. We need you to be calm, disciplined and alert."

Responding to his authority and leadership, the men quickly calmed down.

Concerned that far too few men were being lifted from the beaches, Tennant requested information from his commanders.

"The entire stretch of beach from Dunkirk to La Panne shelves so gradually that the destroyers and large vessels have to anchor a mile off shore, even at high tide, sir."

Charles Cundall's painting of the Dunkirk rescue operation (Imperial War Museum)

APRIL 26th—JUNE 1st 1940

"We don't have enough small craft on the scene, sir. The destroyers have to use their own boats to pick up the men from the beaches and ferry them to the destroyers. The troops are scared and rush the launches when they arrive and try to scramble in from where they're standing in chest-deep water. They're not used to boats, and end up capsizing them."

"It's taking hours and hours to lift only a few hundred men off the beaches."

Back in Dover, the operations room was awash with messages from the destroyers urging them to send more small boats.

Low tide at the mole, soldiers used ladders to board ship (IWM)

Returning to the harbour, Tennant again studied the area. He knew that if he could use the docks, he could evacuate the men faster. But it wasn't feasible; the area was being pulverized by German bombing raids. Then he realized the Luftwaffe was concentrating on the piers and quays and completely ignoring the moles, two long breakwaters that formed the entrance to the harbour. One from the western side and one from the east reached out towards one another, leaving a narrow gap with only enough room for the passage of one ship. The eastern mole, constructed of rock with thick concrete pilings alongside it, was 1,400 yards long. A wooden walkway with wooden railings along the edges ran the full length along the top. The width of the walkway provided barely enough room for four men to walk abreast, and the tides appeared to rise and fall fifteen feet around the mole. It would be risky, transferring the troops at low or high tide, and berthing could be dangerous if the swift tidal currents slammed the vessels against the wooden planking. The mole wasn't built to take such a battering. Tennant decided there was only one way to find out if it would prove sturdy enough to act as a pier.

He ordered a ship to come alongside. In no time at all, this first vessel crammed 950 men on board. At 4:15 a.m. on May 28th, it set sail for England. Sadly, a German plane sank the ship when it was less than half way across The Channel. Nevertheless, Tennant had discovered. the mole worked. It not only worked, it could accommodate several ships at a time, and the clouds of oily, black smoke, belching from the burning oil refinery, hung low over the harbour, hiding the mole from the view of the Luftwaffe. Tennant ordered all vessels to the eastern mole—a decision he hoped would prove to be the turning point at Dunkirk and the salvation of the British Expeditionary Force.

Receiving reports of 5,000 rowdy, leaderless soldiers, forming undisciplined, drunken mobs, which were causing mayhem on the beach at Bray-Dunes, Tennant sent Commanders Kerr and Richardson to Bray-Dunes, along with forty men. He put Commander Clouston, a Canadian, in charge of evacuations at the mole.

Arriving at Bray-Dunes that evening, Richardson alerted Dover that he had found not 5,000, but 25,000 men on the beach and small boats were urgently needed. In the early hours of May 29th, with a storm drawing near, the seas became too rough for evacuation from the beaches.

APRIL 26th–JUNE 1st 1940

Richardson sent the troops to the mole at Dunkirk, only seven miles away, but a marathon for men at the end of their endurance and scarcely able to walk.

After being put into use, the eastern mole proved to be a great success. Destroyers were picking up between 500–900 men in minutes, delivering them to Dover and returning to the mole for more. Commander Clouston towered head and shoulders above the crowds. Using a megaphone, he shouted instructions, skilfully controlling the flow of troops to the streams of arriving ships. Two thousand men an hour were leaving from the mole. On May 28th, a total of 18,527 men safely left France, more than double the previous day's numbers.

Thousands of soldiers converged on the area as news spread of the evacuations at the mole. The morning of the 29th, a steady stream of ships pulled in, quickly loaded, and pulled out. No matter how many men were loaded onto the ships, the lines of men waiting to embark continued to grow, until they stretched the length of the mole and snaked back along the beach. Brigadier Parminter, working alongside Commander Clouston, used a 'hat-check' system. He divided the waiting men into groups of fifty, gave each group a number, and as the number was called, the group stepped onto the mole. At times, the embarkations were going so smoothly, the men had to trot along the mole at the double. The improvement was heartening.

Around 1:30 p.m., the weather started to clear. A change in wind direction sent the heavy pall of smoke inland. Four hundred German aircraft headed for Dunkirk led by one hundred and eighty Stukas. As the twelve vessels at the mole lost their protective cover, German pilots spotted them from overhead—a perfect target. Bombs poured from the skies. The mole was hit. Chunks of concrete hurtled into the air. Swooping down, Stukas machine-gunned troops caught on the crowded walkway. Defenceless and with nowhere to hide, they were easy targets. Hundreds of lives were lost, ships damaged and destroyed as they frantically tried to leave the mole. Two ships sank at their berths. At dusk, after one and a half hours of continuous bombing, the raid ended. In places, the mole had more holes than a rabbit warren, but only the outer side of the mole was obstructed by wreckage. The inner wall was still clear.

Shipping losses on this day were three destroyers and twenty-one other vessels with many others damaged. Despite everything, 47,310 men returned home safely.

Enemy planes bomb the mole and sink a trawler (IWM)

◆ ◆ ◆

On Wednesday, May 29th, Ivy, listening to the wireless, learned about the evacuation at Dunkirk as it was announced to the British public. She knew I was in France, but didn't know where. She said a silent prayer. "I know Norman is in France, but I don't know where. Please God, don't let him be at Dunkirk. Keep him safe. Let him come home."

◆ ◆ ◆

Responding to a public appeal, a motley collection of small craft was brought to Ramsgate from all over the south and east coasts and the River Thames. They came from yachting centres, boatyards, and private moorings to join the naval

APRIL 26th–JUNE 1ˢᵗ 1940

vessels. Owners, many only weekend sailors, insisted on going with their boats. Members of yacht clubs volunteered. Leaving their desks and places of work, civilians came from all over the south of England. Facing grave danger, these unassuming heroes put their lives at risk to save men caught in a desperate plight. Some volunteers used their day off work to save hundreds of lives then quietly returned to work as usual the following day.

Most boats were towed across The English Channel. Few of these little vessels were built for use at sea, but The Channel was kind to them, remaining still and calm while they plied backwards and forwards between the beaches and the larger vessels, ferrying troops to the ships. The small boats provided the only means by which soldiers on the beaches could reach the rescue ships moored so far offshore. Some volunteers worked continuously for forty-eight hours at a stretch before returning to Ramsgate when fuel ran out, or they became too exhausted to carry on.

Only eight small boats were in the first convoy that set out to cross The Channel to the beaches at 10:00 p.m. on May 29ᵗʰ. Gradually, the numbers increased until it was impossible to tell where one convoy ended and another began. Nearly four hundred small craft were involved in the rescue operation. By the time 'Operation Dynamo' ended, they had been instrumental in saving almost 100,000 men from the beaches around Dunkirk.

As Dover's residents listened to the thunder of guns at Dunkirk, newspapers and broadcasters rushed to tell the story of these heroic volunteers. Their activities engendered a surge of pride in the British population. Morale soared. The 'Dunkirk Spirit' developed. People were energized, hopeful and eager to be actively involved in the war against Hitler.

◆ ◆ ◆

I woke up to a dull, cloudy day. The lines of men standing in the sea were still there.

"They must have been there all night," said Tommy.

They certainly didn't seem to be getting away.

That's a bad sign, I thought.

I was taking a wash and shave in a nearby canal when a soldier asked, "You just got here, mate?"

"Yes, we can't figure out what we're supposed to be doing."

"The Royal Navy's going to evacuate us from the beaches soon," he confidently informed us.

Although I desperately wanted to believe him, we hadn't seen many men leaving the beaches so far, and soldiers milling about the area seemed fearful and uncertain. Skulking in the dunes, we could see little evacuation activity. In fact, the only activity was from the German Stukas flying along the beach, dropping bombs and strafing the besieged British soldiers.

"The enemy's pounding at the door, and we're just sitting on our arses in the sand dunes," growled one soldier.

Another piped up. "We're not going to get out of here. Who's kidding who?"

With glum expressions, we watched and waited. Mid-morning an officer from the Royal Engineers stumbled across our group.

"Corporal, you're needed to repair bomb damage at the eastern mole in Dunkirk harbour. Find as many sappers as you can and make your way there."

At last, I thought, *we've got something positive to do. Someone seems to know what needs doing.*

"Scout around," I told the men, "see if you can find some sappers. We'll all meet back at this spot."

We found another sixteen sappers to swell our ranks, then off we marched towards Dunkirk.

Coming to the outskirts of town, we saw a black Citroën screech to a stop beside four French officers standing with their troops. The officers quickly climbed into the car, which then sped off down the road.

"Did you see what I just saw?" asked Tommy.

"The bloody cowards! Those officers want shooting!" I raged in disgust. "They've abandoned their men to God and providence."

"Doesn't it leave a bad taste in your mouth?" said a disgusted sapper.

APRIL 26th—JUNE 1st 1940

Studying the French troops, I saw they were in a sorry state, dressed in ragged uniforms, some without boots. Skin stretched tight over gaunt faces; despairing eyes sunk deep into their sockets with dark shadows beneath testified to the horrors they'd been through. Seeing their officers departing, they became distressed, asking each other, "What do we do?" "Where do we go?"

Concerned, I approached the men. Only one or two spoke a little English. With the few words of French I learned in school and much gesticulating, they understood my message. "Go to Bray-Dunes. Find a British unit that will take you in. They'll look after you."

Moving into Dunkirk, we found the harbour and the eastern mole. The mole seemed to be the place where men were boarding ships to return to England. The day's heavy mist offered protection from the predatory Luftwaffe. There would be no air attacks in these conditions. On the mole, the atmosphere was cheerfully relaxed. Evacuations were proceeding safely and efficiently.

We reported to Commander Clouston who told us to find whatever we could to repair the mole's walkway, severely damaged after the previous day's savage air attacks.

"We'll split up into four groups," I told the men. "Forage for materials such as beams, doors, and floorboards. There're plenty of bomb-damaged buildings in Dunkirk, but if you can't find what you need in those, break into other buildings if you have to."

This was highly dangerous work. German batteries in Calais were firing salvos onto the town, and the Luftwaffe was still delivering bombs. Miraculously, the mole lay just out of reach of the guns. Choking, black smoke filled the air as we moved off through streets littered with rubble, broken glass, burned out trucks, and tangled trolley wires. With no tools or transport, we salvaged what materials we could. We made trip after trip to the mole carrying our plunder, avoiding artillery shells, falling bombs, bomb craters, burning buildings, and masonry toppling down without warning. Backwards and forwards we went, carrying beams and doors taken from damaged buildings to repair the gaps in the mole. It was a good day's work, not only for us, but also for the Royal Navy. A total of 53,823 men were rescued on May 30th.

We worked until dark before proceeding to the beach at Malo-les-Bains, a mile to the east. Munching on hard tack, we discussed our situation. I was glad to be working, better to be busy than just sitting about. It didn't leave much time to worry about how near Gerry was getting.

"They must have us surrounded by now," someone said.

"There're plenty of men getting away in the ships by the looks of it though. We should be all right," another soldier spoke up, hoping he was right.

"The numbers at the mole don't seem to be going down. More and more men keep arriving. We'll never get away," one of the group complained.

"We'd better get used to the idea that they're not going to let us leave in a hurry. They need us to keep the mole in good repair so everybody else can get away," I warned.

We spent another sleepless night disturbed by exploding shells as we hid in the dunes. In the morning, we found a canal to have a wash. I noticed some of the men weren't shaving.

"Get your razor out and have a shave," I ordered.

"Bloody hell, Gus! What's the point? We'll be prisoners of war soon enough," said Tommy.

You might well be right. Keeping my thoughts to myself, I urged, "Let's get down to the mole, lads, and see what needs doing."

◆ ◆ ◆

May 31st was again misty and overcast. These weather conditions, perfect for keeping the Luftwaffe on the ground, did not stop the shelling of Dunkirk. Having found their range, batteries planted east of Gravelines began damaging ships berthed at the mole. It was a nerve-racking dash to the waiting vessels. Occasionally, during the worst of the attacks, frightened soldiers tried to move back off the mole, but discipline was strictly enforced by officers. The men were made

APRIL 26th—JUNE 1st 1940

to run the gauntlet—sometimes at gunpoint, sometimes without making it to the ships.

We watched a flotilla of British destroyers sail westwards past Dunkirk. Training their guns on the German batteries at Gravelines, they fired salvo after salvo, pounding the enemy guns until they fell silent. Then we continued with the repair work. We were more fortunate than most of the weary men around us. We still carried our rifles and rucksacks, which contained a few more days' supply of hard rations. Many of the men waiting to evacuate, both on the mole and on the beaches, had not eaten for days. Before the day ended, 68,014 men arrived in England, free to eat to their hearts' content.

Next morning, the early mist was burning off, promising a clear, sunny day. June 1st also promised to be a day made in hell as German bombers took advantage of this break in the weather. At 5:30 a.m., German Messerschmitts swept in from the east.

Soldiers on Dunkirk beach fire at attacking German planes.
(Imperial War Museum)

I nudged the men awake.

"Come on. Let's be having you. Get ready. Get your breakfast, and let's get down to the harbour."

A CORPORAL'S WAR

Protests and grumbles over, we were all flat on our stomachs, stretching over the edge of the canal about to splash water into our faces, when the planes appeared. Before we could rinse the sleep from our eyes, the beaches were awash with the slaughter of Allied troops mowed down by machine gunfire.

"Gus, if you hadn't have made us get up when you did, we'd have had our chips down there on the beach," said Tommy.

I looked at the bodies strewn along the sands. "They can barely wait for the sun to come up before they're at us. The poor buggers didn't have a chance." Anger suddenly welled up, filling me with fierce determination. "Let's get down to the harbour. The best thing we can do is make sure we help as many men as possible get away so Gerry doesn't get them."

Not every Allied soldier returned from Dunkirk's beaches.
(Imperial War Museum)

Arriving at the harbour, I looked on in horror. Gun flashes and columns of smoke rose over Dunkirk as planes attacked the destroyer Windsor, berthed at the mole.

◆ ◆ ◆

APRIL 26th–JUNE 1st 1940

By 5:00 a.m., the Royal Air Force had forty-eight Spitfires heading towards Dunkirk. Streaks of white crisscrossed the blue sky as the Royal Air Force battled the Luftwaffe. Planes streaming black smoke fell into the sea followed by floating parachutes. Air Chief Marshal Sir Hugh Dowding was trying to spare British planes from further losses, so the protection was spasmodic. British fighters flew only four short patrols a day. By the time the British planes crossed The Channel, they had only enough fuel to engage the enemy for forty minutes before returning home. Pilots often made four sorties each day, but to the men on the ground, experiencing unrelenting Luftwaffe attacks, it felt as if the Royal Air Force had abandoned them. Few soldiers saw anything of the pilots' heroic battles taking place high above them.

The 5:00 a.m. patrol brought down ten German planes before returning to England. It would be 9'o clock before the next patrol arrived. In this period between patrols, the Luftwaffe ruled the skies. As destroyers and minesweepers sailed with their troops from the beaches and the mole, Heinkels and Stukas attacked. When forty Stukas appeared in the sky, every gun in the British fleet opened fire, but by 8:00 a.m., the destroyer *Keith* was hit. The Stukas returned for a second, third, fourth, and fifth attack on the *Keith* before the destroyer finally sank at 9:15. From the mole, men saw the French destroyer *Foudroyant* full of rescued troops, turn over and sink in seconds, victim of another swarm of Stukas.

German air attacks faded away when the Spitfire patrols were in the vicinity, but there were four more periods, during that first day of June, when the Royal Air Force could not provide fighter cover. The Luftwaffe made the most of them, destroying or damaging seventeen ships. Hundreds of men drowned and died in the Luftwaffe frenzy.

Commanders in London, Dover, and Dunkirk felt increasing trepidation at the escalating destroyer losses. They decided to stop using Royal Navy vessels during daylight hours. At 1:45 p.m., all destroyers received orders to return to England immediately.

A CORPORAL'S WAR

Commander Allison, of the destroyer *Worcester*, was entering Dunkirk harbour when the message arrived. Deciding it did not make sense to return to Dover empty, he berthed at the mole.

◆ ◆ ◆

As we watched lines of soldiers disappear onto the destroyer, Brigadier Parminter, aware this would be the last vessel until nightfall, beckoned to me. "We're going to try and get you away. You've done a good job here, Corporal. We're going to need men like you back in England to continue the fight. Now, get your men together. If you and your men can get on that destroyer, get on it."

I called the men to join me. "Hurry up. Get on that ship," I shouted, shoving them down the walkway. "Run. It's leaving any minute."

I took a last look round, making sure everyone had gone then raced down the mole. The destroyer was pulling away. I hesitated. The gap was too wide.

"Jump, you silly bugger! Jump!" yelled a burly sailor at the ship's rail.

So I did. Immediately, I realized I'd made a big mistake. Suspended in mid-air, I found I'd misjudged the distance. I glanced down. The foaming water churned wildly. Lurking beneath that turbulent surface, the destroyer's sharp propeller blades waited to chop me to pieces. With a crash, I slammed up against the ship's rail. Leaning far out, the muscular, thickset sailor had managed to grab my shredded epaulette, flapping loosely from my uniform. With brute strength and a few grunts and groans, he hauled me over the rail, where I fell, a winded, crumpled heap on the deck. Unbridled joy and relief overwhelmed me. I was on the destroyer, safe and on my way home.

Then all hell let loose.

"Get up against the bulkhead!" shouted the sailor.

I stumbled across the deck and pressed against the gray metal. I heard planes. Stukas, thirty to forty of them, diving on the Worcester like a swarm of angry bees. Bombs rained down

APRIL 26th—JUNE 1st 1940

like confetti around the ship. The destroyer, so filled with troops it was top heavy, heeled over wildly at heart-stopping, stomach-lurching angles to evade the falling bombs. Bombs to the rear lifted the stern clear of the water. The massive propellers screamed until the ship crashed down again. Colossal columns of water washed over the ship. *Oh God, it's out of the frying pan into the fire*, I thought, eyes closed tight, body trying to disappear into the bulkhead. By some miracle, not one of the 100 bombs dropped by the German planes made a direct hit on the ship. Shrapnel killed forty-six and wounded another one hundred and eighty before the attacks tapered off. As sanity returned, I opened my eyes and looked round. The planes had disappeared. The *Worcester*, with its crowded decks, was steaming across The Channel to the British coast. *Thank God for the navy!* I may have been exhausted by the day's events, but I was exhilarated. I was returning safely home, one of 64,429 men on this horrific day.

"Look at that, mate," one of the sailors nudged me. "Bet the white cliffs of Dover have never looked so good."

He was right. It was a wonderful sight.

Having failed in battle, we poured off the ship expecting a cold reception. It may have been a defeated army coming home, but a jubilant welcome awaited us. The local populace offered friendly smiles and joyous greetings. Better still, the Red Cross and women volunteers were ready with hot cups of tea, cocoa, sticky buns, and sandwiches. Exhausted and bleary-eyed, hungry if not starving, we soaked up the warm reception. Appreciatively, we smoked the proffered cigarettes, gulped down hot, sweet tea and sandwiches before dragging ourselves onto the waiting trains.

I pushed forward to give my name and number to the clerks. I wanted Ivy to know as soon as possible that I was alive and well. Then I made my way onto the train and collapsed into a corner seat. As the carriage filled up, my eyelids closed.

Darky squeezed through the crowds into the carriage. Making his way along the corridor, he noticed me in the corner of the compartment. He stepped inside, nudged me awake and nodded towards the train on the other side of the platform.

"I thought you'd have been on that train, Gus."

"Why?" I muttered, without bothering to open my eyes.

"It's going to Newcastle."

Suddenly wide-awake, I spun round to look out of the window at the train, then I looked back at the man who had woken me. Jumping up, I hugged Darky while we enthusiastically pounded the living daylights out of each other's back.

"You made it back, you bugger! You made it back!" I yelled full of joy.

"Of course I did," Darky answered, grinning from ear to ear. "Got to collect that pint you owe me. You'd better hurry. That train's leaving any minute."

"Right, see you later, Darky."

I struggled to pull my rucksack from the luggage rack and tried to force my way through the jumbled mass of bodies crowding onto the train. Looking out of the window through the clouds of steam, I saw the Newcastle train pull out of the station. Tears of frustration and disappointment pricked my eyelids as I fell back against the seat, eyes closed, cursing myself for getting on the wrong train. The train started moving. I opened my eyes and looked across at Darky.

"Nice to see you back safe and sound, Darky. Guess I'll be buying you that pint tonight."

JUNE 1940—APRIL 1942.

Dunkirk Leave

At Billericay camp, we ate, slept, and rested to build our strength. If we tried to do anything else, nurses immediately sent us back to our beds with orders to rest. As I snoozed and rested, I missed Winston Churchill's rousing June 4th speech in the House of Commons.

> ". . . we shall defend our island, whatever the cost may be, we shall fight on the beaches, we shall fight on the landing grounds, we shall fight in the fields and in the streets, we shall fight in the hills, we shall never surrender . . ."

Churchill's powerful words reflected the newly emerging Dunkirk Spirit. The complacency which developed during the period of the 'Phoney War' was transformed by the miracle of Dunkirk.

Of the 850 vessels, large and small, that took part in 'Operation Dynamo' 243 were lost and 45 damaged. The Royal Air Force lost 106 fighter planes and the British Expeditionary

Force lost almost all of its equipment—682 tanks, 120,000 vehicles, 2,700 artillery pieces and 90,000 rifles. Over 68,000 men were killed, wounded or taken prisoner. Nevertheless, in the nine desperate days of 'Operation Dynamo', 338,226 men were rescued. The escape of so many brave young men from the clutches of the German Army was a great morale booster. The people were now united and galvanized into action against the enemy. Despite the odds against them, they believed Britain would win this war.

◆ ◆ ◆

Recuperation complete, I was kitted out from head to toe. Then, in my new battle-dress, I was allowed home on leave. Turning the corner of Thorrold Terrace, I could see Ivy in the street talking with Mrs. Small, our elderly neighbour. Ivy, standing with her back towards me, didn't see me coming. Eventually, Mrs. Small's poor eyesight recognized me, or at least my uniform. Tapping Ivy's arm, she nodded in my direction. Ivy turned to look. Squealing with delight, she flung herself into my arms. I thought my heart would burst. Lifting Ivy off her feet, I twirled her round until we were dizzy, and we embraced fiercely as if we would never be parted.

"You're home safe and sound," she murmured, eyes closed, head resting on my shoulder. We were together again, safe and together, at least for a little while. Joan appeared on the doorstep. Seeing me, she gave a joyful cry and ran to join us. That evening was a time for hugging and sharing. The little house glowed in the warmth and happiness we all felt at being together. Once Joan was in bed, I told Ivy of my experiences at Dunkirk. She held my hand firmly in hers while, in a quiet but strained voice, I shared my fears that I would not make it home, my horror at seeing so many of my comrades being killed before my eyes, my sadness at the deaths of so many good men. That night, she held me close as I slept, shuddering and crying out at dreams filled with images so terrifying she could not imagine. Her heart opened wide with the need to love and protect me. The normality of being home filled me with grateful relief.

My mother organized a family get together at her home to celebrate my safe return. My sister, Rene, was there, and Aunt Bessie had travelled from South Shields to see everyone. We arrived early. As we chatted and sipped tea, I noticed my father was withdrawn and quiet.

"Are you all right, Pop?"

"Oh, it's nothing much. Just a little tired of things. The war's getting me down I suppose."

"Tell him what's really going on. It's a disgrace," my mother interrupted.

I bridled with anger as I learned about my father's difficult situation. My father, known to everyone in the family as Pop, was only eighteen years old when he left his native Sweden to travel the world—and travel the world he did, working as a cook on merchant ships. A natural linguist, he taught himself English, Spanish, French, Mandarin Chinese, and German. In 1910, he settled in England, finding work as a ship's chandler on Middlesbrough dock with Messrs Gjertson, Wernstrom, and Co. Because of his employment, Pop knew the River Tees like the back of his hand, as well as the ships and captains who regularly docked in Middlesbrough. He was a foreign national with an intimate knowledge of the river, port, and docks, and if captured, he would be a valuable asset to the enemy.

During World War I, for reasons of security, Pop, his wife, and baby son, (my brother Eric,) were interned and forced to move to Leeds, a town sixty miles away. Returning to Middlesbrough at war's end, they picked up the threads of their lives once more. Bitter about his treatment by the British government, Pop vowed never to become a British citizen. Now, twenty-five years later, it was World War II, and while he had not been interned again, he had been placed under severe restrictions.

"I have to carry a certificate of registration as an alien, at all times," he told me. "That is not so bad, but as soon as war was declared, I was placed under a curfew. I can't leave the house between 8:00 p.m. and 6:00 a.m., and I must report to the police station every day. Then, to add insult to injury, they prohibit me from being in or using a boat on the River Tees—all this while you were in France fighting for King and country. And the saints preserve me from petty bureaucrats," Pop continued, his voice growing louder with anger and frustration, "I even need special permission to use my bicycle at work. What irks me as much, if not more than the restrictions imposed upon me, is dealing with that pompous little official in the town hall. He's an overzealous tyrant. Each time another, more rigorous restriction is imposed, I can tell by the smug expression on his face how he relishes the power he wields over my life."

Disillusioned, disgusted, and embittered, Pop was trying not to let his feelings spoil the party. Angered by this treatment of my father, I promised him, "As soon as I get back to camp, I'm going to see my commanding officer about it. It's just not right."

At that moment, Eric arrived with his wife Mary. Having recently joined the merchant navy, Eric strutted about showing off his dark blue tunic. Always a braggart and full of self-admiration, Eric thought he was God's gift to women. He looked smart and knew it. Showing off the gold braid, which decorated his tunic, he boasted about how much he had paid for each strand. Looking me, his little brother, up and down, Eric took in my new uniform.

"Next time you get a new uniform, you want to make sure it fits," he sneered.

Ivy, knowing how I almost didn't make it home from Dunkirk, was incensed. Quick as a flash, she snapped, "Well, at least Norman got his uniform for free!"

In the stunned silence that followed, you could have heard ice cream melt. Everyone sat motionless, mouths agape with shock. I held Ivy's hand, grinning broadly and feeling proud of her courage. No one could believe that extremely shy and quiet Ivy had put self-centred Eric in his place.

"Eric's rudeness helped Ivy find her tongue," Pop remarked to my mother. Amazed and amused, he started to chuckle. The tension dissolved. Everyone began to laugh too as Pop drolly commented, "I think she got you there, Eric."

On returning to Barton Stacey camp, I went straight to see Major Robinson who quickly arranged for me to see the colonel. Angrily, I told Colonel MacLaren all about the severe restrictions that had been imposed upon my father.

"My father has a son in the merchant navy, a daughter who is a nurse, and another son in the army. If this is how the British government treats the father of one of its soldiers, I don't want to be in the army, sir!" I recklessly concluded.

Fortunately, the colonel agreed that my father's treatment was extreme and inappropriate.

"Leave this with me, Corporal. I'll get back to you when I have some news."

True to his word, the colonel sent me a message within the week. All restrictions on my father had been lifted. I was jubilant. Moments later, I was gloating in satisfaction as I imagined the petty bureaucrat's displeasure at having to inform Pop that he was now free of all restrictions.

"Thank you, Colonel."

Defending the Realm

With the fall of France in June, Britain was beginning a new phase in the war. Germany was on the verge of launching "Operation Sea Lion", a sea-borne invasion of Britain along the south coast. The deliverance at Dunkirk had brought the troops home, but they were not in good shape to defend the country against a determined invasion. Every British Army division was in disarray and without its full complement of men. The British Expeditionary Force had lost almost all of its heavy equipment, transport and personal weapons in France. After returning from Dunkirk, all 62 (C.W.) Company had on training exercises was one rifle between seven men and one machine gun per section. The military was in dire straits: the country's situation grave.

A CORPORAL'S WAR

Winston Churchill personally approached President Roosevelt to plead for arms, aircraft and destroyers. Britain was already buying weapons from private companies in the United States, which was bound by the confines of the Neutrality Act. Now he was asking for urgent shipments of stocks of weapons held in reserve and surplus to the requirements of the American War Department. America responded by sending half a million rifles, 100 million rounds of .30 calibre ammunition, machine guns, and mortars. Some of the rifles were made during World War I; nevertheless, they were speedily distributed to the troops and to the Home Guard.

All available men, young and old, volunteered for the Home Guard. As the weeks passed, the force soon numbered one and a half million men. At first, the only weapons they had were pitchforks, machetes, clubs, pikes, sporting rifles, and shotguns. They trained and drilled, learning how to meet and repel enemy invaders. Concrete pill-boxes were set up at crossroads, signs were taken down. Behind extensive minefields and barbed wire, they kept watch night and day to defend their island.

In industry, men and women worked tirelessly to produce the weapons and equipment needed by the armed forces, particularly British aircraft factories, which were turning out four and a half fighter planes every day.

All effort was concentrated on preventing the enemy from landing. Soldiers, along with civilian contractors, were put to work building anti-invasion defences to protect the country. Roadblocks, tank traps and pill-boxes were thrown up behind the most likely landing areas. In July, 62 (C.W.) Company moved to Axminster, Devon, to undertake construction of the "Taunton Stop Line", returning to a tented camp at Barton Stacey ten days later.

In the meantime, the Battle of Britain commenced July 10th with the Luftwaffe making heavy raids on shipping convoys in The Channel and on military targets in the south of England. The Luftwaffe had already made scattered night raids over England, bombing several towns and cities in a vain attempt to destroy civilian morale. If there was to be an invasion of Britain, the Luftwaffe had to win control of the air space over the English Channel by decimating the Royal Air Force. Reichsmarshall Herman Goering, given that his Luftwaffe strength was double that of the Royal Air Force, firmly believed this could be achieved in five days. In France, close to The Channel, there was a build up of enemy air bases and German divisions ready to act when Britain became defenceless.

The Royal Air Force was all that stood between Britain and the enemy. At this moment in history, the whole future of the country rested on this one branch of the armed forces. Unfortunately for Goering, the commander-in-chief was Air Chief Marshal Sir Hugh Dowding. Dowding was experienced in all aspects of aerial warfare, whereas Goering was not. This balanced out the Luftwaffe's superior numbers. The British also had the advantage of radar to forewarn them of enemy attacks. Plus, when the air battles took place in the skies above Britain, British pilots baling out were landing on native soil soon to fight again. Not so for German pilots who bailed out. If they did not land in The Channel, they landed in the Home Counties of England. By the time their toes touched the ground, they were usually surrounded by members of the Home Guard ready to escort them to the nearest police station. With aircraft production meeting all requirements, Dowding's only concern was that he would not have sufficient pilots for the fighting that lay ahead.

On August 8th, 62 (C.W.) Company moved to Bure Homage, Christchurch, to reconnoitre and mark out proposed projector positions on the south coast. In the ten days we were stationed there, the Luftwaffe joined battle with the Royal Air Force over Portland and other coastal towns. I worried about my family when I heard of Middlesbrough and other industrial towns in the northeast, with their steel works and shipyards, being attacked and bombed. The airfields of Hampshire, Kent and the Thames Estuary also came in for their share of attacks. As 62 (C.W.) Company returned to Barton Stacey on August 18th, the biggest raid of the Battle of Britain was taking place.

Massed formations crossed the coast at Dover to attack the airfields. One hundred bombs fell on Kenley fighter base alone killing fifteen people and injuring thirty-one. Despite all this, the base was back in operation two hours later. The day's fierce fighting ended with seventy-one German aircraft down as opposed to twenty-seven RAF fighters lost and 10 pilots killed.

Two days later, Winston Churchill spoke in the House of Commons to express the nation's gratitude to the Royal Air Force.

"Never in the field of human conflict was so much owed by so many to so few."

August 24th: German pilots bombed London.

August 25th: The night bombers of the Royal Air Force began raids on Berlin in retaliation. This in turn led to a nine-week campaign of terror bombing of London. Diverting the Luftwaffe's attention to London was a huge tactical mistake. Without realising it, German commanders had almost been successful in destroying the Royal Air Force. Now Dowding had a breathing space to recover and come back up to strength with fresh pilots and machines.

Saturday, September 7th, The Blitz began. The enemy was now concentrating on mass bombing raids, mainly against London. For hours and hours at a time, bombs rained down on the East End, the docks, oil tanks and gasworks. Warehouses became blazing infernos. Fires raged throughout the night, guiding German night-time bombers to their target. Rows of working class houses became piles of rubble. Hundreds of people were killed each night the bombers came calling. Rescuers did not finish digging out the dead and wounded from the ruins before the sirens sounded again.

◆ ◆ ◆

As The Blitz on London continued, 62 (C.W.) Company moved to Robertsbridge, Sussex, to build defences in the area. Half the population in the coastal areas had been evacuated inland. We set to, demolishing bomb-damaged buildings in the Rye and Winchelsea areas. We shored and sandbagged buildings in

JUNE 1940—APRIL 1942

and around Hastings. Sappers laid mines all along the south coast. I practised using poison gas, but even during these exercises, I always carried real poison gas in case it was ever needed. To represent the different gases, coloured water was used. I demonstrated to officers how well the gases would work by using the water truck to spray the coloured liquids. The officers, mainly concerned with the effectiveness of the chemicals in halting traffic during a real invasion, watched the demonstrations closely, nodding in satisfaction with this particular method of defence.

Busy on the downs near Hastings, I saw signs of the battles taking place overhead. While the wheat was harvested, new crops sewn, and the hop-pickers worked with gas masks slung over their shoulders, great, wheeling dog-fights took place in

Sgt. French and Sgt. Wellington hold the tail of a Dornier 17 brought down by a 62 Company Bren gun. Robertsbridge September, 1940.

the blue skies above. Vapour trails marked the battlefield. Black dots buzzed in and out of the clouds, dodging attack or chasing enemy planes. Then, from the mêlée, a doomed aircraft would appear, black plumes trailing as it pirouetted from the sky, while the white speck of a parachute glided gently down to earth behind it. Crumpled, burned out wreckage of fallen planes littered the fields. Although I had no personal involvement in the Battle of Britain, I did hear rumours in the village pubs that many a German pilot, who baled out on British soil, was surprised to learn that no German troops had, as yet, invaded the country.

◆ ◆ ◆

The bombing of London continued, as did attacks on Liverpool, Portsmouth, Southampton and the Supermarine Works at Woolston, which was frantically churning out spitfires. Buckingham Palace was hit. Wishing to be Londoners like everyone else, the King and Queen showed remarkable bravery by remaining in residence with their daughters.

On September 15th, considered the day the Battle of Britain was won, one thousand enemy planes, five fighters escorting every bomber, were sent against London. Ferocious, widespread pandemonium filled the skies as Fighter Command sent up everything it had to attack and repel the bomber sorties flown by German aircraft that day. Sixty enemy planes were shot down. The evening news mistakenly informed the public that the RAF had destroyed 185 enemy planes. Although misleading, these high figures were a great morale booster, not only for the Royal Air Force, but for the civilian population too. Despite suffering from severe exhaustion and nervous strain, the heroic boys in blue had risen to the challenge forced upon them.

London was being bombed continually; the people endured. Despite the nightly terrors of Luftwaffe bombs, the loss of loved ones, homes, and possessions, the populace developed a steely resolve, camaraderie, and teamwork to sustain them through the difficulties that lay ahead.

JUNE 1940—APRIL 1942

In its sorties across The Channel, the Royal Air Force damaged 200 barges gathered in the Channel ports, more than one tenth of the enemy invasion fleet. This resulted in Hitler calling off his invasion plans indefinitely. Despite everything Germany had thrown at the Royal Air Force, the Luftwaffe had not established air superiority. The Germans had failed to achieve their objectives. They continued bombing British cities and industrial installations, but no longer with the aim of preparing to invade.

On October 13th, twenty people were killed, 105 wounded in an air raid on Middlesbrough. The heaviest attack of the month came against London two days later. In addition to the usual high-explosive bombs, German aircraft released an additional 70,000 incendiary bombs causing 900 fires. Eight hundred people were wounded and over 400 killed. During the remainder of the war, with The Royal Air Force and anti-aircraft guns ineffective against the night-time bombing raids of the Luftwaffe, German planes struck out far and wide over Britain, attacking industry and communications. There were many casualties and much suffering, yet British resolve did not falter.

Ilfracombe

Early in November, the company moved to Ilfracombe in Devon. Ivy and Joan made the nineteen-hour train journey from Middlesbrough to join me. Travelling with them was Nancy Gardner, whose husband Jimmy was also in 62 (C.W.) Company. It was a long tiring journey, especially for Joan, who'd just turned three. Even though Ivy was excited about spending time with me, it was a dismal, gloomy trip. In the short November days, daylight hours were few. When it grew dark, the weakest of bulbs lit the carriages, and the blinds had to be lowered because of the blackout. Ivy told me how an officious ticket collector did not make the journey any more pleasant.

"How old is this child? Where's her ticket?" he'd demanded, full of self-importance.

"She's three," Ivy meekly replied.

"You should have bought a ticket for her. Children three and over have to have a ticket."

"Oh, I'm sorry. I thought children under five could travel without a ticket," Ivy tried to explain.

As he pressed for payment, his tirade intensified.

"Don't give me that nonsense. You were trying to get away without paying. Well, you can pay up now. You're not getting away with it, missus, not today."

That's when Nancy spoke up.

"Shame on you!" she said. "We're going to see our husbands, who are in the army, fighting for their country. Who knows if this will be the last time we will ever be together, and you're worrying about a ticket?"

Faster than a falling bomb, his demeanour changed in response to Nancy's scolding.

"Don't worry about the ticket, missus. We'll forget all about it," he mollified them, leaving them in peace for the remainder of the journey.

I lived in the barracks until Ivy and Joan arrived, then I billeted out. We moved into lodgings, renting a room in one of the many large, Victorian, terraced houses to be found in the seaside town. They were so different from the working class housing in Middlesbrough, which consisted of cobbled streets packed with small, drab, terraced houses. My house, in common with most working class homes in Middlesbrough, had only four rooms—two up (the bedrooms) and two down (a living room and a scullery,) no bathroom, and the toilet was outside, down the yard.

Ivy enjoyed spending time with a new friend, Irene McMahon, from Blackburn, whose husband, Bill, was in 58 Company R.E. Ivy liked Irene's bright eyes and hearty laughter. She always seemed to be smiling. Nothing ever got her down. In her broad Lancashire accent, she told Ivy saucy jokes over cups of tea in Rosie's Tea Shop and discussed how different life was in the south of England compared to their hometowns. I overheard them talking one night while in the pub. Bill and I were at the bar, buying drinks.

"I'm amazed at how ordinary, working people live in the south of England," said Irene. "They all seem to have bathrooms inside their houses and gardens to grow flowers and vegetables, so different to what we're used to."

"When Norman told me about it, I thought he was exaggerating, but he wasn't, not one bit," said Ivy. "I'll tell you what I enjoy the most, not having to leave a warm fireside to go down the yard on a cold winter's night."

The two women giggled.

"It'll be hard going home. I'm enjoying our luxurious stay in Ilfracombe," said Irene. "Besides, I'd rather be with Bill. We've only been married a few months."

"I wanted to go home almost as soon as I arrived," Ivy confided. "Our first landlady was a mean-spirited woman. She only gave us half a bucket of coal a day for the fire. That's not much to keep a family warm in this weather. When the coal was used up and the room became cold, we had to jump into bed to keep warm."

"Lucky you," said Irene, giggling.

Ivy was still blushing when we returned from the bar. She continued her story.

"That terrible woman was a heartless robber, wasn't she, Norman? She rented a room to two Austrian Jewish women who'd come to England to escape persecution in their own country. She charged them an exorbitant rent. She was so haughty, saying they could well afford it. I was relieved when she told us to find other digs, said she could make more money renting rooms to refugees than from hard up British Tommies and their families. It was the best thing she could have done for us. If I hadn't moved out, I probably wouldn't have met you, and our new landlady is as different from her as chalk from cheese. She can't do enough to make us enjoy our stay, can she? She didn't even blink when Joan developed a bad case of chickenpox."

"Your Joan's an angel. I hope when I have children they'll be just like her. It's better for her here. At least we're keeping safe away from the air raids," said Irene.

"Yes," Ivy agreed. "When we're at home, we hide in the pantry under the stairs during most of them, but I don't know how safe it is. It's quite a ways to the nearest shelter in Collier's field."

"My mother has an Anderson shelter in her back garden," said Bill, taking hold of Irene's hand, "but she lives too far away for it to be any use to Irene."

"I'm going to enjoy this time here as much as I can. It's precious," said Irene.

"It's a treat for us to have you both here," I said. "The winter weather should be a lot milder in Devon, and it's a pleasant change from Price's factory, isn't it, Ivy?"

On New Year's Eve, we went to the local public house to meet our friends.

"I can't believe it's so quiet in here," Ivy said.

Bill McMahon (left) with Corporal Wickman

I called across the saloon, "Hey, landlord, when will people start coming in to celebrate New Year's Eve?"

"Oh, I don't expect many more people here tonight."

I was incredulous. "What do you mean? It's New Year's Eve!"

"Aye, it might well be, but we don't celebrate it like you folks do in the north. To us down here it's just another night."

"I don't believe it," Bill muttered.

I was speechless.

Disappointment was etched on everyone's face.

"What a let down! I was really looking forward to this evening's celebrations," grumbled Darky.

The men approached the bar to order some drinks.

"Doesn't anybody go first footing down here?" asked Blondie.

"What's first footing, and what's so special about New Year's Eve?" the landlord wanted to know.

"New Year's is great. We have parties and celebrate until the early hours of the morning. Everyone has a wonderful time, singing, dancing and getting tipsy," I said.

Darky said, "A minute or two before midnight, a man with dark hair goes outside the house, that's usually me when I'm at home. When it's midnight, he knocks on the door and then comes inside to let in the New Year, bringing a piece of coal and a silver coin for luck."

"People go from house to house to bring the New Year cheer, and in return, they receive a drop of the hard stuff and a piece of dark fruitcake or a mince pie," I told the landlord.

"You won't find any of that nonsense in this part of the world," said the landlord.

It was unbelievable, like being in a foreign country, a miserable one at that. Then to top it all, snow fell on the town for the first time in twenty years. Ivy's face fell. She'd been looking forward to a mild winter in Ilfracombe away from the harsh northern climate of Middlesbrough.

Some days, Ivy and Joan watched me drilling with the rest of the company. Being in charge of maintenance, when drill and parade were over, I marched the maintenance team, about thirty men, through the town to the maintenance depot. More often than not, as we passed Rosie's Tea Shop, I ordered, "Right wheel," and in we all trooped for a cup of tea and buns. Ivy and Joan usually joined me there.

Passing in his car one day, Colonel MacLaren spied us in the café. He ordered his driver to stop the car and find out "What the hell is going on?" and "Who's responsible for all those men being in the tea shop?"

Of course, I ended up being placed on a charge and losing a stripe. My explanation that I only wanted to give the men a chance to warm up before going on to the cold depot didn't hold water with Major Robinson. I took the loss of a stripe in my stride. It was becoming a regular event. A week or so later, I'd get it back; the army was still short of men who were NCO material.

"I think Colonel MacLaren's got it in for me," I told Ivy. "He seems to make a point of passing Rosie's Tea Shop whenever he's out and about in his car."

"Maybe you should stop going into Rosie's on the way to the depot so you don't lose your stripe. One of these days you might lose it for good."

However, the possibility of losing my stripe was no deterrent when I wanted a warming cup of tea.

One afternoon, as I was practising my drilling skills with twelve men, under the watchful eye of Sergeant Wellington, Joan, out walking with Ivy, spotted me and began calling out, "There's my dad! Daddy, Daddy"

It dismayed me to have to ignore her, but there was nothing else I could do. When I returned to our lodgings, I made it up to her by playing with her as much as I could. I knew I'd miss a large part of her growing up if the war continued for any length of time. I stored cherished memories of her joining in singing the company songs at our get-togethers with friends. She knew the words and would sing along:

> Don't turn away the Royal Engineers,
> They're next to the Navy on the sea.

JUNE 1940—APRIL 1942

But if it wasn't for the Royal Engineers,
Where would England be?
  Chorus: *Buggered if I know.*

The highlight of our evenings was cherub-faced Joan singing the chorus with all the gusto she could muster.

◆　◆　◆

Major Robinson liked to keep his men on their toes. Some thought him as mad as a hatter. One evening, I was on guard duty with five sappers at 62 Company's headquarters in the Cliff Hydro Hotel, when the major returned from a meeting.

"Good evening, Corporal."

"Good evening, sir," I replied, saluting.

The major returned the salute then proceeded to give us a lecture.

"I want you to have your gas masks and capes ready at all times. Some soldiers are getting too damned careless for their own good. You are to make sure you put them on immediately a gas warning is given. Do you understand?"

"Yes, sir," we said.

"Good. Carry on, men."

With a nod of satisfaction, Major Robinson entered the hotel. When he was out of earshot, someone said, "He's been to an officers' meeting, hasn't he? Must've had a pep talk about gas masks."

Upstairs in his quarters, a room above the guardroom, the major busied himself filling buckets with cold water. Below, we stood guard, our breath creating white wisps in the freezing night air. Suddenly, the major flung open his bedroom window. Sticking his head out of the window, he began shouting, "Gas! Gas! Gas!"

His head disappeared from view as he moved back into the room. We moved out to look up at his window, wondering what the silly blighter up to. We soon found out. Just as our gaze moved upwards, buckets of icy water cascaded downwards. Everyone was drenched, except me. As soon as the Major started shouting, I knew there was a rabbit away and slipped into my cape and gas mask. The major's head reappeared bellowing, "You're wet, and you're dead! You're all bloody dead! You're all gassed, and you're all on a charge!"

The major galloped down to the guardroom. He was surprised to find me in my cape and gas mask, staying dry.

He turned to my sodden companions and proceeded to read the riot act. "Let this be a warning to you. When someone yells gas, you prepare yourselves immediately. Understood? Dead soldiers are no good to us. Everyone but Corporal Wickman is on a charge."

◆ ◆ ◆

Heavy bombing raids pulverized nearby Portsmouth. With Major Robinson in charge, we drove our trucks to the town to collect families left homeless by the air raids. The sight of distracted men trying to comfort their tearful wives and unnaturally quiet children saddened me. I worried in case the same thing should happen to Joan and Ivy. But I put on a brave face and, following Major Robinson's lead, cheerfully told them, "All right, folks, let's get you in the trucks, and we'll take you somewhere a bit safer than this."

Once back in Ilfracombe, Major Robinson took the convoy of trucks round all the lodging houses in the area. He knocked on doors, and when the proprietors came to the door, the major began his interrogation.

"I've homeless people here who need accommodation. How many rooms have you got in the house? What space is available?"

Some landlords and landladies were unsympathetic, not in the least bit interested in providing accommodation for these unfortunate people.

"Don't come here demanding to know our business. You can clear off. We don't have any room here for evacuees," they told the major in no uncertain terms—not always so politely.

JUNE 1940—APRIL 1942

Undaunted by such hostile responses, Major Robinson would flip open his holster, take out his pistol and point it directly at the belligerent proprietors.

"You seem to misunderstand the situation here. I am not making a request. I am ordering you to find room for some of these people. Think very carefully before you speak. Give the wrong answer and your bed could be the first one available. Now, how many beds do you have for these people?"

The deadly calm fury in his face, the steely resolve in his eyes, and the deceptively quiet tones of his firm voice delivered through lips stiff with rage were so intimidating that the landlords quickly complied with his orders. It was an effective ploy. He always found rooms for everyone in his trucks. I often wondered if the major would have carried out his threats. Fortunately, it never came to that.

◆ ◆ ◆

At the end of January 1941, it was time for Ivy and Joan to return to Middlesbrough. Being on leave, I went with them. The return journey was even worse than the journey south. It was Sunday. Not a refreshment room was open on any of the stations. We spent hours huddled in freezing waiting rooms, hanging about for our connections. As the train left Thornaby station, only three miles from Middlesbrough, we brightened.

"We're almost home, thank goodness," I said, gathering a sleepy Joan in my arms ready to carry her off the train at Middlesbrough station.

"Twenty-two hours to get home. I'll be glad to get off this train," said Ivy.

Relief soon turned to disappointment and worry. As the train slowed and then stopped on the outskirts of the town, the conductor came along the carriage, informing the passengers, "There's an air raid on. The train won't be allowed into the station until the bombing's stopped. Stay seated. We'll have you home as soon as the all clear's given."

It seemed an eternity, but finally we pulled into the station. What a homecoming!

Practice makes Perfect

For 62 Company, 1941 was a year filled with trade and military training. The majority of operations were within a forty-mile radius of Ilfracombe. The company, involved in daytime exercises as well as night-time manoeuvres, spent many a long, bitterly cold night bivouacking in the fields with freezing winds nipping our noses and ears and chapping our lips. The nights I slept under the great stones of prehistoric Stonehenge were the worst. Waking up one morning, I found my groundsheet frozen to the turf. Everyone's hands and feet were numb with cold. Darky said he was chilled to the bone and started jumping up and down, waving his arms to get warm.

The company was engaged in extensive training on Exmoor with the five-inch rocket, or Finch, because its performance was poor and needed improvement. A great deal of effort was put into experiments and figuring out how to overcome the difficulties. Training took place round the clock, but for safety reasons, firing was only allowed during daylight hours.

One experiment involved developing a mortar we could move around and fire from a fifteen-hundredweight truck. I was one of the first drivers to test the new idea. The base of the truck was reinforced, and a special platform built onto it. I drove onto the parade ground for the test to take place. The mortar was fired. The bottom fell out of the truck, which instantly folded up into a 'V' shape under the impetus of the blast. I'd been sitting in the truck and had to go to the hospital to have my bruised back checked out. I wasn't seriously injured, although I did have a sore back for several days. For the Royal Engineers, it was back to the drawing board.

Sometimes practice went well. Occasionally, there were demonstrations to show British and Indian troops what the projectors and gas bombs could do. Explosive shells were used, but instead of poison gases, coloured materials were substituted to produce a memorable, multihued spectacular for the watching soldiers.

On May 20th, 1941, there was a special demonstration on Exmoor by the Chemical Warfare Company. It involved an experimental design of multiple mountings of the Finch. Colonel MacLaren, Commander of the Chemical Warfare troops, stood in front of a battery of these rockets. With his back to them, he shouted his orders. Lifting his arm high above his head he yelled, "Fire!" and brought his arm down. Soldiers fired the rockets, which soared over the colonel's head. The sappers assembled another battery of rockets.

The colonel lifted his arm again and shouted, "Fire!"

One of the platforms collapsed on firing. The shell bounced along the ground, breaking up into pieces as it travelled towards the colonel. Seeing the danger, a horrified murmur rose from the watching soldiers, turning into a roar of warning powerless to prevent a fragment striking the colonel in the back. Medical officers arrived on the scene in minutes, but despite all their efforts, Colonel MacLaren died fifty minutes later, where he had fallen. I was shocked and saddened. Even though I'd had some run-ins with the colonel, I liked and respected him as a man and as an officer. Two days later, with the officers, NCOs, and men of the group lining the streets of their respective stations, the coffin carrying Colonel MacLaren's body was taken from Lynton to his home on Salisbury Plain. Each of us gave half-a-crown to the collection to provide an obelisk as a memorial for him on the moors near Minehead. It's still there to this day.

The training continued until the spring of 1942, when I received word that I was being posted overseas.

◆   ◆   ◆

I walked along Thorrold Terrace, knowing that this home leave would be bittersweet. Ivy and I had been expecting the army to send me away soon. Now the time had arrived, my heart was heavy. A posting overseas meant five years abroad with no chance of returning to England during that time.

Walking through the front door, I called, "Hello, sweetheart. I'm home."

Ivy and Joan kissed and hugged me tightly. I was thrilled to be home. We sat at the kitchen table. Joan sat on my lap, her head on my chest, hugging me as hard as she could. At four and a half, Joan was daddy's little girl. Ivy filled the kettle with water to make a cup of tea.

"How long have you got?" she asked.

"Fourteen days."

"Fourteen days? That's a long leave." She stopped suddenly, kettle in her hand. "Oh, I . . . You're being sent overseas." Her voice was flat with misery. She lit the gas under the kettle then came and stood behind me, her chin resting on the top of my head, her arms round my neck.

"When?" she asked.

I reached up with my free arm to squeeze and rub Ivy's shoulder, my other arm held Joan close.

"Some time in April. I've been issued with tropical kit, so I'm going to either the Middle East or India."

With heavy hearts, we held one another in a family embrace. I knew Ivy felt as wretched as I did as we considered the loneliness of the coming years. The kettle's shrill whistle pierced our thoughts. Abstractedly, Ivy patted my shoulder before moving to the stove to turn the kettle off.

"We've got fourteen days, Ivy. Let's make them special. It's got to last us a long time."

We made the most of our precious time together, knowing that once I left, it would be five long years before we would see each other again. The few days I was home, we created memories to cherish. Braving the cold March weather, we went to Albert Park and strolled round the lake. Even though rationing restricted our food supply, we managed to spare some stale bread for Joan to feed to the ducks. Ivy carried a paper bag containing small pieces of bread, and I held Joan up so she could throw the pieces over the fence surrounding the lake. We smiled as she wriggled and screamed with excitement when dozens of ducks zoomed in from all directions to gobble up the unexpected feast.

JUNE 1940—APRIL 1942

When we became chilled, we went into The Dorman Memorial Museum built as a memorial to soldiers in the Green Howards who had died in the South Africa War. The exhibits in the animal room fascinated Joan. She gazed wide-eyed at antelope heads displayed on the walls, trophies from officers' hunting expeditions. A gory panorama, inside a large glass case, dominated one of the rooms. Joan pressed close to me for safety and stared at the taxidermist's masterpiece of a snarling, black-maned lion standing with its front paws on the body of a zebra, whose throat had been ripped out.

Well-wrapped up against the cold, blustery weather, we caught the bus to Redcar to walk along golden sands and the deserted seafront promenade. We went for tea and played cards in my parents' house. We even managed an evening at the cinema. Alone at night, in the privacy of our bedroom, we savoured tender, poignant, moments, creating indestructible bonds of love to withstand the long separation we were facing.

The day of my departure, we took Joan to Ivy's mother, while we went to the railway station. I knelt down in front of Joan.

"Come on, sweetheart. Give your dad a big hug." I squeezed her tightly. "It's going to be some time before I see you again," I muttered into her soft, dark hair, kissing the top of her head.

Stretching her small arms round my neck, Joan returned my embrace.

"See you soon, Daddy," she said, her face solemn as she kissed my cheek.

But not soon enough, I thought. After five years away, would she remember who I was by the time I returned?

Ivy's mother, a warm-hearted no-nonsense Yorkshire woman, patted my arm.

"Take care, lad. Come 'ome safe. We'll be waiting for yer."

I picked up my kit bag, and taking hold of Ivy's hand, we slowly walked to the market place to meet my mother who was going with us to the railway station.

At least two dozen soldiers were on the platform, going off to war. Nancy Gardner was there, saying goodbye to her husband, Jimmy. Six other Middlesbrough lads from my company were leaving too. The typical British stiff upper lip was well in evidence. The atmosphere was subdued and restrained. A few people were attempting jokes and brightness, but for other wives and mothers there was sniffing of noses and dabbing of eyes with handkerchiefs. Some couples clung tightly to each other, tenderly whispering endearments. Dramatic shows of emotion were held at bay; nobody wanted the boys to be going away upset. Ivy clung to my arm, being quiet and brave. My mother was also quiet. Her eyes kept studying me, taking mental snapshots of my face, ready to recall when needed. Then, over the Tannoy loudspeaker system, we heard Vera Lynn's voice, singing the words of her popular song *We'll Meet Again*.

Muffled sobbing from women, whose men were about to leave, joined her words, echoing hollowly around the platform. Handkerchiefs, hastily pulled from handbags and pockets, wiped noses and dabbed away tears. The train pulled into the station, clouds of steam hissing, wheels and brakes squealing.

"Just come home safe. We'll be here, waiting for you," Ivy told me, after a long lingering kiss.

My mother, her eyes brimming with tears, simply said, "Goodbye, son. Take care."

I hugged and kissed them both. All around, farewells were taking place, quick hugs, pecks on cheeks, passionate kisses and embraces. Carriage doors clunked on closing; windows were quickly lowered; soldiers squeezed together leaning out.

"Take care of yourself."

"Don't worry about us, just come home safe."

"Write to me."

"Ta ta, sweetheart. Don't cry. It's not the end of the world."

But of course, for some of us, it was.

Moving along the platform, the railway worker checked all the doors were shut. The guard blew his whistle. Slowly, the train pulled out of the station. Hanging far out of the windows, we waved and blew kisses. Handkerchiefs, which had been pulled out of pockets and handbags to wipe away tears, were soon waving aloft in hands held high above heads, until the

JUNE 1940—APRIL 1942

train disappeared from sight. Loved ones left behind straggled out of the station. The deserted platform, only moments before filled with life, activity and emotion, stood bereft and empty.

APRIL 1942—DECEMBER 1942.

The Cape Town Castle

April 14th, 1942, tugs gently guided the *Cape Town Castle* from Mersey docks out into the estuary. As the crowded troopship embarked on the first leg of its dangerous voyage, I stood at the rail with my friends.

"I'm shaking with excitement, Darky. We're starting the adventure of a lifetime," I said.

"Me too. I just hope we get to where ever we're supposed to be going in one piece. We've got a dangerous trip ahead of us."

"I'm not going to worry about that right now, and even though I'm as miserable as sin about leaving Ivy and Joan, I'm thrilled to be seeing something of the big wide world."

"That's the ticket, Gus. Don't let anything dampen your spirits," said Hinny. "It's a great opportunity."

"We've got the army to thank for this. They'd better have decent beer where we're going or I'll be putting in a complaint," said Mac, partly joking, mostly serious. Everyone knew Mac took his drinking pleasures seriously.

Joining up with escorting destroyers and other ships to form a convoy, the *Cape Town Castle* sailed north round Ireland then headed west across the grey Atlantic waters. Travelling almost to the American coastline before heading south and then zigzagging its way across the Atlantic, the convoy managed to avoid encounters with prowling German submarines. Ships stretched out as far as the eye could see. Their many funnels billowed black smoke that was left behind to drift lazily across the horizon. To make the convoy less conspicuous, the ships were painted dark grey, and a blackout was in effect.

The *Cape Town Castle's* passengers were servicemen from the British Army, the Royal Air Force, and some nurses. Accommodations were congested. We hooted with laughter when we saw our sleeping quarters.

"Bloody hell! It's wall to wall hammocks."

"Is this where we've got to sleep for the next few weeks?"

"Look at the way they've strung them one above the other. There's barely room to breathe."

There was much hilarity that first night as we struggled into the hammocks.

I finally got settled in mine.

"Well at least they're comfortable. Let's hope it's easy to stay put if the seas become rough."

"No taking deep breaths, Gus," said Darky in the hammock above. "We're so close together that if you expand your chest, you'll knock me out of my hammock."

"And no letting it rip, Darky. Remember it's your friend down here. I don't want to be gassed out," I shot back at him.

We slept in our clothes. There seemed to be a shortage of water. We were only allowed to swill our faces and use one mug full of water to shave. Days were spent reading, snoozing, talking, playing cards, and lounging on deck. Sometimes, we ran round the deck for exercise. In the evenings, there was community singing to the accompaniment of a couple of harmonicas and a piano. We sang with gusto. Baritones and tenors, as well as voices flat and off-key, belted out songs. Some men sang solos. I sang one of George Formby's popular songs, and my friends promptly dubbed me the 'golden-voiced tenor'. Strains of 'Roll out the Barrel' and 'Run Rabbit Run' were carried afar by the sea breeze, and to really lift our spirits, we always ended with a rip roaring rendition of a favourite song such as 'Bless 'em All'.

As the ship headed south, the weather grew hotter. We changed into tropical kit, and the crew erected awnings to provide shade. When we got the chance, we enjoyed the warm sunshine and fresh sea breezes by stripping down to our shorts and snoozing on the decks under the awnings. One of my naps almost put me on a charge. I slept for several hours, safely in the shade so I thought, but then the ship changed course, leaving me unprotected from the sun's fiery rays.

Hinny and Darky found me fast asleep, oblivious to my predicament. Hinny shook me awake.

"Gus, come on wake up. You're being fried to a crisp."

"You daft bugger!" said Darky, his voice tinged with concern. "You're as red as a boiled lobster."

I sat up and looked at myself. I was beginning to feel sorer than a hiker's blistered heel.

"You should go and see the Medical Officer. You might get sunstroke."

"No. I'll suffer in silence. I don't want to be put on a charge just because I've got a bit of sunburn."

And suffer I did for the next five days, first with excruciating soreness followed by irritating itchiness until I began to peel. Sitting on the deck, I passed the time pulling large sheets of dry skin from my body then watched it gently float away when I tossed it overboard.

Fifteen days after leaving Liverpool, the ship arrived at Freetown, West Africa. With the blackout lifted while the ship was anchored in the harbour to take on supplies, our spirits rose, relieved to be free of those long evenings on deck, sitting in the dark."

"Now, all we need is to be allowed to leave the ship," I said, looking at the shore with longing.

We leaned over the ship's rail as natives in tiny dugout canoes came alongside to sell fruit and dive for coins we threw into the clear blue waters. During the four days we lay at anchor, we saw plenty of small craft buzzing around the harbour. Two aircraft carriers, the *Van Galen* and the *Albatross*, were anchored nearby. Planes, screaming about the skies, disturbed this bustling, but otherwise peaceful, harbour.

APRIL 1942—DECEMBER 1942

"Maybe they're practising manoeuvres to be ready for action in Burma," I said.

"Aye. Now that we're here in Freetown, we know we're not going to the Middle East or North Africa," said Tommy.

"So it's got to be India and Burma for us too," said Darky.

"Most of the men seem to have found their sea-legs now. There's not so much moaning and groaning and throwing up, so they should enjoy the rest of the voyage more," I said, pleased that I hadn't suffered from sea sickness.

One afternoon, a tropical storm blew in. From black skies, heavy rain sheeted down. We made the most of this fine opportunity for a shower, stripping off our clothes to bathe in the refreshing downpour. It certainly dispelled the strong, stale, body odours and revived the ship for a while.

Clean and refreshed, I lounged on deck, deep in thought.

"What are you thinking?" asked Darky.

"Just something my dad said. He was in the merchant navy years ago. Went all round the world before settling in Middlesbrough. Before we left, he told me to go on my travels with an open mind and an open heart. 'You may pass that way only once in your lifetime,' he said. 'Learn what you can from the people and their cultures. Don't waste time wishing you were back home. If you do, later in life you'll regret not making the most of your opportunities while you were away.'"

"That's good advice to follow."

"Oh, I know. Are you as excited as I am, Darky? I've always wanted to travel after hearing some of Pop's stories. I'm going to miss Ivy and Joan so much, and yet it's really exciting. I'm fulfilling a dream."

"I'm excited same as you, but I'm nervous as well. It's going to be so different to what we're used to." Then in a brighter, more positive tone of voice, Darky continued. "But that's all right. It's not as if we're going out there on our own. Hell, we've got the army to take care of us," he finished with a mischievous gleam in his eye.

We burst out laughing.

"I hope they do a better job of feeding us than these cooks do. I'm sick of this manky food," I said.

"You know the army better than that, Gus. I'd say you're being a bit unreasonable, wouldn't you?"

Heading south after leaving Freetown, the ship crossed the equator on May 5th. We were again hot and sticky and bored with the monotony of the journey. To provide some entertainment, officers organized boxing matches between the various army units. For a few hours, boredom was left behind as the excitement of the competitions had us cheering and rooting for our champions.

Those evenings when I felt the occasional pang of homesickness, I stood by the deck rail looking out at the blackness of the ocean stretching into infinity, watching the phosphorescence in the waters below or the gleam of moonlight on the waves. Even though I tried to focus my mind on Pop's advice, my heart refused to obey, feeling as black and as empty as the expanse of water before me. Ivy and Joan were the phosphorescence, the only brightness and colour in my world—and I was separated from them, thousands of miles and five years away from them. I pictured myself at home with Ivy, sitting in front of the fire, watching her knitting, while the clock ticked reassuringly on the mantelpiece. I imagined Joan on my knee, coyly giggling with pleasure, as I coaxed her to sing the new song she had learned. Unshed tears threatened to overflow. *I'm getting maudlin, Ivy, but five years.... It's a long, long time to be away from you.*

Darky usually sought me out after allowing me some quiet time.

"Come on, Gus. Come and join the lads. We're having a game of cards. I don't like to see you so miserable."

You're not married, Darky. How can you imagine how wretched I feel?

"Come on, mate. Remember what your dad said and come inside."

The weather turned cool and dull. We changed back into battle-dress. During the night of May 15th, we heard two explosions. I wondered if ships further back in the convoy had encountered some mines. There were no more mishaps before the ship sailed into Durban, South Africa, in the early hours of May 18th.

Welcome to Durban

The town, ablaze with lights, looked inviting after the tedium of the past five weeks. Excitement filled the air, as we bustled about preparing our kit for the four days we would spend ashore. Disembarking at 1:30 p.m., we marched the three miles to Durban's racecourse where we were to sleep in the grandstand. But this didn't worry us. We were off the ship and on dry land. No seasickness here and a town just waiting to be explored. The townspeople, delighted to see British soldiers, gave us a warm welcome, cheering and waving as we marched past. We knew we were in for a wonderful time in Durban.

Excitement woke me early to a beautiful day. Powerful, prancing racehorses exercising on the course captured my attention. Black jockeys perched in saddles, noses bent low over the horses' necks, backsides pointed to the heavens. Natives arrived early, pestering us to buy fruit. I wandered around, munching on the juiciest grapes I'd ever tasted.

Civilians started arriving at the racecourse. I watched as a smartly dressed, middle-aged couple stepped from their gleaming, black Humber. The man, with silver-grey hair and dark, horned rimmed glasses, was short and chubby. The woman with him, dressed in a sky blue dress with white, polka dot trim and matching hat, was as thin as a beanpole. Her dark, sharp eyes darted here and there, observing the scenes around her with interest.

"Can I help you?" I asked.

"Yes, I'm Doctor Stewart Wilson and this is my wife. We'd like to invite some of the men to go for a drive this morning to see a little of South Africa while they're here."

"Oh, I'd like to do that. All right if I bring a couple of friends?"

"It would be our pleasure," replied the doctor.

I sought out Darky and Blondie. "Come on. Drop what you're doing. We're going for a drive."

We settled into the Humber's comfortable, leather seats, and Dr. Wilson whisked us away to explore Natal. The smooth ride of the luxury car was a huge improvement to the bone-jarring trucks I was used to driving. Proudly, Dr. and Mrs. Wilson pointed out various landmarks. Heading towards Pietermaritzburg, we drove along Old Main Road, which ran along the crest of the hills. The scenery was magnificent. To allow us a better look, Dr. Wilson stopped the car near Drummond.

"Here's a good place to look at the view. This area," he said, pointing north, "is called Valley of a Thousand Hills. Those collections of huts dotting the hillsides are Zulu kraals or homesteads. This is where the Zulu live when they don't live in town."

We took in the panorama before us. Densely folding hills and bush-covered valleys stretched as far as the eye could see. Blue-tinged hills marked the distant horizon. The beehive-shaped huts with their thatched roofs appeared quaint, whimsical.

"The seasons are backside first here, aren't they? Isn't it coming up to winter now?" asked Darky.

"Yes, Durban has a subtropical climate, but we're moving into our dry time of year. In another month or two, these hills will be quite brown."

The vastness of the wide, empty landscape riveted my attention. "What a view. It's beautiful. England seems so small and compact in comparison to this. South Africa is such a big country."

"We like it," said Dr. Wilson. "My parents emigrated here from Scotland when I was a young boy. I'd never leave here now. We have a good life. Come on. Let's go further inland. I'd like you to see Pietermaritzburg before we return to Durban. We can find a café and have a cup of tea."

As we continued our journey, Dr. Wilson described the region.

APRIL 1942—DECEMBER 1942

"This road we're on now is the N3. If we keep driving west for three hundred miles, we'll arrive in Johannesburg. I saw the natives at the racecourse selling fruit. Natal's climate is excellent for growing mangoes, grapes and pineapple. Make the most of it. It's probably the best fruit in the world."

A signpost at the side of the road signalled our arrival at Pietermaritzburg. The charming, colonial town with its wide, tree-lined streets was filled with old, redbrick Victorian buildings. Our heads were turning to the left, right, looking up and peering all around.

"I feel almost at home," said Blondie. "It looks very English."

It reminds me of some of the big houses in Linthorpe, Middlesbrough, I thought, hit by a sudden pang of homesickness. I pictured Ivy in Middlesbrough, dodging Luftwaffe bombs, bringing up Joan all by herself and toiling away in Price's factory, while I was here, seeing the sights of a breathtaking country on the other side of the world. It didn't seem right.

Darky's voice jolted me from my reverie.

"Come on, Gus. We're going to that café on the corner of Market Square."

Refreshed by cake and several cups of hot tea, Dr. and Mrs. Wilson decided it was time to return to Durban.

Dropping us back at the racecourse, Dr. Wilson said, "I'm sure you young men will be wanting to explore the delights Durban has to offer."

Mrs. Wilson invited us to tea at their apartment the next afternoon.

"We have a few people coming. You'll enjoy yourselves I'm sure."

I shook their hands.

"We had a good time this morning. It was a great drive out. Thank you. We'll see you tomorrow."

Darky and I collected our pay, bought huge bunches of black grapes, and set off to see what Durban had to offer. Devouring the luscious fruit as we walked along the streets, we absorbed the colourful foreignness of Durban. Vegetation, the likes of which we never saw in England, was lush and dense. Date palms provided a tropical flavour. Bougainvillea and hibiscus—magenta, purple, yellow, and red—sprayed the town with colour. We passed black men, working in gardens and cleaning cars. Zulus, faces shining with sweat, hauled rickshaws and passengers along the Durban thoroughfares. Near the harbour, we found Indian bazaars and spice shops, with narrow doorways leading to dim interiors. Indian women, immigrant traders, wore the colourful saris of their native land.

First port of call was a bar, where we enjoyed a beer or two, or three, or even four—certainly enough to make us happy. Thirst assuaged, food became the next priority. We found it at the Victoria League canteen, good food as well! The people of Durban generously invited soldiers to their homes for dinner, including me, Darky and Blondie. After passing an enjoyable afternoon at the Metro cinema, watching Mickey Rooney in *Babes on Broadway*, we went looking for Mr. and Mrs. Foster's flat, our dinner hosts for the evening.

Summoned by the doorbell, Mrs. Foster opened the ornate wooden door leading into the apartment. She was a large, strongly built woman with dark hair styled into a short bob. With a welcoming smile, she ushered us inside.

"Come in, boys. It's so good of you to arrive on time."

The apartment was much larger than I expected. Mr. Foster came forward to shake our hands, his canary yellow hair a startling contrast to his florid complexion.

"We're so pleased you could make it. It's a pleasure for us to help a soldier feel at home. Our son Henry is in the army too. He's in Libya at the moment."

"Are those his trophies?" I asked, spotting the silver cups proudly displayed on the sideboard.

"Yes. Henry's a great sportsman. He won most of them in fishing competitions, and there's a few for athletics."

We sat on the overstuffed, leather chesterfield beneath three brightly painted pheasants made of pottery, hanging on the wall. Arranged in a line one after another, the birds appeared to be flying up and away. As we drank the glasses of beer brought by the Bantu maid, Mrs. Foster bustled in and out making sure the maid was preparing everything exactly as she wanted. It was not too long before we were called into the dining room where a beautifully laid table greeted us. Mrs. Foster was pulling out all stops. Each place at the table was bedecked with her best Spode china. Matching tureens, full of steaming vegetables, were crammed into the centre of the table. Mr. Foster carved the joint, a large piece of succulent sirloin. Plates were piled high with roast beef, roast potatoes, carrots, roast onions, green beans and even Yorkshire puddings. Darky, Blondie and I exchanged glances at the large portions of food on our plates. I couldn't stop grinning with pleasure and must have looked like the cat that got the cream.

"You've done us proud, Mrs. Foster. This is great," I complimented our hostess.

"People on rationing, back in England, would give their eye teeth to be tucking into a meal like this," said Blondie.

Keeping a straight face, Darky added, "It's nearly as good as the grub we got on board ship."

There was an awkward moment's silence until Mrs. Foster laughed with delight.

"Darky, stop pulling my leg, you naughty man," she playfully reprimanded him. "I knew you boys would enjoy some good home cooking."

"Henry's always telling us in his letters how awful the food is in the army and how he can't wait to come home for some of his mother's cooking," said Mr. Foster.

For the next hour and a half we ate our fill of delicious food, exchanged chitchat, talked about the war, home, families, South Africa, Durban and the highlight of the season—the forthcoming July Handicap.

Taking leave of the Fosters, we walked to Marine Parade where there was an open-air dance. We jitterbugged and boogied for the next two hours with the young ladies of Durban, intent on having fun, living for the moment, forgetting that this was just a pleasant few days interlude. Moving on from the dance, we explored the side shows along the seafront before heading back to the racecourse. On the way, we stopped at a fruit stall and, for only a couple of pennies, bought more grapes. We tossed the plump, purple fruit into our mouths one at a time, crushing them between our teeth to allow the sweet juices to trickle down our throats as we walked through the brightly-lit streets,. A man in an Austin pulled up beside us.

"Would you boys like a lift?"

What a great town, I thought.

The arrival of the natives to sell their fruit marked the beginning of a new day. I spent the morning feasting on grapes, bananas and ice cream until I strolled into town with Blondie and Darky, where we wandered round the streets and peered into shops. We took in the sights, riding in rickshaws along Marine Parade. Then, leaving Darky behind, Blondie and I went to the home of Dr. and Mrs. Wilson to keep our appointment for afternoon tea. Darky was otherwise engaged, captivated by a pretty, young woman, who seemed equally enthralled with him.

At Dr. Wilson's apartment, the doctor and his wife greeted us like long lost friends. Handing us each a glass of sherry, Mrs. Wilson introduced us to the other guests already comfortably settled in the living room. I looked around. A glossy, black, grand piano dominated the large room. Against the far wall stood a handsome, dark oak Welsh dresser decorated with blue and white Delft plates propped up in rows along each shelf. A tall, mahogany, grandfather clock, standing in the hall, pendulum sedately ticking, acted as sentinel to the proceedings. I studied the pen and ink drawings hanging on the wall. They were all characters from Dickens' books—Mr. Micawber, Fagin, Scrooge, Nicholas Nickleby. One of the other guests, introducing himself as Tom, came to join me.

"They're an interesting looking bunch, aren't they?"

"Dickens certainly knew how to create colourful characters." I said.

I watched the plump, black housekeeper walking to and fro, busy preparing the veranda for our tea party. Then I looked down at the subtle colours of the expensive, Persian carpet beneath my feet. "I'm pleased we're eating out on the veranda,"

APRIL 1942—DECEMBER 1942

I told Tom. "I'd hate to drop any crumbs on this beautiful rug. You seem to live very well here."

Our conversation was interrupted while we moved through the French doors to the veranda outside. Once seated, I took in the delicious spread Mrs. Wilson had provided. The table was crammed with sandwiches delicately cut into triangles, scones, sausage rolls, shortcake, chocolate cake, and my favourite, macaroons. The conversation continued, as Mrs. Wilson poured tea from the well-polished, silver tea service.

"Norman was noticing that we're still living in relative ease and comfort despite the war," Tom announced to the gathering.

"That's true. Compared to what Europe is experiencing, we have it easy here," said Dr. Wilson.

A prim looking woman defensively reminded us, "We do have petrol rationing."

"Oh, there are ways round that. It's no problem really. All in all, we do quite well," Dr. Wilson responded, completely free of guilt at the war's lack of disruption to his comfortable lifestyle.

"When we go to the beach, we see British convoys passing up and down the coast at least once a week. We sit and count the ships. Usually, twenty to thirty at a time go by," added another guest, Doris.

"Our young men are joining the forces and going off to fight," the prim woman persisted.

"All young men everywhere are going off to fight. We have two of them here as our guests," said Mrs. Wilson, determined her tea party conversation was not going to deteriorate into an argument.

Dr. Wilson obviously sensed his wife's concern and swiftly changed the topic of conversation. Pointing out the view of the harbour the veranda offered, he showed off his gleaming brass telescope, which he used to study the various ships and yachts in the docks. Blondie and I peered down the telescope at the view and found the *Cape Town Castle*.

Lively, interesting conversation filled the remainder of the afternoon. We heard how industries had changed to meet the war needs. South Africa was without arms when it declared war on Germany, September 4th, 1939. The mining companies' engineering shops, the railway workshops and even the Royal Mint were quickly converted into munitions factories. The Royal Mint was churning out bullets; steelworks were making mortars and shells, as well as steel plate for armoured vehicles. Families worried about their sons and husbands sent off to war. Despite these woes, South Africans knew their lives were only marginally affected by the war. I was touched by how generously they opened their homes and hearts to young soldiers from foreign lands taking respite in Durban before moving on to perils unknown and unimaginable. As a last act of kindness, when we took our leave, Mrs. Wilson drove us to the Victoria League Club where we were to meet Darky.

We nudged each other when we saw Darky sitting with friends from 62 Company and no lady-friend in sight.

"Where's the young lady, then?" I asked.

"Short romance," said Darky, laughing.

The three of us left the club to spend the rest of the evening at the Playhouse watching an Old Mother Riley film and listening to a Welsh choir singing a few songs for the boys. Then it was back to the racecourse, scoffing grapes and spitting out the seeds as we ambled along.

I was on guard duty all the next day until 6:00 p.m. Upon dismounting the guard, I met up with Darky and off we went to the Victoria League Club.

"It was a really tough guard duty," I told them, "probably one of the toughest."

"Why, what happened?"

"Oh, I had to sit there all day eating grapes, bananas and ice cream and reading South African magazines . . ."

Realising he'd been had, Darky gave me a playful shove.

"You bugger! You had me going there for a minute."

The club was packed, too crowded to be enjoyable. We decided to move on to an ice cream parlour for a banana split. Inside, we found Hinny and Blondie with Michael, a South African soldier they'd befriended.

APRIL 1942–DECEMBER 1942

"One of my friends is having a party at his flat. Would you like to go?" asked Michael.

"Do birds fly?" said Darky. "This is our last night in town before we get back on that sardine can. We'd love to come, wouldn't we, fellas?"

The flat was filled with people talking and laughing. Joe Loss, playing *In the Mood*, volume turned low, made it easy to hold a conversation while we drank coffee and ate cake. This was much better than the Victoria Club. The host organized party games—musical chairs, pass the parcel, pin the tail on the donkey. These innocent games, enjoyed as children, had never been so lively and entertaining as they were on this night, in this flat, in a foreign land, a long, long way from childhood. Later, with the volume turned up, we danced to the latest swing music. Everyone had a great time. Even the neighbours didn't complain. It seemed as if civilians wanted the young men serving their country to have a joyful, carefree time while at home, away from the dangers on the front line.

We strolled back to the racecourse. The next day we would be packing up and leaving, but that night we savoured our happy memories of Durban.

The following day, in battle-dress uniform, we marched in full order through the town, sweating under the hot, bright sun. People once again waved and cheered, and took photographs. It was a memorable farewell to a memorable country.

Destination India.

Ploughing along at a decent rate of knots, we quickly fell back into the same old routine—reading, arguing, discussing, playing cards, lounging about and becoming brown as berries under the hellish-hot sun. Leaning over the rails, I shared pleasurable hours with Darky, watching flying fish and porpoises racing alongside the ship. I took snapshots, with my Kodak Box Brownie, to send to Ivy. On May 27th, the ship sailed into the Madagascar Straits, a dangerous place where

German submarines lurked in the depths intent on ambushing Allied convoys making their way up the coast of East Africa. On two occasions, when German U-boats were tailing the ship, submarine alerts interrupted the long boring days.

As soon as the alarm sounded for action stations, everyone scrambled to get out on deck to avoid being locked in. The NCOs reported to the officer in charge. From his rota, he selected the NCOs whose turn it was to go to the lower decks to seal the bulkhead chambers. On one of these occasions, my name was called. Stepping into the chamber, I pulled the lever to lock the doors. The chamber was sealed off with me locked inside. In the pitch darkness, I sat and waited out the two hours until the alert ended. I've never felt so alone in my whole life. I was trapped in the chamber until a ship's officer came along to open the door to let me out. I didn't like it. With no means of escape if the ship was torpedoed, I'd have had it. On the decks, soldiers sat in the dark and waited. Some men sang to ease the tension. There was nothing else to do but wait and see if they would be attacked.

Leaving the Madagascar Straits, the *Cape Town Castle* sailed into the Indian Ocean. Submarine alerts were left behind. Monotonous days continued. Colonel Bolton organized a whist drive and gave out prizes. We attended church services, played deck quoits and spent evenings listening to the piano on E deck. One evening, we even got a chance to dance with the nurses on board.

Finally, on June 7th, from out on the Arabian Sea, we sighted the coast of India. In the unbearable heat, the shipped dropped anchor in Bombay harbour. We spent the next three days watching the shore and the activity in the harbour, itching to disembark. Excitement rippled through the ranks when a tug was spotted approaching the ship to guide it to its berth. We had been granted one day's shore leave, and we were impatient to explore this strange new land. With the ship docked, the wooden gangplank creaked and groaned under hasty footsteps, scrambling down to firm ground.

All dressed up and ready for a day on the town, me, Hinny, Blondie, Tommy, Mac, Sergeant Wellington and Darky

APRIL 1942—DECEMBER 1942

briskly walked away from the docks. Immediately, every one of our senses was assaulted. Bombay reeked of fish drying in the sun—Bombay Duck in the making. The stench of rotting vegetation, exotic spices and excrement filled the air.

"It smells like Schellenberg's glue and hide factory has moved from Middlesbrough to Bombay," I said, wrinkling my nose at the strong odours wafting our way.

We were hounded by beggars calling, *"baksheesh, sahib, baksheesh, anna, anna, sahib"*. It was hard to deal with this situation. Begging had never been a part of our experience. We had been warned on board the ship not to give to the beggars, or we would end up being surrounded by dozens of them pestering for money. Although my heart went out to these poor people, some of them blind, some deformed, others without limbs, we walked on.

Old crumbling tenements flanked narrow lanes. Snake charmers and street dentists were found on every corner. Busy bazaars sold everything under the sun. Tethered to the ground by cables, barrage balloons floated above the city, a precaution against low-level Japanese air attack.

"Bombay's interesting; filthy, but interesting," was my verdict.

"I want a good meal with all the trimmings," said Darky with feeling.

"After the lousy food on board ship, I should say so," said Sergeant Wellington.

We searched for a place to eat. I detected the aroma of mouth-watering food and walking to the corner of the street, I found what we were looking for.

"There's a Chinese restaurant. Let's see what they've got," I said, eager to put some decent food in my stomach.

We wolfed down enormous mixed grills with chops, eggs, lashings of chips and all the trimmings followed by mountains of ice cream and copious iced drinks.

"I'm as full as a poisoned pup," said Blondie, a satisfied grin on his face.

"Time to see the town, lads," I said, ushering them out of the restaurant to explore Bombay. Wandering through the streets, the heat was insufferable, but we were lucky enough to find an open-air swimming pool where we spent several refreshing hours, frolicking in the water.

"This was a real treat after the difficulties we've had trying to keep clean on board ship," I said, towelling myself dry.

"I'm as clean as a whistle," said Darky.

"And smelling as sweet as a daisy," we chimed in.

Final touch to the evening was a visit to the Metro cinema before returning to the ship.

Next day began with a 4:00 a.m. wake up call. It was hell as thousands of men scrambled to stow hammocks and bedding in the holds, get their kit ready, and eat breakfast before leaving the ship at 7:20. We marched to the railway station. Victoria Terminus was a massive, imposing building of Victorian Gothic architecture. Its ornate walls, spires, domes, and arched windows were guarded by grey, stone British lions perched on lofty pedestals, standing by the sides of the wrought iron gate at the main entrance. Outside the station were ranks of ghoda-ghadis, gaudily painted carriages pulled by bony horses, adorned with rosettes and flowers. Inside the Terminus, we squatted on the stone floor of the station's main concourse to wait for the train. Hundreds of people were in the station, some milling around, some sitting patiently, waiting for the arrival of their trains. Most Indian men were dressed in white cotton robes. An occasional figure was dressed in more western attire of white shirt and dark trousers. All the women were dressed in colourful saris. While we waited in the stifling heat, vendors made the most of the opportunity, selling us dates, bananas, and drinks. At last, at 12:15 the train arrived. We'd no sooner boarded the train, than it was moving out of the station, carrying us past tightly packed tenements and Bombay slums, shimmering in the heat and swarming with flies. We were glued to the windows, catching glimpses of women squatting in doorways, preparing food surrounded by skinny children. Bony dogs prowled the narrow dirt paths between the rows of mud huts. An occasional scrawny chicken scratched at the dirt.

We left the city behind. The train started to travel up a gradient as if we were going into the hills.

APRIL 1942–DECEMBER 1942

"Oh-oh! We need to watch out. We're not the only passengers on this train," said Darky.

He was right. The train was full of ants. It made for an uncomfortable journey, until we rolled into Deolali station one hundred and twenty-five miles and three and a half hours later.

Deolali

From the station, we were marched to a training and replacement camp. Rifles and ammunition were handed in, exchanged for blankets and mosquito nets. The enlisted men's barracks were austere, devoid of one touch of luxury. Each building had a veranda. When it was raining hard, this was the place where morning parade was held.

We settled in, wondering what lay ahead. I wasn't expecting the pleasant surprise awaiting me. Early the next morning, an Indian boy roused me from a deep sleep. I, and all the other sleepy-eyed soldiers in the barracks, found our boots cleaned and water already poured into a bowl for washing. As soon as I got up, the boy, who was called Kutcha, made my bed. There were several boys to each barrack room. Each soldier paid their boy one rupee a week for making beds, putting up mosquito nets, cleaning equipment and boots, as well as washing and ironing the men's clothes. These highly prized jobs were passed from father to son. Having a servant to look after our needs was a completely new experience for us working-class men.

"I felt like a lord when I woke up this morning. I wasn't expecting to be looked after like this. It's a real treat," I told Darky, while we lazed about in the heat our first day in Deolali.

Darky was amazed too.

"My mother doesn't even look after me this well."

"It feels strange having a servant do for me. I'm not sure that I'm comfortable with these goings on," said Hinny.

We laughed at his discomfort; we were loving every minute of it.

"Make the most of it. We don't know how long this will last," I said.

"It's my birthday today. Having that boy Chola fussing round and waking up to find my boots nice and clean was a fine birthday present," said Darky, cheerfully.

"Twenty-fourth?" I asked.

"Yes. Let's go out and celebrate tonight."

"Can't. I'm on armoury guard this evening and all day tomorrow."

"Pity. You'll miss the fun."

It started to rain. The monsoon was on its way.

Sunday was our day off. Darky and I decided to go horse-riding. At eight annas an hour, it seemed to be a bargain. Undaunted by the fact that neither of us had been on a horse before, off we trotted. I was not a natural horseman, yet despite slipping perilously to the side several times, I managed to stay on my horse. In the afternoon, we went to the bazaar. I bought two vests and three handkerchiefs. Darky treated himself to new swimming trunks.

"That was a ferocious bout of haggling, Gus. Where did you learn to argue like that?" said Darky, impressed with my bartering skills.

"I was just having a bit of fun. Anyway, you drive a hard bargain yourself. I thought the shopkeeper was going to tear his hair out."

"Look there's a photographer's studio. Let's have our photos taken."

Photographs taken, we returned to camp and got indoors just in time to avoid getting soaked in a heavy downpour. From the shelter of the veranda, we watched the spectacular show of lightning in the night sky. We'd never seen anything like it in England.

We settled into army routine. Mornings were spent in physical training and toughening up exercises. Before breakfast, it was a three-mile run. After breakfast, it was route marches, which were more like nature lessons as we examined lizards, ants, beetles, centipedes, plants, but fortunately, no snakes in this new and strange environment. Soon we were

APRIL 1942–DECEMBER 1942

marching ten miles a day. The heat was so excruciating, we usually took an afternoon siesta. By June 19th, five men were in hospital after collapsing from heatstroke.

Within a week of arriving in Deolali, the army decided to make sure everyone knew how to swim. The sergeant-major assembled 62 Company beside the swimming pool.

"Look at the size of him. He's got to be well over six feet and built like a battle ship," I muttered under my breath to Darky. I was 5' 9", the average height for an Englishman in the 1940s.

"All right, you lot. Any man who doesn't know how to swim, step forward," the sergeant-major bellowed.

I stepped forward. Glancing around, I saw that only a handful of men had moved.

"You don't know how to swim, Corporal?"

"No, Sergeant-Major."

Without further ado, the sergeant-major picked me up and threw me into the pool.

"Now, bloody well swim to the side, or drown," he yelled, before moving on to the next hapless victim.

With much thrashing, gurgling and spluttering, I managed to reach the side of the pool. Clinging tightly, I coughed and gasped for air, all the while spitting out water brought up from my lungs. I was a fast learner. Within two weeks, I was swimming a mean sidestroke with my rifle slung across my back.

Every four or five days, I wrote to Ivy, my mother or Aunt Bessie. I painted pictures with words, telling them about this fascinating new land and how the monsoon rains came every afternoon between 4:30 and 7:30 p.m. I told them of having a servant boy called Kutcha and sent them a photograph of myself and some of the men with the grinning boy. I told how, in the evenings, I would stroll with Darky along the dry riverbeds called *wadis*, exploring the area around the camp, or that sometimes, we joined impromptu games of football, until it was too dark to see the ball. I wrote them about how we often went to the garrison cinema where, half way through the film, they stopped the projector so the *char-wallas* could come round selling tea from silver urns.

After breakfast on our next day off, I went with Darky, Blondie and Hinny for a walk along the riverbank. Coming across a fig tree and a mango tree heavily laden with fruit, Darky's eyes lit up.

"Look! Do you see what I see?"

"Doesn't it make your mouth water?" said Blondie.

"No good just staring," I said. "I'm going to pick some. Get ready to catch when I throw them down."

I trotted over to the mango tree and began to climb. Darky ran to the fig tree. We stretched along the branches, trying to reach the fruit, and then we began to curse.

"What's the matter, Gus?" called Hinny.

Darky and I scrambled down as fast as we could, jumping the last few feet in our haste to get out of the trees.

"What is it?" Blondie asked, as we frantically brushed off our clothes.

"Ants. Give us a hand. We're getting bitten to death here," I said.

We ripped off our clothes and shook them hard.

"It's been a long time since I saw you move so fast, Gus," said Blondie, chuckling.

"You'd have moved too with ants in your pants. They could've given us a nasty injury," I said, with a chuckle.

"Too bad the ants got there first," said Blondie. "I've never eaten mangos before."

We set off along the riverbank, taking one last wistful look at the juicy, ripe fruit.

That night, sitting in the NAAFI, having a relaxing drink, we listened to the news broadcast on the wireless. Groans of concern and disappointment filled the air as the speaker announced, "Tobruk has fallen. The Allied troops defending the town have surrendered."

"Makes you wonder how long this war's going to last," I said. "What the hell are we doing in this God forsaken hole when we could be fighting in Africa?"

APRIL 1942—DECEMBER 1942

My friends murmured their agreement. They too wondered what we were supposed to be achieving here in India.

Toughening exercises were building up, but presented no problems to our group, which was easily able to meet the challenge. One day, we were sent on a two-and-a-half mile run before breakfast. After parade, it was a ten-mile route march in the blazing sun. The afternoon was spent napping until *tiffin*. Fortified with tea and cakes, we participated in a fast game of hockey. Darky, with his killer instinct as an attacking player, was a force to be reckoned with. Nothing and no one could stop him from scoring goals. All this exercise wasn't enough to tire us out. Game over, we walked two miles to the cinema to see *Captain Blood* and walked the two miles back again. We were fit and in our prime.

One of the jobs we undertook on a regular weekly basis was to de-bug the *charpoys* or beds. The *charpoys* consisted of a wooden frame with jute ropes fastened across to support the sleeping occupant. Using ropes, we lowered the beds into large vats of boiling water to kill any bedbugs that might be lurking in the cracks.

When it managed to stay dry for a few hours, I took the section on foot drills after *tiffin*. By the end of June, it was raining heavily most days. In the inclement weather, the cinema became a favourite evening pastime. It was here we escaped from reality and the loneliness of being far from home, laughing with Red Skelton in *Whistling in the Dark*, listening to Deanna Durban singing in *It started with Eve*, and watching Gary Cooper in *Sergeant York*.

While it poured outside, I attended lectures inside. Lieutenant Curtis gave a lecture about Indian politics. "India has been a British colony since 1858," he told us. "Although we have introduced many economic and social benefits to this country over the years, such as the road and railway systems and the British system of law, there have always been factions who resent British rule. These factions formed the Indian National Congress with the aim of gaining independence from Britain. Within this movement are both moderates and extremists. The moderates are seeking gradual reform within the structure of the law and government. The extremists are hostile to British rule and are prepared to use violence to achieve independence. You will hear the name of Mohandas Gandhi. By organizing peaceful civil disobedience as a way of defying the law, he has united the Indian people as never before. Tens of thousands of non-co-operators and protesters have been jailed following his lead. Although Ghandi is still highly regarded, leadership of the Indian National Congress party has now passed into the hands of younger men such as Jawaharlal Nehru.

"A further split developed in the independence movement when the All India Muslim League was founded. This organization demands an independent homeland for Islam and is fighting for a partitioned India. These two groups, the Indian National Congress and the All India Muslim League, sometimes agree to work together, and sometimes they are totally opposed on how to be free of British rule. Instead of preparing for battle, many of our units are being used for internal security duties, helping the police restore order during the violent clashes which keep breaking out between Muslims and Hindus; or, they're involved in quelling riots and dispersing demonstrations against the government. Indians generally want the British to leave. Be prepared to encounter some hostility when you are out and about and keep your wits about you."

As a driver, my lectures consisted of learning about the internal combustion engine usually from Lieutenant Lind, more commonly known as 'Dr. Moto'. The whole section received lectures on Mills bombs, trench mortar, gas and its effectiveness in combat. We learned skills in tying knots and lashings. I gave a lecture on maintenance to the drivers. We participated in lively debates on topics such as "Should a Soldier be a Jack of all Trades or Master of None?" We were kept busy, busy, busy. In the daytime, it was lectures, training, lectures, route marching, lectures, drilling, more lectures, more foot slogging. Evenings were filled with baseball games, football, hockey matches and darts competitions against some of the other sections, and of course, there were the frequent trips to the cinema.

Hinny and I went on a cadre class under the regimental sergeant-major. After several days of drilling in the pouring rain, I'd had enough. Soaking wet and seething with anger, I complained to Hinny.

"Its bloody ridiculous! We're drilling like mugs, while men are dying in Libya just because they did too much drill and not enough practice with weapons."

"I'm sick of foot slogging in the pouring rain too," said Hinny, "but we're getting quite nifty at it now, aren't we?"

Begrudgingly, I admitted that we were starting to look good now that we were all moving in unison. Still, I'd rather have been doing something more useful such as weapons training.

July 12th, it was jabs in arms for typhoid and cholera inoculations. Despite complaints that our arms hurt like hell, we didn't escape more foot drill the next day, but at least the sun was shining for a change.

July 17th, our fifth wedding anniversary. Ivy was on my mind all day. I hoped she was all right. I hadn't received a letter from her in three weeks. That afternoon I lay on my bed, hands linked behind my head, feeling homesick and lonely. I'd been in the army exactly three years—not bad considering I only joined up for six months. My thoughts drifted back over the past few years.

I've used up at least a couple of my nine lives in France and at Dunkirk. I've built defences along the south coast to protect good old England from the Hun, all the while dodging bombs and wreckage from the Battle of Britain. And I've been trained and trained and trained again for the privilege of languishing in the heat and humidity of Deolali. That's the army for you. Oh, Ivy, I've been thinking about you all day and how life might have been, should have been. We were only sixteen when we fell in love, and I promised you the world. So far, I haven't done very well, have I? We struggled a lot when we first married. There wasn't much money in the kitty to help us build a home together, but we managed it, even though I was out of work a lot. What did we start out with? A bed, a chest of drawers, a table and some chairs, but with all the love we had, we didn't need anything else. I promised you we'd have a wonderful life together—you, me, our children—and now we're thousands of miles apart. Five years we've been married, two perfect years together and three with the army ruling our lives. It wasn't what I imagined for us—only being able to have a family life on those weekends when I managed to be on leave. And now look at us. I'm stuck in India, up to my knees in mud, with no idea when I'll be coming home. I love you. Always will. There's nothing I want more than to be at home with you, lying by your side and holding you tight. I stopped thinking to compose myself. My eyes were moist, and I had a choking lump in my throat. That evening, feeling pensive and wistful, I wrote a letter to Ivy. "My Darling," it began, "I can't help thinking of you tonight . . ."

The rain returned with a vengeance. More drilling and rifle bashing, not to mention field signals in sheeting rain. The mood of the men was becoming bleak. Darky, cheerful as ever, rushed me to the cinema where we enjoyed watching *Arizona*. Later, at the Majestic café, we hungrily tucked into egg and chips. Darky could see that I was feeling low and missing Ivy. The weather, the lousy meals and the conditions at camp didn't help. Darky listened sympathetically while I got things off my chest.

"I'm fed up to the teeth. I missed going on a mechanics course through R.S.M. class. I'm sick of always having to scrub equipment. The camp's a disgusting pigsty, nothing but a mud-hole. What a lousy place this is."

Darky continued in the same vein.

"Don't forget the food, or should I say the poor excuse for what the army calls food. My evening meal was so bad I threw it out, couldn't eat it."

"Me too," I said. "And I'm fed up with mosquito bites. Were you there when the C.O. caught ninety percent of the barracks with their mosquito nets up? He was furious. Confined them to barracks for two days."

"I was digging drainage ditches yesterday," Darky said, adding fuel to the fire, "up to my eyeballs in mud."

APRIL 1942—DECEMBER 1942

"I'm thoroughly browned off with this rotten monsoon weather. It's been raining for days. Doesn't it ever stop here? One consolation, we can't sink much lower."

"You've forgotten something."

"What's that?"

"The flies in the bread. What I wouldn't give to eat a nice slice of white bread from Meredith's bakery without baked flies in it."

Darky was drooling, a far away look in his eyes.

"You'll just have to eat your heart out, Darky. There's no way the cooks can stop the flies getting into the dough. Pretend they're currants." I started to chuckle. "A right pair we are. We've done nothing but moan since we came in here. Let's go back to camp."

We walked outside. Darky grimaced as if in pain.

"It's still bloody well raining."

A scowl of disgust swept his face. Then a reluctant grin twitched at his mouth. Soon we were laughing so hard our eyes were wet with tears. The grumbling session had done us good. We were still smiling when we arrived back at camp.

Entering the barracks, we heard the latest news.

"There's rumours flying of an invasion of France," said Hinny.

My spirits lifted. *Maybe we'll return to England soon.*

Mohandas Gandhi and Jawaharlal Nehru, leaders of the National Congress Party, were arrested August 9th. Riots broke out in Bombay and Nasik. There was also trouble in Baghur village. Soldiers of 62 Company were standing by in battle-dress order. 2 Section was sent off to Nasik to quell the riots. HQ Section was standing by ready to go. Next day, 1 Section joined 2 Section in Nasik. HQ Section was still standing by. *Things must be really bad there.*

There was a remarkable improvement in the quality of the food. I wondered if complaints had reached the ears of Major-General Witt when he inspected the camp a few weeks previously.

I was in the barracks, sitting on my bed surrounded by letters, when Hinny and Blondie found me.

"What's this then, Gus? Did you steal the post bag?" asked Hinny.

"Have you seen the smile on his face?" said Blondie.

"I've received ten letters in the past three days. Thought I'd read through them again. Ivy's working shifts at the Malleable steel works in Stockton, driving a gantry crane. They're making bomb casings, tank parts and booms for minesweepers.

"Here," I handed Blondie a photograph. "She's sent a photo of herself in her turban and boiler suit. Says she hates going home in the black out. The works' bus drops her off round the corner and then she runs like hell to get home. Says it's creepy with no lights on anywhere. They're still getting air raids in the northeast. A bomb wrecked Middlesbrough Co-op and the Emporium in July, but she doesn't say if anyone was hurt. I'll have to write and tell her I passed the army swimming test and that I'm getting suntanned."

"Are you sure it's not rust?" Hinny pulled my leg.

We were moving into a tented camp. I was put in charge of a party of men who spent several days loading shingle onto bullock carts. Then we loaded tents at the Indian Engineer's camp and erected them in South Deolali. It was hot, sticky work in temperatures well over one hundred degrees, and it was a welcome pleasure to cool off at the swimming baths for a few hours in the afternoons. We moved into the new camp. There were only seven men in my tent, the original group and Cliff Brough, so there was plenty of room and it was comfortable. The next day, we dug a drainage ditch round the tent. It had been sunny the past few days, but the monsoon weather was not over yet.

We were in high spirits and hopeful of an early return to England after hearing reports of an Allied landing on the French coast with tanks and artillery in action.

I wrote letters home to my mother, Ivy, and Aunt Bessie. "It's hellish hot here," I told them, "but we manage to go to the swimming baths most days to cool off. I've been buying a few things in the bazaars. I enjoy haggling with the Indian shopkeepers to get the prices down. It's a big production just

APRIL 1942–DECEMBER 1942

to buy a pair of shoes and some stockings. Some of the Indians in the street are angry and hostile to us. They've had enough of British rule and want us out of India. They shout at us, but don't physically attack us. We just shoulder them aside to get past, and to be on the safe side, we never go out without bayonets in our belts—just in case. The other day, the camp commandant rode by before morning parade. A bloke in 58 Company failed to salute him. We had a laugh when we heard the commandant bawling him out saying, 'No wonder the Japs got through Burma. The British Army's got its eyes shut.'

"A few days ago, HQ Section played Group HQ at football and won 4-1. It was a great game. Then yesterday, after *tiffin*, we went down to the aerodrome ground to play against 67 HQ. I got crocked. My arms are badly grazed, and my hips are bruised. I'm so stiff, I can hardly move—and to cap it all we lost 3-0. I had to go on sick to get my arms dressed. Most afternoons, I have a nap or go swimming. Oh, I nearly forgot. I passed my cadre classes."

We were all disgruntled about the food, the consensus being that army meals could only be described as putrid. The weather continued hot and clammy. It started to rain again. It rained so much, the place was thick with mud, and flooding was a strong possibility. We dug deeper drainage trenches round the tent.

Along with some other NCOs and officers, I was taken to a military hospital to see patients with sexually transmitted diseases, especially those with syphilis, so that we could see for ourselves the effects of the disease. We started by going to the wards where patients were in the early stages of the disease, before moving on to the terminal cases. It was horrific, seeing the state of the men in the last stages of syphilis. I'll never forget it as long as I live.

At the end of the tour, the Medical Officer in charge of the hospital spoke to us.

"You've seen with your own eyes the terrible, debilitating effects of this disease, for which we have no cure. I want you to return to your camps and tell the men what you've seen. Warn them against using the brothels, or going with any women here. It's the only way to steer clear of infection."

That evening we played solo and listened to Mac play the mouth organ.

"Could anyone eat their midday meal today?" asked Tommy.

"No, it was those horrible yams again," said Darky. "Must've run out of potatoes. I threw mine out."

"Anyone going to the bazaar tomorrow? We can get some decent grub at the Majestic Café," said Hinny

"I'll come with you," said Mac. "The food's really going down the nick in this camp. I keep buying egg and chips in the NAAFI just to keep my strength up."

"I went with the NCOs and officers to the hospital today. They showed us what happens if you catch syphilis," I said. "It was horrible, heartbreaking—and there's no cure. If you get infected, it starts with small ulcers on your penis, although they can appear anywhere—on your mouth, hand, eyelids. Then you'll start getting fevers, headaches, rashes, swellings under the armpits, and your hair will fall out in clumps. After several years, your brain, heart, and nervous system are affected. You'll become paralysed and even insane. Some of the men told us they would rather go and fight and risk being killed fighting the Japs, than wait to die of syphilis. They knew what was coming, and they were frightened."

"Trust Gus to cheer us up," jibed Mac.

"Gus is right to tell us," said Hinny. "We're all mates here. It would be upsetting if one of us caught it."

"It's best to keep away from Indian women and brothels altogether," said Tommy.

"You're just a dirty rotten spoilsport, Gus, telling us about that just as we've settled into a game of cards," said Darky, laughing.

"Let's change the subject," said Blondie. "What did you think of the talks we gave yesterday?"

"What? Those ten minute talks that we gave to the rest of the section about anything we fancied?" said Cliff, dealing cards.

APRIL 1942—DECEMBER 1942

"No, the Prime Minister's talk in the House of Commons, you twerp," said Mac, pausing in his mouth organ playing.

"I thought they were good," I said. "Who'd have thought Sergeant Green knew so much about bird watching?"

"Pity they wouldn't let us talk about women," said Darky.

Tommy threw a pillow at him and scoffed, "What do you know about women?"

"Less than he knows about playing cards," I said, spreading my winning hand out on the table. "Come on. Pay up, Darky."

Transport Detail.

The many hockey games and football matches against other Engineering sections, coupled with a reduction in the rainfall now that we were into September, was helping to keep morale high.

Darky came by the tent, where I was busy packing my kit.

"I've been looking for you. Are you coming down to see the hockey match?"

"Can't play tonight, Darky. All the drivers have to report at 2100 hours. We're going to Bombay to bring back some trucks. Have a good game though."

Blondie and I were among the forty drivers gathered for parade and then marched off to Deolali station. Captain Cave was in charge. We travelled all night. Like everyone else, I didn't sleep much. The train kept stopping, and the journey seemed to take forever. I woke up at 5:00 a.m. to another hot day. Two and a half hours later, the train arrived in Bombay. Trucks were waiting to take us to the docks where we wasted no time munching bacon sandwiches bought from a mobile canteen. We hung around the docks all morning, but the ship we were waiting for had not yet come into port.

Frustrated, Captain Cave told us, "Take a break, men. You have permission to go and explore Bombay. There's nothing doing here. Be back for 1600 hours."

A group of us entered the crush of sweaty crowds in the city centre market area. We found the larger bazaars all crowded together, the array of merchandise testifying to the industriousness of Bombay's citizens. Some streets were full of people selling shoes; in other streets, vendors specialized in selling clothing, or all manner of souvenirs for servicemen to send home to wives, girlfriends, or family. There were intricately carved figurines, lacquered brassware, inlaid boxes made of sandalwood, jewellery and trinkets to satisfy every bargain hunter. The narrow streets, lined with open-fronted shops, were filled from end to end with groaning stalls crammed full to overflowing with goods piled high. Poorer peddlers squatted on the floor, selling their wares from cloths spread out on the pavement. I found the exotic atmosphere—the babble of voices speaking incomprehensible languages, the milling multitudes going about their daily tasks—fascinating. But within a short time, we were driven to seek refuge in the Sir Alwyn Ezra Canteen for *tiffin*, our senses overwhelmed by the heat, the heavy scent of spices and the smell of cooking food from the many restaurants and cheap food stalls.

We returned to the docks only to discover there were no new developments. Nothing had arrived. While we waited, we enjoyed a refreshing shower at Ballard's pier and ate bread and jam washed down by mugs of steaming tea. When it became obvious that nothing would be accomplished that day, we marched through Bombay to Colaba camp situated on a peninsula south of the city centre. Here, there were white colonial houses for the officers and brick barracks for the troops. Shade trees lined the avenues. We moved into a tented camp available for transient troops.

After a wash and a shave, I returned to Bombay city centre accompanied by Blondie. We found a dance and had a lively time jitterbugging to the latest swinging music from America—music from Tommy Dorsey, Glen Miller, Benny Goodman and Frank Sinatra. I danced with an Indian Army nurse. She was a wonderful dancer with a natural feel for rhythm, which at times left me feeling ungainly. At 10:30 p.m., the dancing stopped. After an iced drink and supper, Blondie and I walked back to Colaba and, upon entering the tent, fell

APRIL 1942—DECEMBER 1942

exhausted into our beds. Fifteen minutes later, I was up again, striking matches to kill the bedbugs that were eating me alive. I gave it up as a bad job. The tent was crawling with bedbugs. Blondie was sound asleep, oblivious to the assault on his body. Repulsed, I went outside where I spent the night sitting on a wall smoking cigarettes.

In the morning, Blondie staggered sleepily from the tent to find me still sitting on the wall.

"You must have been up bright and early."

"Up bright and early? I didn't sleep a wink last night. The tent's full of bedbugs."

He looked down at his welt-covered body.

"Bloody hell! I'm a mess. Let's get some breakfast, then we'll get the buggers out of the bedding before we leave for the docks."

Along with the other drivers, I hung around the docks, waiting for the vehicles to be brought out of the holds. The water truck finally surfaced and was deposited on the quayside during the afternoon.

"What a sorry state the old girl's in," I muttered to Blondie. "Look at her. She's covered in dirt and looks totally neglected. My work's going to be cut out getting her shipshape."

The few vehicles that came up from the holds were parked on the docks overnight. There was no pay for us, but by borrowing five chips apiece from Captain Cave, we managed a night out at the Regal cinema.

Back at camp, I discovered my bed was still crawling with bedbugs. I stomped out of the tent in disgust and slung a blanket over the guy ropes for a makeshift bed, where I swiftly fell into oblivion until Blondie shook me awake the next morning.

We found Captain Cave before breakfast to tell him about the bedbugs. He frowned in displeasure.

"You have bedbugs in your tent you say? That won't do. That won't do at all. I'll not have my men suffering such conditions in a British Army camp. Leave it with me."

The Captain wasted no time in relaying this information to the camp commandant, who immediately organized vats of boiling water for 62 Company's men to dip and debug the beds.

Then it was off to the docks for a busy day ferrying the trucks to the car park. After the trucks' long sea journey, there was as much towing as driving. The weather was scorching, and we worked in only shorts and plimsolls. The effect of the sun's rays was soon revealed on our backs, ranging from Blondie's lobster red to Dick Wright's burnt umber.

With the workday over, Blondie and I, accompanied by Wilf Jackson, Cliff Brough, and two other drivers, went into Bombay where we bumped into more of 62 Company, seeing what mischief they could get up to.

"Let's go and see these brothels they're on about. They're supposed to be like cages," said Cliff.

"I'll go," I said, "but only for a look see. I'm not going in."

"We've all got more sense than that. Nobody's going in, right?" Blondie dared them with sham threats of a clenched fist. "I don't want any of my mates catching V.D."

"Ooooh, Blondie's being firm. We'd better behave ourselves," we mocked. Feigned groans of disappointment and sulky pouted lips were our response to Blondie's admonition, but at heart, no one really wanted to go through the shabby doors of the brothels.

Making our way through the slums of Grant road and the bazaars, still bustling even at this late hour, the group reached Kamatipura, Bombay's red light district. The brothels were in small, filthy buildings huddled together along the streets and twisting lanes. The stuccoed walls were grey, mostly devoid of paint and stained black with mould. Long ago, someone had painted several of the buildings turquoise. The paint, now peeling off, added to the area's air of sleaziness. Some of the entrance doors were painted cerulean blue, but the paintwork—chipped, gouged and battered—did not look at all inviting. I could see why they were known as "the cages". Behind the small barred windows of one brothel, pretty, young women paraded for passers-by. Round the corner in Foras Road, bored prostitutes leaned out from behind gaudy curtains at upstairs windows, trying to make eye contact with us, enticing us to come inside with waves and smiles.

"Hey, Gus, I think she likes you," said Wilf about one prostitute, who persisted in calling for my attention.

"Not bloody likely," I said, laughing.

"She's got more chance of rolling a snowball in hell," said Blondie.

"You're wasting your time, love," Cliff called up to her.

I'd had enough of exploring.

"Come on. We've satisfied our curiosity. Let's get back to camp."

Now that the beds were bug free, I slept soundly. I needed to. After a day spent tinkering with the trucks to get them running, I was placed on car park duty late in the afternoon. India was beset by civil unrest. Only the previous month, a crowd had stoned a Bombay police station and tried to set it on fire. Five people were killed and twenty injured when police fired into the crowd. More riots had followed. Supporters of the National Congress Party might find a car park full of British Army trucks a tempting target to sabotage.

During the evening, a British government official, returning home from a party, saw my lonely vigil in the car park.

"Good evening, Corporal. Looks like you have a long night ahead of you."

"Oh, I'll be all right as long as I keep moving. The hardest part is keeping awake, especially when you've been out in the hot sun all day. It tends to make you sleepy."

"Why don't you come over to my flat for a drink? It's just over there. You can see it from here. It will be a break for you."

I didn't need to be asked twice. It was a welcome, but short break, time to savour a small glass of whisky, smoke a cigarette, and some pleasant small talk with a lonely man longing to return to his homeland. But, duty called. Heavy rain during the night was reassuring. There wouldn't be many mischief-makers out and about in that deluge.

Dismounting the guard at 8:45 a.m., I had the rest of the day off. The morning I spent sleeping; the afternoon I explored the city on my own. On the way to the city centre, I went to the entrance to the port of Bombay, The Gateway of India, a honey-coloured, basalt monument on Apollo Bunder. Passing beneath its arched portals, I approached the quayside. For five minutes, I stared longingly out at the harbour and wondered how long it would be before I was on a ship and on my way home? I strolled past the town hall with its columns and Greek porticos. I spent a full ten minutes standing across the road from Victoria Terminus, admiring its grandeur and architectural detail. Passing the Flora Fountain, situated at a busy intersection, surrounded by prosperous shops and offices, I wandered under the ornate entrance into Crawford market overflowing with all manner of fruits and vegetables, some of which I recognized and some I didn't.

By now, I was thirsty and decided to drink some tea in a nearby café. It was a tough, low-life joint. Mine was the only white face there. The almost tangible, silent resentment and hostility of the other patrons brought out my stubborn streak. I lingered a long time over my tea, determined not to be scared off by scowling, sullen faces. Eventually, with studied nonchalance, I sauntered out of the café. Out on the street, I looked over my shoulder to make sure I wasn't being followed and gave a heartfelt sigh of relief as I quickly walked from the area without incident.

I returned to camp to meet up with Blondie. Then it was off again for more exploring, supper at the Services canteen, and a visit to the cinema to see *Reap the Wild Wind*. When the show was over and the National Anthem finished, we made our way through the crowd flowing from the foyer.

"That was a damned good picture," I said.

"The lads said it was good. They were right," Blondie agreed.

Happy and satisfied with our outing, we climbed into a gharry, one of the many horse-drawn carriages waiting outside the cinema. The leather seat covering was torn and split. The smell of hay and horse fodder, coupled with the smell of the driver, who probably used the carriage to sleep in, assailed our nostrils, but in no way detracted from our pleasure as we watched the city's activities on the way to Colaba.

We spent the next two days working on the vehicles, test driving and preparing them for the road journey back to Deolali. One week after arriving in Bombay, we were on our way out of the city in a truck convoy. Cliff Brough rode with me in the water truck. It was a hot, sticky, jolting drive along the dusty road, rutted and potholed from the heavy downpours. As we neared Deolali, the trucks toiled up the hilly roads. The views were wonderful of farmers working in fields, craggy green hills, lakes and villages perched high on the hillsides.

Eleven hours after leaving Bombay, I was relieved to arrive at Deolali. During the last five hours of the journey, I'd been driving with a nagging toothache, which promptly ceased the moment the dentist extracted the guilty tooth the next morning.

Now that the transport had arrived in camp, drivers were spared further participation in the toughening up courses. Instead, we worked putting the vehicles in trim and checking the section's tools and equipment. Lieutenant Lind and Captain Cave presented more lectures, some interesting, some not.

On September 24th, we were shocked and saddened to learn that Driver "Crasher" Prail had died of typhoid during the night. His close friends carried the coffin into the red brick church of Deolali camp for the funeral service. Afterwards, at the graveside, along with dozens of men gathered to pay their last respects, I watched as the coffin containing Driver Prail's remains was lowered into its resting-place in the shadows of several shade trees beside the church.

"It so bloody unfair that Crasher died of some silly disease after coming through Dunkirk without a scratch," I said.

"Who would have thought it? Aren't all those inoculations supposed to protect you from that sort of stuff," said Blondie.

"You'll have to save your coppers now. They're getting up a collection for his widow," Tommy told us. "It's a poor substitute for a husband, but I'm sure it'll be a help to her."

Camp Moves.

Upon the dispersal of 1 Chemical Warfare Group R.E., we packed the tents they had been using and sent them off to South Deolali. In the scalding heat, the drivers continued to work on their vehicles, cooling off with frequent trips to the swimming baths. I wrote another airgraph to Ivy, the second in three days.

"Darling, I spent the morning packing my kit and loading trucks. 62 Company officers accused the officer in charge of food supplies at Deolali of filching our food rations. They found a way to prove it and complained to the camp commandant. His response was to tell our officers, 'if you think you can do better yourselves, you can leave the camp'—so we did. We ate our last deplorable meal in Deolali at midday. Then we drove about thirty miles to South Deolali, well away from the transit camp.

"We're back into tents, eight men to a tent. The scenery is beautiful. We're on top of the hills, so we can see for miles. As I'm writing this letter, there's plenty of livestock in the tent now that it's dark. I've already caught a locust and a dragonfly the size of a small plane. I've just had one tooth taken out, now another's got to go. At this rate, I might be toothless by the time I get home. We bought pith helmets yesterday to protect our heads from the sun while we're working outside in the heat. It's worse than working at the coke ovens at Lackenby steelworks. How is your work at Malleable steelworks? I hope you're over the shock of cutting off your workmate's thumb with the gantry crane. The fool shouldn't have put it where you could run over it. Knowing you and your soft heart, I'm sure you'll be upset with yourself for months, but don't worry, I know it wasn't your fault. I love you and miss you."

◆ ◆ ◆

The first morning in our new independently run camp, we ate a tasty, well-cooked breakfast of eggs, sausage and tomatoes.

APRIL 1942—DECEMBER 1942

Lunch, *tiffin* and supper were delicious too. The move was working out well, at least until the morning we awoke to discover there was no water. Unable to wash, shave or shower, everyone grumbled, "Might have been lousy food in the transit camp, but at least we could get washed." But it was only a temporary hiccup, and normal water supply was restored before the day ended.

By the beginning of October, the evenings were becoming chilly. 361 Chemical Warfare Maintenance Company joined the Royal Engineers at Deolali South. A bus service was provided to take us into Deolali town for recreational activities. The road into town was extremely dusty. I was detailed to drive the water tanker along the road, to spray it with water to keep the dust down.

I was put in charge of collecting rations, which entailed driving a truck twice daily into Deolali to collect meat, vegetables, bread and ice. In the unbearable heat, I drove with the windows down. This was not pleasant, as I soon became covered with a gritty layer of dust kicked up from passing trucks. It was hot, thirsty work, but there were always ample supplies of refreshing cups of tea to drink, while I waited for the truck to be loaded, and treats to nibble as I helped myself to tomatoes and fruit from the rations on the return journeys.

◆ ◆ ◆

I wrote to Ivy telling her about my work as rations NCO.

"It's a cushy number apart from the dusty ride," I told her. "Whenever I go into Deolali, I usually make time to wander round the bazaars and do some shopping. While I was at the Indian Army Service Corps the other day, I met a corporal in the Royal Army Medical Corps. We were together in 106 Battery at Carlisle. We had a good natter while we waited our turn to load up on rations."

I hesitated wondering if I should tell her about my narrow escape.

"You would think I would be safe collecting and delivering the company's rations, but I had a near squeak two days ago in the flour store. Some heavy sacks of flour fell on me. Luckily, a couple of blokes were nearby and soon lifted them off. I was left quite winded, but otherwise unhurt. As usual, I am sitting in the tent writing this letter. It's evening, and I can hear the Indians playing their drums. It's little things like these that make me feel a long way from home.

"Yesterday was the Muslim feast of the New Year. All the Muslims were dressed up to the nines. It was so colourful and picturesque. The women wore brightly coloured tunics over the baggy trousers they wear to keep their legs hidden, and then I saw a beautiful sky blue one, which matched the colour of your eyes and thought how lovely you would look in it. Both the men and women wore dopattas, silk or cotton scarves worn as shawls, which glittered in the sunlight from silver and gold threads woven into the fabric. I took some snaps, and I'll send them to you as soon as I get them developed. I went for a swim in the Darna River with Darky. I don't think there are any crocodiles in it?? Then we watched the Muslims' New Year concert from the riverbank.

"I've finished being rations NCO, which is a pity because I enjoyed getting out of camp and exploring the bazaars each time I went into Deolali. I was on the carpet at 4:15 this afternoon, put on a charge again, which makes a round half dozen. The major doesn't approve of my taking the truck for my personal use, but he only gave me a reprimand this time—must be learning I'm not likely to mend my ways.

"When I've finished this letter, I'll write a telegram to Joan for her fifth birthday. I hope it will be a nice surprise for her. It's been a long time since we were all together. I hope she remembers who I am when I eventually return home. Write soon, sweetheart. I love you and miss you."

◆　◆　◆

The following day was busy. Taking the truck to the river, I washed off the thick layers of dust, which had accumulated during my frequent trips for rations. On my return to camp, I was ordered to bring water from Deolali for tea and supper as the camp was once again without water. At 8:30 p.m., I was sent for further water supplies. By the time I completed my

APRIL 1942—DECEMBER 1942

orders, it was almost midnight. Frustrated and tired, I rushed to send off Joan's telegram before falling into bed.

The company was scurrying about getting ready for a move to Juhu beach camp, Santa Cruz, near Bombay. I was put in charge of getting the motor transport in good shape for the drive south. Tool kits were organized for each vehicle. Drivers painted their trucks. Through it all, I was becoming more and more disgruntled as officers changed priorities, changed orders and countermanded previous instructions.

Sergeant Wellington came by with yet another change of orders. I threw my dirty rag to the ground in temper.

"I'm thoroughly disgusted with this company. Our officers are a pack of incompetent nitwits. God help us if they have to lead us in action. I've spent the whole day dashing round like an old hen trying to satisfy their orders. First they want us to paint the trucks, then they want us to concentrate on preparing them for the trip, and now they want me to do something entirely different!"

"Are we finished now, Corporal?" Sergeant Wellington asked in a droll tone of voice.

"Yes, Sergeant."

"Then get on with it. We're moving out in two days."

October 19th, the road party moved out—twenty-four trucks, me in the water truck and twelve motorcycles. The main body of the company moved by rail two days later. Once at Juhu, the units would be employed on camp structures and road building in Combat Training Centres near Bombay.

After a dusty drive, the road party arrived at Thana at 4:00 p.m. With no beds available for us, we had to sleep on the floor. In the NAAFI, we talked with some soldiers who thought we were lucky blighters to be going to Juhu.

"It's paradise by the sea," they told us.

"Yeh," someone else piped up, his tone of voice envious. "It's full of coconut palms with long stretches of golden sand. You can fall asleep listening to the sounds of the Indian Ocean surf crashing onto the beach."

"That sounds all right," I said.

"All right? It sounds great!" said Blondie.

We were in high spirits next morning when we set off for our final destination. That afternoon, the convoy rumbled to a halt in what looked like paradise. I eagerly climbed down from my truck. Wide-eyed and with broad smiles of delight, we gaped at the beach and the ocean in disbelief.

"This is bloody marvellous!" said Blondie.

The camp at Juhu beach

The bracing sea breezes dried our sweaty clothes and foreheads. Palm trees creaked in the wind and above our heads, palm fronds swished briskly with each gust. All the frustrations of the previous few days were forgotten.

"All right, Sergeant, set the men to work. We've got a camp to prepare," said Lieutenant Lind.

Over the next two days, we erected tents ready for the arrival of the main party. Guard duty was a unique experience. I lay under the palms listening to Hawaiian music then cooled off with a dip in the sea. It was so beautiful I couldn't wait to tell Ivy how tough I was having it.

Shanta Kumar Morajee

My daily duties included foraging for water supplies in the surrounding area. Driving into Juhu village to fill up the water truck, I spotted a well in the garden of a large house. I pulled

APRIL 1942—DECEMBER 1942

up and began to take on water. While I waited, I smoked a cigarette and looked round the peaceful garden with its footpaths, trellised arbours, statues and exotic plants. Hearing footsteps behind me, I turned and discovered a man I judged to be in his late thirties walking towards me. He was dressed in a white, long-sleeved Nehru tunic, which buttoned down the front and ended below his knees. Beneath the tunic, he wore narrow-legged white cotton trousers. On his head was a Gandhi cap, also of white, homespun cotton.

"What are you doing in my garden?" the man asked in Indian-accented English, his voice gentle and quizzical.

"I'm just getting some water for the British Army. That's all right, isn't it?"

"Yes. That is permitted. You may take all the water you need." The man examined the water truck and watched as it was filling from the well before he began speaking again. "Today is the first anniversary of my father's death, and you are the first person I have spoken to today. This makes you my friend, a special friend. Will you be staying in the area for some time?"

"Yes. Our camp is beside the beach."

"Come into my house, I have something for you. I am a businessman. I am well known here and in Bombay."

I followed him into the house. He signed the back of some business cards and handed them to me.

"I am giving you these cards. When you and your friends go to a restaurant, or cinema, or some other place of entertainment, you may show these cards. You will be given preferential treatment and a special price. If you get into any trouble, show one of these cards; it will help you. The authorities will recognize my name."

I read one of the cards.

"Your name is Shanta Kumar Morajee?"

"Yes. I own a trading company, and I have a fleet of ships that sail round the coast between Bombay and Calcutta. I own much land in and around Bombay. You will be well treated. You may visit my house whenever you wish. Not your friends, only you. But I allow no alcohol in my house. No drinking, no drinking at all."

"Oh, that's all right. I don't need to drink to enjoy myself."

"Then you are very welcome."

That evening, I told my friends about my meeting with Shanta Kumar Morajee.

"You're going to his house?" asked Darky. "What for?"

"It should be interesting to talk to a well-educated Indian. Hopefully, I'll learn something about India and its customs. After all, it looks like we're going to be here for some time."

"I wouldn't mind coming with you," said Hinny. "Are you sure he said only you could go?"

"'Fraid so."

"If he ever changes his mind about that, tell him we'd all like to come along too," said Blondie.

After supper, I walked to Shanta's house. It was large and airy. Decorative wooden panelling covered large areas of the walls. Curtains and sofa coverings were of brightly coloured fabric in deep blues, turquoise, rose reds, with golden stripes and elaborate designs of elephants and trees. Shiny brass ornaments were plentiful in all the rooms.

Sipping fruit juices and nibbling a fudge-like sweet called *barfi*, I listened as Shanta talked about Indian culture and explained what was happening in the snapshots he brought out for me to look at. There were photographs of an Indian prince riding in state to Congress sitting in a howdah, atop an ornately decorated elephant. In front, a turbaned *mahout* was riding on the elephant's neck. I studied photographs of the interior of Mysore Palace in southern India, one of the largest palaces in the country. I was amazed to learn it had a carved silver door and a solid gold throne. There were such big contrasts in this country—the opulent buildings, the slums, the wealthy and the miserable beggars calling *"baksheesh"*. Shanta told me about the diversity of lifestyles and religions in his country. It was enough to draw me back again and again to learn more.

The next day, after a morning fetching water and a relaxing afternoon swimming in the sea and sunbathing under

APRIL 1942—DECEMBER 1942

Shanta Kumar Morajee at home with friends

the palms, I again visited Shanta Kumar. We listened to the wireless, drank iced tea and ate cream cakes. I showed Shanta a small postcard I'd bought in September when I was in Bombay. The picture was entitled 'The Parsi Tower of Silence.'

"Do you know what this is?" I asked.

"Oh yes. This is one of the circular walled enclosures called dakhmas, or 'receptacles for the dead' for the followers of Zoroaster, the Parsis. When the funeral service is over, bearers carry the corpse into the enclosure and lay it out naked for the vultures. Once the vultures have picked the flesh off the body, the clean bones are thrown into the central pit. For the Parsis, it is the most sanitary way to dispose of their dead. Would you like to go and see one? The dakhmas are in Bombay on Malabar Hill."

"Yes I would. Tomorrow's Saturday. I'll be free after 9:30 in the morning."

Arriving at Shanta's house, I was ushered into his grey Wolseley and ferried into Bombay, twelve miles away. We drove to Malabar Hill where the forest's dense vegetation hid the dakhmas from public view. We were not allowed to go through the gateway into the dakhma, but perched on the enclosure's stone walls and surrounding trees, I could see large, well-fed vultures, plump as Christmas geese, patiently waiting for the next meal.

Shanta dropped me off near the bazaars, while he went to a business meeting. I gleefully indulged in some outrageous haggling with the shopkeepers while buying a snapshot album and some socks. After a lunch of chicken and salad in a Chinese restaurant, I had refreshing swim at Breach Candy baths. A satisfying day off was completed with a visit to the cinema and supper in a Hindu café before catching the train to Santa Cruz. Leaving the station, I found an army truck, waiting to ferry soldiers to Juhu.

My army duties at Juhu beach were not demanding. Once I'd found water and supplied it to the camp and a nearby Royal Artillery unit, I spent my days tinkering with the truck, changing the oil and checking the carburettor. Afterwards, as I soaked in the sunshine and swam in the Arabian Sea to cool off, I felt content and full of gratitude. Apart from a bout of *dhobi* rash, life was idyllic, and I had another interesting evening with Shanta Kumar to look forward to.

◆   ◆   ◆

"I'm astonished by the variety of temples, mosques and churches in Bombay," I told my new friend. "Tell me about your religion."

"As you know, I am Hindu like most of the people who live in Bombay, but then there are Muslims, Buddhists, Christians, Jews, Parsis, Sikhs and Jews. We are most tolerant of all religions in this country."

"Yes, but what does it mean to be Hindu?"

"Hindus believe there is one supreme god called Brahman, who is present in all things and who gives all living things life, just like Christians believe God is omniscient and omnipresent. We also believe there are many aspects of that God. We worship Shiva, that part of Brahman that destroys the old and useless so that new can be created. Then we have Brahma, the creator God. He recreates the world after Shiva destroys it.

APRIL 1942–DECEMBER 1942

We also have Vishnu, God of protection, who sustains and preserves creation."

"What about the god with the elephant's head?"

"Ah, Ganesha. Ganesha is the god of foresight. He removes all obstacles. We pray to him for the wellbeing of our future. Hindus believe in reincarnation. We believe we live many lifetimes. The kind of life I am living now will affect the kind of life I will have when I am reincarnated. In each lifetime, we learn more and increase our understanding, until the day comes when we no longer need to reincarnate."

"Why are cows sacred to Hindus?"

"The cow is a sacred animal because it represents God in all living things. It is also an animal that gives much and takes very little. Hindus aspire to the same ideal. We are vegetarian too. We believe that eating meat prevents our spiritual growth."

"I noticed you have a shrine in your house."

"Yes. As part of our daily duties, we Hindus tend to our shrines. We clean it and place fresh fruit and flowers there. Every day, my family prays and chants before the shrine."

Shanta took an old cigar box off the shelf.

"I have told you enough about my religion. Let me show you what is happening in India."

Taking out some photographs, he showed me photographs of a crowd, carrying banners in the streets of Bombay to protest the arrest of Gandhi and Nehru in August.

"The protests were peaceful in accordance with Gandhi's policy of non-violent opposition to the British government in the 'Quit India' campaign," Shanta explained, "yet you can clearly see the police wielding truncheons and beating protesters to disperse the crowd. This violent repression does not endear the British government to us."

"Do *you* want the British out of India?"

"Yes, of course. I hate the British. They have taken over my country. It is time for India to form its own government and for Indians to rule their own country. I am a member of the National Congress Party. I have no personal animosity towards the British soldiers—they are just trying to do their job. Indeed, you are my special friend, but politically, it is time for the British government to relinquish its hold on India." He paused, then asked, "What do you and your friends think about our struggle for independence?"

"Most of us understand why you don't want to be ruled by a foreign power. If that were happening to us in Britain, we wouldn't like it. Heck, we're fighting Hitler to prevent that from happening. So, yes, we do understand why you want us out. We just wish we didn't have to get caught up in battling civilians when violence breaks out."

"Another evening, when it is not so late, I will tell you more about Indian politics."

Leaving Shanta's house, I strolled back to camp under the bright moonlight. It was pleasantly cool. My thoughts were of Shanta Kumar. He was such a charming, interesting man, and I was pleased to be his friend. I was learning a lot about India.

◆ ◆ ◆

The following Saturday morning, Shanta gave Darky and me a lift into Bombay where we enjoyed a day shopping, visiting the cinema, eating a hearty lunch of steak, egg and chips, and later, tea in the Coffee Club. Returning to camp at the end of the day, we caught a bus to Byculla. During the walk to Dadar station from the bus stop, I felt uneasy.

"Keep your eyes open, Darky. It doesn't feel very safe here. We're the only white men in the area."

"I know," said Darky. "I keep expecting a knife in my back any minute."

We stayed alert and watchful, but managed to board the train to Santa Cruz without incident. When we arrived at Santa Cruz, a lift in an army truck back to Juhu saved us a five-mile hike from the station.

November was a busy month. Not only was I supplying water to 62 Company and the Royal Artillery, the Signals and Royal Air Force were added to my delivery list. On top of that, when 1, 2 and 3 Sections of 62 Company moved to Marve to construct a bridge over Acksa Creek, I travelled the ten miles from Juhu to deliver water to them. On one trip, I cooled down

APRIL 1942–DECEMBER 1942

with a swim in the creek with Darky, who told me the men were working twenty-four hours a day in shifts to complete the bridge.

In Juhu, the steamroller arrived; the unit could now tarmacadam the roads. Despite my busy schedule, I found time to

Part of 62 Company hard at work building Acksa bridge, Marve, near Bombay, 1942

cool off with a swim in the ocean each afternoon and time to visit Shanta several times each week. Listening to the wireless at Shanta's house November 5th, we heard good news from Egypt—Monty was leading a victorious campaign at El Alamein. I cheered and said, "Carry on Eighth Army. Pound them into the ground. Let's get this war over so we can go home. I'm feeling homesick."

Two weeks later, the wireless was still broadcasting good news of the fighting in North Africa, as well as the destruction of part of the Japanese fleet in the Pacific by the Americans.

The evenings I spent in camp, I played cards with my friends or wrote airgraphs and sent snapshots to Ivy, my mother and Aunt Bessie. I told them how the seas off Juhu beach claimed the lives of two men from the Royal Army Medical Corps, who were caught in a treacherous undertow. I shared how I spent my days off, travelling into Bombay and going to one of the many cinemas to see films such as *How Green was my Valley*. I told them of the dances I attended at

Bombay town hall with the lads and how we went for *tiffin* in the Services Canteen, lunch in St. John's Institute, tea and cakes in the Coffee Club. And I told them how much I missed them and wished I were home.

◆ ◆ ◆

One of the evenings I went to Shanta's home, I met some of Shanta's friends, including the editor of *The Bombay Journal*. As Shanta's wife passed sweetmeats round on silver trays and brought in a large jug of fruit juice, I was asked if I knew anything about the political situation in India.

"Well, yes," I told them. "We received a lecture when we were at Deolali. I know that Indians want independence. We were told how Gandhi encouraged the people to be involved in civil disobedience and make peaceful protests. But also there is friction and conflict between Hindus and Muslims."

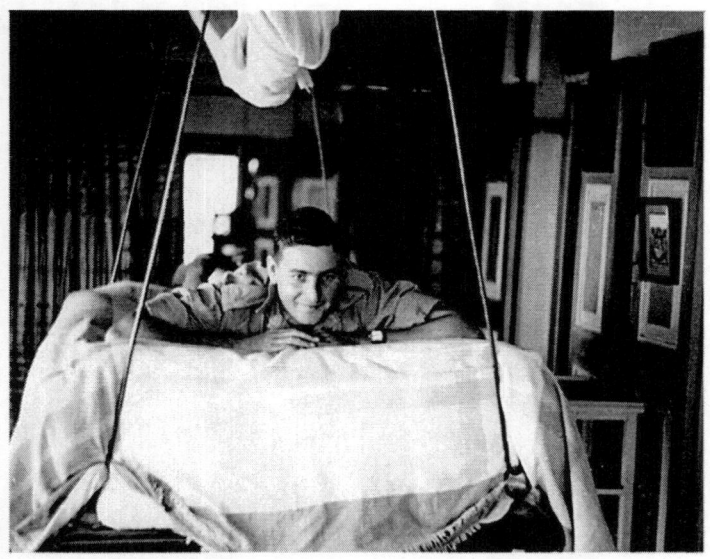

Norman relaxing in Shanta Kumar Morajee's house.

"Very good. It is wise to have some understanding of the events taking place here, but that is not the whole story," said Shanta.

APRIL 1942—DECEMBER 1942

"No. Gandhi is looked upon as a saint," someone else continued. "That is why he is called Mahatma or great soul. Gandhi brought all the Indian people together with a sense of purpose through his courage and determination."

"He is most astute. He knows how to create images," said the editor, "and he knows how to use newspapers and cameras to promote his cause. He makes himself available to the press, and his greatest campaigns for independence are carefully planned to create dramatic impact on the people and world opinion."

"How does he do that?" I asked.

Shanta took up the thread.

"Here is one example. The government had a monopoly on the manufacture of salt. Gandhi announced that he would defy British law by making salt. At sixty-one years of age, he set out on foot to march two hundred and forty miles from his ashram to the sea, accompanied by scores of his supporters and, of course, a contingent of reporters. As he walked along, thousands of people joined him. Newspaper stories reporting the events captured people's imaginations. On reaching the sea, Gandhi made his symbolic gesture by picking up salt from the shore. Salt making spread like wild fire all over India as did the civil disobedience campaign."

"His ability to inspire the masses is awesome," another guest continued, "but let us not forget what a wily politician he is. He never tried to stop the extremists. He relied on their terrorist activities to produce situations which he hoped would make his own non-violent bids for independence more acceptable to the British government."

"In 1940, the people were clamouring for independence. Incidents of passive resistance increased," said Shanta. "Jawaharlal Nehru and over twenty thousand congress supporters were jailed. There were so many congress leaders in jail that Muslims moved into the vacant positions of power; power they used to fight for the partitioning of India. Mohammed Ali Jinnah, leader of the Muslim League, out manoeuvred us. On August 8th, Congress passed the Quit India resolution. Gandhi and other Congress leaders were arrested.

Violence erupted. Protesters tore up railway tracks, attacked stations, post offices. Anything that was symbolic of British rule was destroyed and set on fire. Clashes broke out between Muslims and Hindus. Hundreds of people died."

"So that's what the riots were about in Nasik. Some of our units had to go and deal with the trouble a few months ago."

"Yes. That is so."

"And you, Shanta. Are you involved in all this?"

"Yes. I, and my friends here, we are all involved in plans and political manoeuvrings to remove British rule from India once and for all. You might call us subversives. If I were ever stopped on the street by the authorities, and they examined the contents of my briefcase, I would be arrested and sent to jail like Nehru and Gandhi."

I was speechless and honoured that he trusted me enough to tell me this. I never told a soul.

◆ ◆ ◆

At the beginning of December, I began two weeks leave in Bombay and booked into the Salvation Army Hotel. On the second day of my leave, I was strolling round the town when I bumped into Cliff Brough, who was exploring Bombay on his day off. We spent the day together. Bombay was awash with American soldiers on leave, intent on having a lively time. Everywhere we looked, we saw boisterous, rowdy, Americans turning the town inside out, ruffling feathers, keeping the MPs busy with an occasional brawl involving British soldiers and sailors.

We were amazed at their brash ways and self-assurance.

"There must be thousands of them here," Cliff complained.

"All causing mayhem and chaos," I said. "They're nutters."

The next evening, I spent three hours with four of these hooligans and had a great time. I found their invincible attitude, confidence and liveliness infectious. British soldiers were quiet and reserved in comparison. It wasn't that they lacked confidence; they just expressed it in a more subdued way.

APRIL 1942–DECEMBER 1942

After reading the morning newspaper on the hotel's sun-drenched veranda, I took a leisurely walk to The Gateway of India and sat for thirty minutes underneath the centre arch. Although homesick, I was full of the wonder of it all. *Fancy me being here, under this Gateway to India. Me, an ordinary working class lad running round the British Empire, going to Africa, whooping it up in Bombay, making friends with Shanta Kumar. It's hard to believe all this has happened in a few short months. Life's really wonderful at times.* I wished Ivy could be with me. The best I could do was to describe it all in my letters.

I spent my leave in Bombay dancing at the Bombay Club, Greens, the town hall, and the Sports Club. I even returned to Byculla for the Royal Air Force dance, getting a lift back to my hotel in the red caps' truck. I went to some of the many cinemas in Bombay, the Regal, Metro, New Empire, Excelsior, Eros and the Strand to see the latest releases. I ate and snoozed and wrote airgraphs home.

Darky arrived at the hotel for his leave. Over the next few days, more men from 62 Company trickled into town. Together we went to the races. At Mahalakshmi racecourse, the scenes were colourful. Barefoot grooms in white uniforms led the well-groomed thoroughbreds, with their gleaming coats, round the paddock. The grandstand was full of affluent people studiously following their horses with binoculars as they thundered round the track. I watched the well-to-do race goers shrug light-heartedly when they lost their bets or clap gleefully when they won. Working class people, huddled opposite the clubhouse beyond the racetrack, revealed more anxiety about their bets with tense faces, teeth chewing lips, and crestfallen faces as their horses trailed the field. Everyone, those carefree and those apprehensive, enjoyed the spectacle of vividly attired jockeys and prancing thoroughbreds. Never having seen horse-racing before, I soaked up the atmosphere.

December 8th was a day full of incidents. After breakfast, we watched the march past of the crew of the Bengal, an Indian Navy minesweeper, which had docked in Bombay. We felt proud of being in the forces. Two hours later, as we wandered through the streets, we noticed a column of thick, black smoke rising over the centre of the city.

"What's happening there?" I asked a passer-by.

"A school is on fire, sahib. It is very bad," the man said.

"Poor devils! I hope no children are hurt." I turned to my friends. "Let's see if there's anything we can do to help."

We hurried towards the billowing smoke. A crowd had gathered, concern visible on each face. The fire department spewed water into the building, which was well ablaze. Every once in a while, some inner wall collapsed, sending a burst of sparks and smoke high into the air. Looking around, I noticed the school's pupils congregated well behind the crowd. Teachers calmly controlled the crying youngsters, who appeared shocked and frightened.

"Did they all get out?" I asked a policeman.

"No, sahib. Some of the children and one of the teachers did not get out of the building. They are probably dead. They cannot survive in there," he said, nodding towards the inferno.

A wave of sadness swept over me. I needed to move away from the scene.

"Come on, lads. Let's go. There's nothing we can do here."

Late in the afternoon, I interrupted my leave to catch the train back to Juhu to say hello to Captain Stewart Anderson from Redcar, a town only eight miles from my home town. Then it was back to the foray for beer drinking, dancing and cinemas.

My last day of leave was December 14th. After sending my kit back to camp on a truck, I spent a quiet day meandering through the streets and visiting the Prince of Wales Museum and, of course, another cinema. Before catching the train at Churchgate station, I popped into the Coffee Club to celebrate my twenty-fourth birthday, which I'd forgotten four days earlier. Inside, I struck up a conversation with a quiet, unassuming American merchant seaman.

Spotting an empty seat at the sailor's table, I went over. "Hello, can I sit with you?"

"Sure, pull up a chair." He offered his hand. "I'm Homer Inglis from Houston, Texas."

"I'm Gus. I'm on my last few hours of leave before I catch the train back to Juhu beach."

"First time I've been to Bombay, but then this is my first trip anywhere," Homer confided.

"My father was in the merchant navy years ago. He travelled all over the Far East. My brother and my uncles are merchant sailors now," I said.

I was having difficulty tearing my eyes away from Homer's inflamed skin peeping out from behind his shirt where the top three buttons were unfastened.

"Is that a new tattoo you have there?"

"Sure is," said Homer proudly. "Look at this. It's as sore as hell, but worth every rupee."

He unbuttoned his shirt to reveal, etched on his smooth, hairless chest, a spectacular picture of the American eagle, wings outstretched across the pectorals, battling a writhing snake, which it was holding down with its talons.

I gasped, partly in admiration for the scope of this work of art, partly because Homer seemed so young to be permanently marking himself with such a large tattoo and partly because his chest seemed to be so sore.

"Homer, it's beautiful, but it's so permanent. How old are you? What if you decide later that you don't want it?"

"Me? I'm twenty, and I'll never get tired of this tattoo. I'm from a small farming community. Nobody, but nobody has a tattoo like this in the area. I'll be the envy of every guy around," he said, pleased with himself. "Haven't you gotten one while you've been here?"

"No, I've never fancied getting a tattoo."

Homer buttoned up his shirt. I was interested in his life in Texas, and he wanted to know about my life in England. We talked about our different life experiences all evening, until I left for the 9:00 p.m. train back to camp.

Arriving at Juhu, I heard the shocking news on the wireless. Someone had thrown a bomb into the Coffee Club, killing a sailor and injuring some soldiers. I was engulfed in sorrow and prayed that Homer survived to be able to show off his tattoo to his friends. It was a near thing for me too. I must have only missed the attack by a few minutes. I couldn't believe how lucky I had been.

Christmas in Deolali

With a sad farewell to paradise, we left Juhu for Deolali on the morning of December 16th. I'd been caught by surprise, only finding out we were moving off when I returned from leave. I was disappointed and upset because I hadn't had time to say goodbye to Shanta. I hoped he would not think too badly of me for leaving without a farewell.

It was a hellish run, on crumbling mountain roads, as bumpy as riding a bucking bronco and as dusty as having a shower in ash. Nine hours of driving brought us to MacLaren Camp, South Deolali. The whole group, including the units from Marve, had already returned.

A few days later, all NCOs paraded in the Commanding Officer's office. Major Robinson had been promoted to Lieutenant-Colonel of 51 Indian Chemical Warfare Group R.E. Captain Cave, promoted to acting major, was taking over command of 62 Company. I shook hands with newly promoted Lieutenant-Colonel Robinson.

"I'm sorry to see you go, sir, but I'm pleased they've seen fit to promote you. Good luck, sir."

I began to feel sick and listless, yet my days were as busy as ever. New Chevrolet trucks and Norton motorcycles arrived. I was allocated a new three-ton water truck. The days were full as we worked to bring the vehicles up to optimum performance and reliability.

Trying to write letters home before Christmas, I felt so much under the weather, I couldn't concentrate. I was placed on sick leave and would have rested on my bed, except with my dysentery, I had to keep running to the lavatory. While I was feeling rotten, the rest of the company was involved in mortar and other training exercises.

APRIL 1942–DECEMBER 1942

Christmas Eve arrived, and I was no better. All I could manage to eat was a small amount of bread and butter. Feeling weak, I rested in bed as much as I could and spent the evening in the tent. It was the worst Christmas Eve I have ever experienced. Ivy was at home, thousands of miles away; I was sitting in an Indian Army camp in South Deolali.

Mine wasn't the only miserable face in camp. Everyone was despondent during this first Christmas away from England. The atmosphere in the camp was decidedly flat. The men, normally eager for lively diversions and creating fun, sat morosely round the NAAFI tables. Like me, they all felt far from home. There would be no watching children opening presents on Christmas morning. We were sitting in a place we did not want to be, our hearts and minds elsewhere. I felt maudlin. We all felt maudlin and oh, so lonely. A tidal wave of sorrow swamped the camp.

Sitting by the campfire that night, a drunken soldier began to sing in his rich baritone voice:

> *There'll be bluebirds over*
> *The white cliffs of Dover*
> *Tomorrow, just you wait and see.*
>
> *There'll be love and laughter*
> *And peace ever after*
> *Tomorrow when the world is free . . .*

The song's lyrics tugged at our homesick hearts, sending some of us into the tents to seek privacy. Men lay on beds, arms folded behind their heads, unseeing eyes staring at the canvas roof or squeezed tight shut, eyelashes glistening with unbidden tears.

I lay on my side on top of my bed, staring at a photograph of Ivy and Joan. My aching heart, feeling like a ton weight inside my chest, pained my sick body. I could hear muffled sobbing in a nearby tent. "Merry bloody Christmas," I muttered, as I forced myself into the escape from emptiness that sleep would bring.

A CORPORAL'S WAR

There was a noticeable lack of cheer on Christmas morning. Everyone was still down in the dumps. I returned to my tent after breakfast, *to wait for what?* I thought. *Bugger all, that's what.* The cooks did well, providing us with a tasty traditional Christmas dinner. Major Cave gave a boring speech. Still not feeling well, I slept most of the afternoon away.

That evening, I listened to the King's speech on the NAAFI's wireless followed by a classical music and jazz broadcast from Ceylon. Then I joined the lads singing round the campfire. A couple of drunks sang solos. I listened to the racket for a while before going to the tent where I lay on my bed and tried to cheer myself up. It was the worst Christmas I'd ever spent. Even so, we had a lot to be thankful for. We hadn't been involved in any heavy fighting since Dunkirk. We weren't in North Africa or living on the streets like the beggars in Bombay. It could have been much worse.

Having got past the sadness of Christmas, Boxing Day was livelier. The company held a mock group parade. Some men shaved their heads and wore sheets as if they were Tibetan monks; others dressed in sheets, imitating the followers of Gandhi. Norman Stock and friends smeared their bodies with war paint, carried spears, and wore grass skirts, pretending to be African natives and won first prize for fancy dress.

Christmas fancy dress parade 1942

Following the fancy dress parade, the company held sporting events. I took part in the tug of war, but I wasn't on the winning team. Feeling weak again, I spent the rest of the

APRIL 1942—DECEMBER 1942

day playing cards, writing airgraphs and listening to the wireless.

New Year's Eve was spent cleaning the water truck. I began to feel ill again as the dysentery returned. Unfortunately, I didn't manage to escape guard duty that night. All the lads were in bed early to be well rested for company training exercises on New Year's Day. It was a quiet, pitch-black night, too quiet for New Year's Eve.

1943

Madras

It was time to move on, eastwards toward the rising sun.

Leaving Deolali South, the company moved off to Madras, an 849-mile journey by road in a fifty-six-vehicle convoy. I was given permission to be last in line. Still suffering from amoebic dysentery, I frequently had to leap from the truck and dive into the bushes. It was an exhausting journey for a sick man. Five days later, the convoy arrived at Bangalore, where we paused for a day to do some maintenance on the trucks before going on to Madras. By now, I was experiencing severe abdominal pain, diarrhoea and dehydration, but I was determined to stay with the company. I wasn't going to be left behind to finish the war with strangers. I'd been with my friends in 62 Company for three and a half years. I intended to see the end of the war with them and no one else. They were too valuable to lose to an attack of dysentery.

We reached Madras at the beginning of February. Seriously ill by now, I collapsed and was taken to the British Military hospital despite my protests.

I pressed the doctor, "How long will I need to be here? I don't want to lose my company."

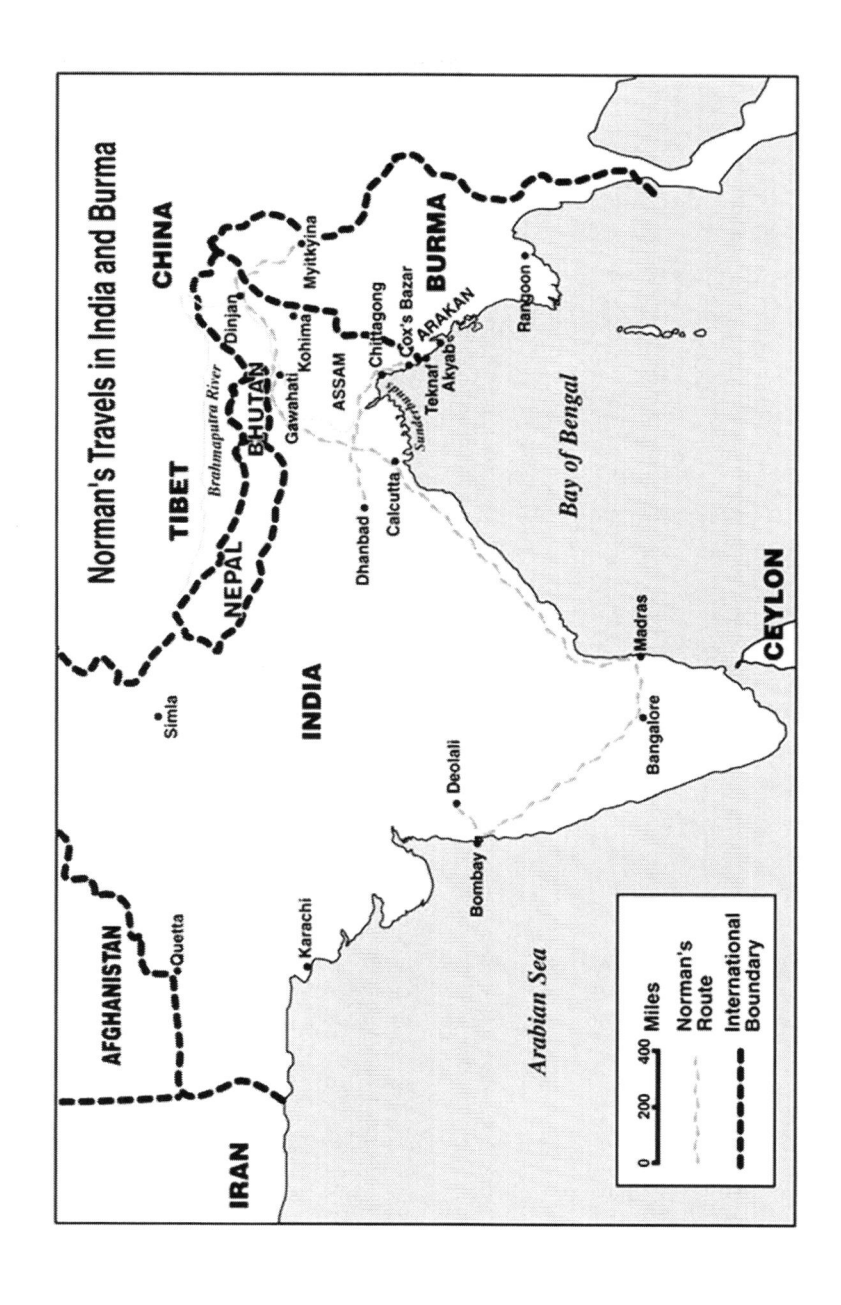

1943

Norman's Travels in India and Burma

"Don't worry about that now. You are very ill. You have an extremely serious case of dysentery," the young, bespectacled, Indian doctor informed me. "Come with me. We will look after you."

I was admitted to a ward crammed with beds and walls painted bright blue. I was the only European on the ward; all the other patients were Indian. As the two-week course of emetine injections took effect, I started to feel well enough to take more interest in my surroundings. I was amused to discover that during the day the Indian patients sat on their beds while they socialized and played cards, but when it was time to sleep, they abandoned their beds, preferring to sleep on the floor. I felt the odd man out for staying in bed to sleep, as the Indians unrolled rush mats and settled down in the spaces between the beds. I was prescribed a further two-week course of treatment and worried anew about being left behind by my company.

"We must be sure you are fit and well before returning you to your army duties," the doctor insisted.

The doctor discharged me from his care after five weeks. My concern about losing my company turned to relief. It was still in Madras and was going to remain there for several more weeks for weapons training, field firing, demolition work and participation in army exercises with 51 Indian Infantry Brigade.

The unit's stay in Madras was not all work. We were quick to create interesting diversions in our leisure time.

"I hear the Indian Army nurses here in Madras have a reputation for being good hockey players," I told the group gathered round the table in the NAAFI.

"Is that so?" said Darky. "I guess we'll have to show them how to really play, won't we?"

"Tommy's the sports rep. We'll get him to challenge them to a game," an enthusiastic Hinny joined in.

The nurses, eager to show the Royal Engineers what they could do, set a date for the end of the week. Darky, the most aggressive hockey player in the unit, was centre forward; I played half-back.

1943

"Now listen lads," Sergeant Wellington spoke to the team before the game, "you have to remember you're playing a ladies' team. Take it easy on them."

"Of course we will," Darky answered. "They'll be a push over. We'll go gently, so they don't look too bad when they lose."

Our cocky side ran out onto the parade ground confident that we were already the victors. The nurses, faces beaming with excitement, trotted casually to their positions.

The Royal Engineers won the coin toss but magnanimously allowed the fair sex to choose which end to attack in the first half. Realising the soldiers thought women would be no match for them, the nurses lowered their heads at Darky's smugness and patronising gesture. Smiling impishly, they glanced knowingly at one another.

What's the saying? Ignorance is bliss?

They bullied off. One tap, two tap, three tap. The nurses' team centre forward deftly took the ball. The action raged as the nurses moved quickly to dominate the game. Our team attacked vigorously, trying to take control of the ball. Darky took a serious tumble that left a horrendous graze on his cheek and blood trickling from his left nostril. The women sparkled, scoring some wonderful goals. To shouts of encouragement from the spectators, I delivered a snappy pass to Darky, who walloped the ball into the goal.

In the sweltering heat, we were soon soaked in sweat. At half-time, the Engineers were trailing by five goals. Bruised and battered, we discussed our situation before play resumed.

"Who's the clot who said we'd better go gently with them. They're slaughtering us."

"Come on, fellas. Let's show them what we can do when we really mean business. Don't hold back."

The fast, hard-hitting game continued. It was rough play as both sides summoned all the grit and heart they could muster to keep up a forceful attack. We tried to salvage the game. With time slipping away, Darky broke loose with the ball and fired into the net to cheering and hollering from the spectators. The nurses retaliated, scoring three goals in quick succession. The crowd erupted. Then it was over.

Reeling from the defeat, we staggered from the field, pride and bodies bashed and beaten. Darky, covered in cuts, abrasions, and sporting shins bearing dark blue bruises, ended up needing a week on sick leave to recover from the game.

At the refreshment table, the players tucked into tea and sandwiches.

"You went through us like a dose of salts," I told the nurse next to me.

"You gave it your best shot," she smiled, disarmingly. "Hockey is India's passion, you know. Our national hockey team's already won four Olympic gold medals for India."

Dabbing the blood away from his nose with a spit-dampened handkerchief and grimacing in pain, Darky limped towards us.

"We thought we needed to be gentle with you. Were we ever wrong. You gave us a good game. Mind you, we're going to take some stick from the boys now that we've been beaten by a women's team."

The nurse smiled sweetly and looked at his wounds.

"You know, if you wanted to catch a nurse's attention, there are better ways than almost getting yourself killed," she flirted with him.

Surprised and flustered, Darky coughed and spluttered as he choked on his sandwich. I burst out laughing and pounded Darky's back to clear the blockage.

Darky was right. The Royal Engineer's hockey team certainly took some ribbing from the men in the unit. We were met with comments such as, "Fancy being beaten by a group of women." "What's going on? Are you getting soft?" "Don't get discouraged, lads. We'll find some school kids for you to play against next time."

The jibes continued until we left Madras on May 17th. Before leaving, 62 (Chemical Warfare) Company was disbanded and reorganized as 62 Field Squadron Royal Engineers.

1943

Assam

The next two weeks we travelled by train to north Assam, land of tigers and one-horned rhinos. Carried along on flatbed cars, each truck had an experienced driver sitting in the cab for the whole journey. It wasn't the most comfortable of journeys. The rest of the company enjoyed the luxury of sitting in carriages. Each mealtime, the train would stop to allow the cooks to prepare food and make tea, using hot water out of the train's engine.

We arrived at Amingaon on the mighty Brahmaputra River near Gawahati at 1200 hours, only to discover there was no bridge over the river, which at this point was one and a quarter miles wide. The ferrying of men and trucks started six hours later and continued until transfers were completed at 0400 hours. Now on the eastern banks of the Brahmaputra, we moved into Pandu transit camp, where we languished for five days owing to an accident on the railway. Finally, at 2300 hours, May 28th, the squadron entrained and left Pandu.

Sleeping in the cab of a truck, on a moving train, doesn't provide for a restful night, but as I struggled out of the fog of sleep one morning, I sat bolt upright, captivated by the scenery, catching glimpses of feeding deer and startled antelope as the train chugged along the narrow gauge railway track, hemmed in by wild jungle.

When the train halted for meals to be served, there were no facilities available to cater for even our most basic needs. Relieving ourselves required a trek into the bush.

"Makes you wonder what conditions are going to be like at camp when we get there," said Blondie.

"Makes you wonder where the hell we're going," I said. "Do you know what we're doing here, Sarge?" I called to Sergeant Wellington.

"Not yet, Gus. They'll tell us in good time."

"It looks like we're going to the back of beyond," said Mac.

"How's the trip going, Gus?" asked Darky.

"It's a bit rough cramped up in the cab all day, and the heat coming through the windshield is horrendous. Keep your fingers crossed I don't die from heat stroke like poor Joe Maddocks back at Kharagpur. Looking at the views and watching people working in the fields and seeing all the wild animals keeps my mind off the discomfort."

"Looks as if we're going into mountain country," said Blondie, nodding towards 3,000 foot high jungle-covered hills to the east.

"It seems to be all jungle and small rural villages. I guess we're not going to have much nightlife to write home about. No Bombay cinemas, or dances here," Darky moaned.

Thirty-six hours after leaving Pandu, the train reached its final destination at Dilsum sidings. We moved into temporary quarters at Chabua. That first night, I lay on my bed wondering what the army had in store for us and why we were in this wild country.

◆ ◆ ◆

The reason for our presence in Assam dated back to the Japanese invasion of China. By 1942, China had been fighting the Japanese for four years and the United States had been supplying arms and materiel to China through her southern ports. When the Japanese cut off supplies along the coast, China was forced to build the Burma Road. Western aid was then shipped to the Burmese port of Rangoon, moved by rail and river to northern Burma from where it was ferried by truck 700 miles along the Burma Road into China.

After the bombing of Pearl Harbour in December 1941, America declared war against Japan. American General "Vinegar" Joe Stilwell was sent to China and Burma in February 1942. He was to be senior American military representative to the China-Burma-India theatre of war. One of his responsibilities was to keep the Burma Road open from Lashio to Kunming and keep it in Allied hands in order to keep aid flowing into China. There were over one million Japanese troops battling in China, and every Japanese soldier that was kept busy there was one less soldier fighting the Allied Front in the Pacific.

The Japanese, seemingly intent on conquering the whole of Asia, raced down the Malayan peninsula to attack Singapore. The British Army's traditional fighting tactics of using roads and vehicles were no match for Japanese troops trained in jungle warfare, and in February 1942, the 130,000 British soldiers in Singapore surrendered. It was the greatest disaster in British military history.

The Japanese Army swarmed into Burma from Thailand, took Rangoon and charged northward to cut the Burma Road. The British military in Burma was an army of occupation, not a fighting force. They had little chance of success against the fierce, experienced fighters of the Japanese Army. With the Japanese overwhelming the British in battle after battle, General Alexander decided to abandon Rangoon and withdraw overland to India. The longest retreat in British military history began with the Japanese continually harrying the British during their 900-mile trek to the Indian border. Of the 42,000 soldiers of the British-Indian Army withdrawing to India, only 12,000, in a pitiable condition, reached the safety of Assam.

Aggressive Stilwell detested the British for retreating and leaving him with no option but to flee as well. He led a band of 114 people 240 miles through disease infested jungle, across rivers and over mountains in monsoon conditions, before staggering gaunt and starved into India.

While the British press described the retreat as "an heroic, voluntary withdrawal" and "a glorious retreat", Stilwell's response was testy. "I claim we got a hell of a licking. We got run out of Burma, and it's as humiliating as hell. I think we ought to find what caused it, go back and retake Burma."

He was determined to recapture Burma and build an overland route from India through northern Burma to China.

For the British, it was a humiliating defeat by well-trained jungle-fighting forces. Returning soldiers, telling stories of the enemy being fanatical fighters who would rather die than surrender, created an image of Japanese troops who were ferocious and invincible. Morale within the British Army plummeted. Many soldiers deserted; others stopped taking anti-malarial drugs, preferring to be ill in hospital rather than fight an enemy they feared in the dreaded jungle.

The Japanese occupied Burma except for a small area in the far north-east. Having stretched their lines of supply, they did not attempt to invade India, believing the jungle-clad, mountainous terrain between India and Burma to be impenetrable.

For the Americans, it was imperative to keep supplies moving into China to keep her in the war and forcing Japan to keep a well-trained and well-equipped force tied up there. With the Burma Road and southern Chinese ports unavailable, the only way to carry aid to China was by air from Assam over 'The Hump', the nickname given to the Himalayan foothills, which lay between Assam and China.

The United States Army Air Force began a regular air service between the two countries, flying military supplies into China and bringing back reinforcements for the diminished Chinese force General Stilwell had led out of Burma and which he was reforming in Assam. In order for this air service to continue and expand, the construction of 200 new airfields, workshops, warehouses, offices and other buildings for the American bases was urgently needed along with accommodations for 30,000 American troops.

◆ ◆ ◆

We soon learned we had been brought to the area to build airfields for the United States Army Air Force. The squadron was split up into four sections with one section assigned to each of four airfields—Chabua, Dinjan, Mohanbari and Sookerating. Squadron headquarters were situated at Chabua airfield used by the Americans to fly supplies into China. My troop was assigned to Dinjan airfield, which at that time consisted of tangled, overgrown virgin jungle. The whole squadron was spread out over a radius of forty miles and supplies for each unit were to be drawn from the supply depot in Dibrugarh thirty miles away.

1943

We were expecting to live in field conditions so we were pleasantly surprised to find native huts called *bash*as provided for our living accommodation. The *bashas* were constructed using a bamboo frame with woven bamboo and palm leaves for the walls. The floors were compacted dirt, and the thatched roofs crawled with a myriad of insects. We soon discovered that rats, lizards, snakes, and insects would vie for a place in these dwellings. No sooner had we stowed our gear and organized our quarters than the briefing sessions began.

Bamboo basha

Sergeant Goodwin spoke first.

"Listen carefully, men. There's a lot to take in. We have a lot of hard work ahead of us to build this airfield, seeing as how it's still jungle out there. The airfields are top priority, so we'll be working twenty-four hours round the clock to get the job done. You will get two half days off each week. However, what you can do on those half days off is limited. All villages are out of bounds, owing to malaria and infectious diseases in them. All restaurants, so called hotels, and eating-houses are out of bounds, except the Chinese restaurant "Comrade" at Dibrugarh. The "Chunking" and "Wakoo" are out of bounds until further orders, owing to an outbreak of smallpox."

This information was met with groans.

"You are a spoilsport, Sarge," someone called out.

"Better a spoilsport than a coffin bearer, lad. Now, malaria is likely to be as big an enemy as the Japanese, so anti-malarial precautions will be strictly enforced. From 1830 hours to 0600 hours long sleeves and long trousers must be worn, even in this heat. All mosquito nets to be down and tucked in by 1830 hours and rooms sprayed with the flit guns at dusk."

"What flit guns are those, Sarge?"

"You'll be picking them up after this briefing session. A squad will be organized to clean up the area around the campsite and do everything possible to prevent mosquitoes from breeding.

"This area is subject to periodical air raids by the Japanese. Alarm posts will be detailed, and steel helmets and respirators must be kept handy at night. Full blackout conditions apply from dusk to dawn. Night guard duty—watch out for anyone trying to sabotage the vehicles or pilfer from the stores, apparently that sort of thing is rife round here. And finally . . ."

Muted cheers erupted behind me.

With a touch of sarcasm, Sergeant Goodwin asked, "What's the matter, lads? In a rush to go out on the town? Anyway, as I was saying, the Commander of General Reserve Engineer Force orders you to keep a high standard of smartness, both on works and especially walking out after duty. You are not, repeat not, to copy the slovenly and unsoldierly habits of the American transport drivers you'll see around here. Now, Lieutenant Curtis has something to say."

Lieutenant Curtis stepped forward.

"You can see we're out in the wilds. There are no canteen contractors here, so each troop will have to organize its own canteen and appoint someone to run it. The Commander of the Royal Engineers is going to provide a hut and some furniture, and a *pani-wallah* will be provided to do the washing up and help out generally. In the meantime, until we can get a more permanent canteen organized, we are going to set up some mobile canteens to keep us going. I think that's all I need to say at the moment."

1943

"Everyone dismissed apart from the drivers," said Sergeant Goodwin.

Sergeant Wellington stood up to address the drivers.

"You've received a lot of information this afternoon, so I'll keep this brief."

"Good for you, Sarge."

"Put a sock in it, Jackson, and let me get on. We're at the end of the supply line here in north Assam. In all likelihood, we'll have a lot of trouble getting the spares that we need, so you must keep your vehicles well maintained. And drive carefully. I have it on good authority that this place has some of the heaviest rainfall in the world. The monsoon season is just starting, so it won't be long before the roads are in bad condition, and some may even be washed away. Also, stay away from Americans driving heavy vehicles. They drive too fast, and they're selfish, inconsiderate road hogs. Give them a wide berth. Avoid making any unnecessary trips in your vehicles; they may have to last us until the end of the war. That's all, men."

While wells were being drilled through the ninety feet of subsoil in the Brahmaputra valley, and bulldozers cleared virgin jungle to prepare for the construction of Dinjan airfield,

The mobile canteen was a welcome sight in North Assam where there were no facilities in June 1943 (IWM)

I volunteered to drive the mobile canteen. For one month, with Mrs. Fortesque, a slim, energetic tea-planter's wife, I travelled round the various British, American and Indian camps, airfields and hospitals in the area.

Wherever we stopped, servicemen hurried over to buy homemade cakes, biscuits, sandwiches and drinks. It was not only refreshments that made the mobile canteen's appearance such a welcome sight. Homesick soldiers, missing the company of wives, mothers and sisters left behind in England, relished the motherly attention Mrs. Fortesque lavished upon them at each site.

Women and children, employed by the British Army, break rocks for road building.

With the ground levelled, construction of Dinjan airfield began in earnest. The tea planters' Board of Labour found the workers, and soon the air was filled with the noise of hundreds of Indian *coolies*, both male and female, hoeing and chipping at the stony earth with primitive tools. Heavy equipment was in limited supply and was reserved for only the toughest of tasks. My job, with a team of six sappers, was to supervise the unloading of building materials at the railway sidings. Construction moved smoothly. The airfield began to take shape, with runways big enough for B25 bombers. Hangers, storage units, gun towers, and accommodations for American and Allied troops living around the airfield were sprouting up. It was all coming together. Top brass were pleased with the speedy progress. Then an uninvited guest came to the show.

Equipment in North Assam was in short supply. 62 Company R.E. was fortunate to have a bitumen sprayer to use in building airfields.
(Imperial War Museum)

Encounter with a Goddess.

I slid behind the wheel of my truck and set off towards the siding with my crew of sappers in the back. As the truck trundled along the track, I wished it were not my turn to work the late shift. I was still stunned by the news I'd received that afternoon. Rene was dead—of pneumonia. She was only twenty-two. It was hard to believe I would never see my sister again. Once at the siding, my reluctance at being there evaporated. The work of unloading shale and gravel from the railway wagons and transferring it into trucks ran smoothly. By keeping busy, I kept my mind off Rene. It would not be such a bad night after all.

Darkness closed in as I smoked a cigarette. Deep in thought, it was some time before I realized the *coolies* were stealing away from the siding. Tossing the cigarette aside, I grabbed my rifle.

"Hey, get back to work! Where the hell do you think you're going? Come on now, get back!" I ordered, as I tried to halt the exodus.

With downcast eyes, the men ignored my orders, hurriedly dodging past me. Catching sight of Sanjay, the Indian foreman, I demanded, "What the blazes is going on?"

"Sorry, Corporal Sahib. I tell you. The woman has come, and the men will not work now that it is dark."

"What woman? What are you talking about?"

"It is the woman with no feet, Corporal Sahib."

The foreman was almost dancing in agitation at being delayed.

"Sorry, sir. She is here. I must go."

Blackness enveloped the siding. Deserted by my *coolies*, alone except for the crew, I was completely nonplussed. Stirring myself, I strode to the truck and opened the door. "How the hell do I explain this to the C.O.?"

I ordered the sappers into the truck. Then, breaking all speed records for an army truck on the washed out roads of north Assam, I lurched and jounced back to camp to report to my commanding officer.

"It's not good enough, Corporal. You have to get them working somehow. It's imperative we keep working round the clock. We need those materials down at the airfield."

Oh sure, I thought as I left Major Cave's office. *Easier said than done.* With no chance of any work being accomplished at the siding that night, I went to the canteen looking for Darky, who was working at the siding on the day shift. As he listened to my tale, Darky shook his head in disbelief.

"Beats me, mate. I've never heard of the likes of that before."

Arriving at the siding the next afternoon, I went to the foreman.

"Will the men work tonight?"

"No, Corporal Sahib. She is here."

"Tell me what the men are afraid of."

1943

"The woman is now here, sahib. She is a woman with no feet. No, sorry, sahib. She is a woman with her feet on backwards. Sometimes, she comes as a large cat. The men will not go anywhere near her. If they do, they will die. She walks backwards and calls to them, '*Idher aao, idher aao*'. This means come here, come here. If they go, they are never seen again. People believe she is a phantom, a goddess. This happens here in Assam."

At nightfall, the *coolies* fled. I didn't try to stop them. I knew it would be useless. Once again, I returned my men to camp and reported to Major Cave.

"Damn it!" Major Cave exploded, slamming the desk with his fist. "I don't care what you do, but we have to get these men back to work. See to it."

I met with Darky to tell him the latest developments.

"We'd better do something about it then, hadn't we?" said Darky. "I'm on late shift next week. I want it all sorted out by then."

"What have you got in mind?"

"Get your rifle and plenty of ammo. We're going to the siding. We'll sit up all night if we have to waiting for this . . . this . . . whatever it is."

That night nothing happened. The second night was also uneventful. Sitting in the *basha* at the siding on the third night, we were alert, waiting. We listened for any alien sound other than the usual jungle cacophony of rustling leaves as animals scuttled about, the incessant croaking of frogs and the occasional screech of an animal falling prey to a hungry predator. In the humidity of the night, sweat beaded up on our tense brows and upper lips. Then about midnight, I heard it—a cat howling.

The sound gave us the creeps. Fear gripped our guts. Darky adjusted his hands firmly round his rifle as I carefully opened the door. Looking out into the darkness, we could just make out the shape of a large black cat standing in the middle of the siding. Stealthily, silently, it moved into the shadows towards the piles of shale beside the track. Slowly, I closed the door. Tension and trepidation filled the *basha*. Our hearts pounded loudly. Hairs on arms prickled like porcupine quills as we struggled to control our erratic breathing.

"If it starts howling again, I'm going to shoot it," muttered Darky annoyed that he had, just for a moment, almost lost his nerve. He checked his rifle again.

Standing by the door, breathing deeply, rifles at the ready, we steeled ourselves for action.

It called again. *"Idher aao, idher aao."*

My eyes locked onto Darky's. With a curt nod, we charged from the *basha* firing off round after round at the cat, by moonlight clearly visible in the middle of the railway track. Bullets thudded into the animal's body. Adrenaline pumping, we continued firing until the rifles clicked empty. Keeping our eyes on the track ahead, we fumbled more bullets into the rifles with trembling fingers and walked cautiously along the track, until we came to the spot where we expected to find the cat dead, but found nothing. No blood, no corpse, just splinters in the wooden railway sleepers and marks in the gravel where the bullets had struck.

"Where the hell is it? I know I hit it," said Darky.

We scouted around for a few more minutes, but there was no cat to be found.

The eeriness of the place gnawed at my nerves.

"Let's get the hell out of here."

Darky didn't need telling twice. As if the devil himself was after us, we scrambled into the truck and bolted down the road. Darky started to chuckle. Before long, he was roaring with laughter, rocking in his seat, holding his ribs and slapping his knees. I stopped the truck and looked at him in amazement. Then I too began to snigger before bursting into hearty laughter. Tension and fear melted away.

"Fine pair we are," I chortled. "I almost wet myself."

"Me too. I nearly filled my pants," added Darky.

We burst out laughing anew. Hysteria over, we calmed down, thoughtfully drawing deeply on our cigarettes, as we pondered the night's events.

"What do you make of it, Darky?"

"Buggered if I know. I've never believed in ghosts and that sort of stuff."

"There should have been a dead cat up there. It couldn't have just been wounded and crawled away. It was hit too many times, so where was its body? We didn't imagine it, did we?"

"I don't know, Gus. I don't understand it."

"I guess there's a lot more to life than we really know. The *coolies* knew something was up. It'll be interesting to see if they'll work tomorrow night—I mean tonight," I said, looking at my watch. I started the truck.

"Let's not say anything to anybody about this, Gus. They'll think we're crackers."

We returned to camp having made a pact to say nothing about our escapade at the siding—at least for the time being.

When I arrived at the siding for the evening shift, the foreman hurried across.

"Sahib, she has gone."

"Who's gone?"

"She, the goddess, she has gone. She was not wanted here. She was told she had to go."

"So, what will happen now?"

"The men are back at work, sahib. They will work tonight and every night from now on."

I smiled to myself. *Wonderful how being on the receiving end of a few bullets can make someone feel unwelcome, even a goddess.*

"Tell the men I'm pleased they are ready to work hard. I'm glad this nonsense is over."

Throughout the rest of the shift, I puzzled over it. Was it only coincidence that the men returned to work this evening, or did we really chase a ghostly goddess away last night? I guess I'll never know.

Pastimes in the Valley

In my letters home, I told Ivy about my life in Assam.

"We're living out in the wilds in bamboo huts called *bash*as. They're dry and comfortable even though the monsoon has arrived, and it rains heavily at times. When it rains, it really comes down. The road to Sessa camp was washed away last week after taking a beating from the Royal Artillery towing in their guns, and a lot of roads are impassable right now. Our *basha* backs onto the jungle. We can almost reach out and touch it from our veranda.

"There are lots of restrictions on what we can and can't do and where we can and can't go. Although it's against orders, I go off exploring with Darky. We put on our knapsacks, pick up some 'K' rations, grab our rifles, (just in case we come up against any trouble) and then off we step into the jungle. It can be dangerous. Because the foliage is so thick, it's easy to become disoriented and lose your way, but we've done all right so far. We've come across sacred shrines and native villages hidden well away from the airfield area that no one has ever seen before. We found places where the women rolled their own *cheroots*. Using sign language to communicate, we managed to buy some. For only two rupees, we can fill our knapsacks with cheroots, which last us for weeks. It's much cheaper than buying cigarettes from the canteen, and anyway, there's a shortage of cigs in the NAAFI. The natives are friendly towards us. We never feel unsafe or in any danger. They are warm, wonderful people.

"As soon as we enter the jungle, it's a different world. The plant life is beautiful. Clover-coloured wild orchids hang from trees like giant catkins, and yellow flowers, looking like lilies, peep out from the undergrowth. Monkeys chatter overhead in the tall trees. Birds and parakeets with brilliant plumage flutter over our heads squawking in alarm as we disturb them by moving through the foliage, which is so dense in places, we have to hack our way through with machetes. The animals are fascinating. I managed to get a snapshot of an antelope just outside our *basha* before some noisy clot scared it away. I love it here. Some of the men can't stand the heat and humidity, but it doesn't seem to bother me, although, the leeches can be a pest when we're in the forest. We use cigarettes to burn them off before they suck us dry of blood.

1943

"You'll be surprised to learn I've taken up fishing. I go off into the jungle to some ponds I found about ten miles from Dinjan. Native boys set me up for a day's fishing by providing me with some bait for ten annas. They bring me a hollow, bamboo tube about fifteen inches long, plugged up at both ends. Inside, now don't scream in horror, there are usually fifty huge cockroaches, not worms, for me to fasten to the hook. I know I've given you the creeps, but you can stop shuddering now, I won't mention my bait again.

"It's interesting the people you meet in the jungle. I was fishing one afternoon when I heard a voice from behind me say in perfect English, 'Are you having a good day's fishing?' I looked round and was amazed to find it was a native talking to me in my own language and speaking it better than I do. He told me he'd been to school in England, but before I got the chance to have a really good talk with him, I felt a tug on the line. I turned to pull in the fish all the while talking to him over my shoulder, asking him how he liked England, but there was no reply. When I looked round, he'd gone, vanished, melted away into the jungle. I never saw him again.

"I never go back to camp without a load of fish slung over my shoulder. I take them straight to the cookhouse. Anything that gives us a break from soy sausages and bully beef is a wonderful treat.

"The food is poor here. We're short of even basic things such as milk for our tea, bread, flour to make cakes and even, would you believe, razorblades. We're told it's because of the difficulties involved in moving supplies from Calcutta to here, but the Americans seem to have plenty of good food. Unfortunately, on our pay, we can't afford to buy anything in their PX.

"In July, we became 62 Field Company instead of a squadron. Sergeant Wellington was promoted to C.Q.M.S. (Company Quarter Master Sergeant). We celebrated by having a party in our *basha*. I got a bit merry and a bit boisterous, but it was harmless fun, and that's all I am going to tell you about it.

"We're using elephants on the airfield works for lifting heavy timbers or dragging heavy construction materials to different locations. A corporal from Middlesbrough is in charge of one of the elephants. He let me have a ride. It was great. The elephant bent his leg so I could climb up on his back, and I rode him for ten minutes. If you think they're big animals when you stand next to them, they're an awful lot bigger when you're up on their backs.

"All in all, we're not getting into any serious mischief here. We play cards and drink a few beers in the *basha*, and tinker with our trucks and motorcycles, listen to the wireless, and have lots of discussions on what's happening in Europe, but most of all we miss home. I'm making the most of having to be here. I'm not sitting and moaning, but it doesn't alter the fact that I miss you, and I would rather be with you than anywhere else in the whole world. Roll on the end of the war so I can come home to you. I love you, always."

Elephants were used to carry timbers during construction at Dinjan airfield.

Flying the Hump

With little in the way of entertainment in Dinjan, we were spending yet another evening in the *basha* talking and playing

1943

cards. As Cliff dealt a hand, I asked, "Does anyone fancy flying into China to see what it's like?"

"What, in one of those rickety old buckets? Haven't you seen the burned out plane wrecks at the end of the runway in Chabua?" said Darky, his tone of voice indicating he thought I'd lost my marbles.

"Well, that's only when they try to land," I joked. "Just kidding, Darky, just kidding," I quickly added seeing the look of horror on Darky's face. "The American planes are fine. Their wheels don't drop off like they do on those decrepit Chinese planes that have started using Dinjan airfield. Seriously, I know there's some risk, but they seem to do okay. The pilots keep making the trip. None of us has ever been to China. Let's do it while we've got the chance. What do you say?"

"Never been to China? Gus, I've never been on a blooming plane!" Darky protested.

"Neither have I. What do you think?"

"I wouldn't mind going," Hinny offered.

"It'd be something to write home about. God knows there's sod all else happening here," said Tommy.

"Go on then, Gus. See if you can fix us up with a trip," said Darky, surrendering to the enthusiasm of his mates.

In the following days, as I made the rounds with the water truck, I asked about flights to China at the various airfields in the area. I struck it lucky at Chabua. Joe, a young fresh-faced American pilot with nicotine-stained fingers, agreed to take us as long as we gave him something to sell on the black market. Unknown to the commanders of Air Transport Command, this pilot was part of a small contingent of the American Army Air Force, hell bent on its own missions when flying to Chungking; the risk of a court-martial didn't deter them from smuggling cigarettes, chocolate, and other saleable items into China.

The day of the flight, I was the only one of my group who could go. Darky was stuck with guard duty, Blondie was in hospital with a fever, and everyone else was working. I drove to Chabua airfield. It was early morning. My shirt was already dark with sweat from the heat and humidity in the steaming Brahmaputra Valley. I carried my great coat to wear, once I was on the plane. Hidden deep in its pockets were six bars of chocolate, three bars of soap, and a few packs of cigarettes.

I went looking for Joe and discovered that two other American servicemen, one a pilot, were also making the trip.

"Hi, Corporal, this is Chuck and Gene. They're my business partners. They'll be keeping you company during the flight," said Joe, introducing his companions. "Have you got the stuff I asked for?"

I handed over my contraband.

"First flight? How do you feel about going over 'The Hump'?" asked Gene.

"The Hump?" I repeated, mystified.

"Yeah, 'The Hump'. It's the nickname we've given the Himalayas. We'll be flying over them to get to China."

"Oh, I'm really looking forward to it."

"Let's hope you don't puke. It's a rough ride," said Chuck. His expression was hostile, seemingly taking exception to my presence.

"Don't worry about Chuck," said Gene, cheerfully. "He thinks we could do without taking along a Limey soldier, as he put it, on our first trip to China. Besides, it's too early in the morning for him to be civil."

I climbed in after the two Americans and took my seat on the aluminium benches, which ran along each side of the fuselage. There were no parachutes despite the dangers involved in flying 'The Hump'. Between June and December 1943, 155 airplanes crashed with 168 crew fatalities. This total didn't include passengers who also lost their lives. The flight path from Assam into China went over the Naga Hills, inhabited by the Naga headhunting tribes, then over the precipitous peaks of the Patkai Range to the east of Chabua. After that came the 20,000 foot eastern ranges of the Himalayas called the Santsung Mountains.

Treacherous weather waited in ambush for planes flying 'The Hump'. Severe thunderstorms sprang up from nowhere. Clouds rolled in to cover the peaks. Violent, life threatening turbulence threw planes around without mercy.

1943

Blissfully ignorant of the hazards I was about to face, I was itching to be off. I didn't wait long. The Dakota's engines roared into life, and the plane taxied to the take off point. Picking up speed, the Dakota rattled and lurched along the rough surface of the runway. Already wondering if I'd made a mistake in deciding to visit China, I clenched my teeth, as much to stop them from jolting loose as anything. I clung to my seat. Looking across the fuselage to Gene, I shouted over the noise, "Is it always like this?"

The airman nodded and smiled.

"Sure as hell is," he shouted back. "Take it easy, soldier."

"Oh, I'm fine," I answered, forcing confidence into my voice.

Suddenly, the jolting stopped as the pilot nudged the plane into the air. Here it was, my first flight. The plane climbed steeply, carrying me off to the blue skies above. I hoped I wasn't going to meet my Maker. Below, neatly laid out tea gardens fell away to be replaced by the jungle's dense green canopy slashed by the passage of an occasional river. A large part of this jungle was uncharted, a blank, white patch on the map. Even if the crew of a downed plane bailed out safely, the chances of them ever emerging from that wild, green hell were almost non-existent.

The drone of the plane's engines was reassuring. Unable to compete with the noise, I settled into my seat. There would be no interesting conversations to pass the time on the long journey. As the plane soared higher, icing conditions set in at 15,000 feet. My teeth began to chatter. Less than an hour before, I had been wet with sweat—but then I was still on the ground. I put on my great coat and relaxed my tense muscles.

The view through the windows to the north was of the Himalaya's snow-capped peaks, stretching far into the distance. I marvelled at their imposing, barren magnificence. I felt I was flying over the top of the world.

Passing over the high mountains, the plane began to lurch, pummelled by eighty-knot winds. Then the plane, caught in a downdraft, shuddering as if it would fall apart, plummeted towards the ground at three thousand feet per minute. Wrestling with the controls, Joe regained mastery over the plane. Banking steeply between two peaks, he managed to avoid slamming into a mountainside. Bruised from being flung from my seat, I didn't know if I was more relieved to be flying on the level again, or by not throwing up now that my stomach was stuck in my throat.

"Way to go, Joe! Nice bit of flying," the two American passengers shouted to the pilot through the doorway to the cockpit as they settled back in their seats. Eugene hollered across to me, "You okay?"

I nodded, a wry smile on my lips.

I thought I was having a rough ride, but at least I was spared another of the dangers of 'The Hump' flights—Japanese attacks. These didn't begin until several months later in October 1943, when four American planes were lost.

Over 700 miles and almost six hours later, the plane began its descent. Dropping rapidly, it landed with a jolt on Chungking's rough gravel, constructed by thousands of labouring Chinese using the most basic of tools.

"You did all right there, soldier. I was surprised you didn't puke all over the plane when it got a bit rough," said Chuck, with begrudged admiration.

"The name's Gus," I said, "and don't think I didn't come close to sharing my breakfast with you back there."

The Americans were still laughing at this as we gathered outside the plane in the bright sunlight. Because it was the first time in China for all of us, we decided to stick together while exploring Chungking.

When Japan invaded China, the city became the temporary seat of government of Chiang Kai-shek, leader of the Chinese Republic. For this reason alone, I was expecting a city that was attractive, pleasant, worthy of receiving dignitaries from other governments, but it was not to be. Chungking was a bruised and battered city fortress, a grey drab place perched on the hillsides overlooking the Chang River. The once white walls and buildings were now painted black, camouflage against Japanese bombing raids. Shops and buildings reduced to rubble were quickly rebuilt in flimsy fashion to once again ply their trade. Its steep, winding streets teemed with small, black-

1943

haired people going about their business—people walking, talking, laughing, arguing, hurrying, scurrying, limping, staggering, children relieving themselves in the gutter as the occasional rickshaw, cart or bus passed by. Clouds of dust raised by traffic clogged the air. Breathing was unpleasant, the atmosphere polluted by odious fumes from the belching black exhausts of buses fuelled with alcohol. Other smells pervaded the air, ferociously attacking the senses—filth, the stench of filth, caused by foul, unsanitary practices of people who defiled their homes by defecating around the exterior of their houses, squalid dwellings besieged with stinking excrement.

Our stroll round the morass of filth that was Chungking was brief. In less than an hour, we were ready to leave.

"I've had enough. Let's go back to the airfield," said Gene in disgust.

"There ain't nothing worth seeing here. It's a dump, a dirty, filthy dump. Let's go," Chuck spat out, lips curled back in distaste.

There was no argument. All we wanted was get as far away as possible from the loathsome place.

Joe, always the entrepreneur, suggested we get some chow down at the airfield and then see what business he could drum up selling or swapping the loot.

"There's bound to be some airfield personnel who want to make an easy buck."

Stomachs filled, business completed, we made the return journey to Assam, this time with less excitement. The weather was kinder and the turbulence insignificant, at least for a 'Hump' flight.

Back on the ground, I removed my great coat to be more comfortable in the valley's muggy night air.

"Was it a profitable trip for you then?" I asked my new-found friends.

"We didn't do as well as we hoped," Joe answered for the group, "but we'll try another time. How about you? Glad you came?"

A CORPORAL'S WAR'

"Oh, definitely! Mind you, I won't be doing it again. Once was enough. Thanks for the ride, Joe. It was quite an experience."

Fearsome Jungle, Fearsome People

As if we didn't work hard enough, building airfields and roads in the heat and humidity, at the end of our shifts, we would borrow a truck for a tour of the airfields—Dinjan, Mohanbari or Tinsukia—to volunteer our services as kickers.

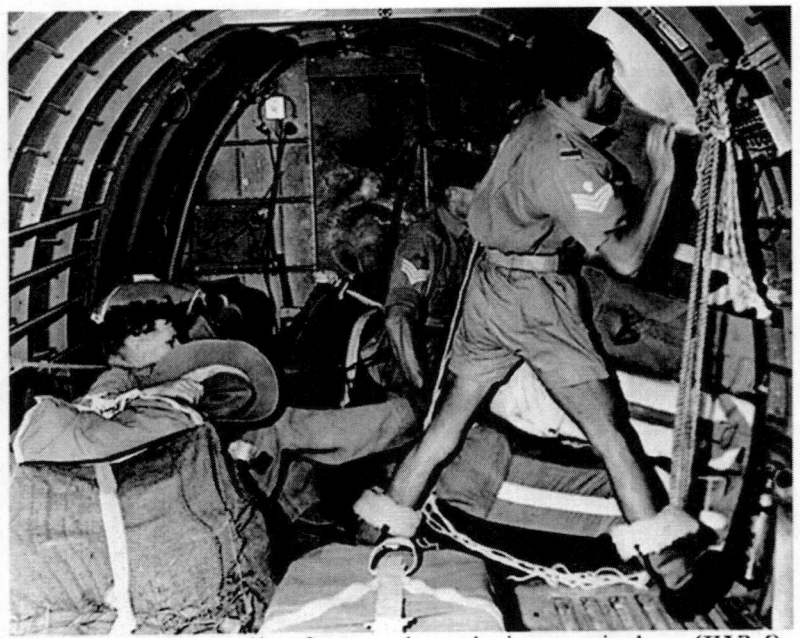

Kickers push supplies from a plane during an air drop (IWM)

The Royal Air Force flew three and four-hour missions to drop supplies to allied troops in Burma's enemy-occupied territory. Here, General Stilwell's Chinese units were fighting their way forward into north Burma ahead of American Engineers building the Ledo Road, and Special Forces were causing havoc to Japanese communications and supply lines.

1943

There was a shortage of kickers to push supplies from the planes, and we were pleased to fill our spare time doing something to help. Dakotas were the planes in use, being the most suitable aircraft for the slow flying speeds necessary for supply drops.

The airfields were hives of activity as workers loaded aircraft. We always tried to fly in planes that had British pilots. We'd seen how American airmen gauged the weight of the loads for take-off by sizing up how squashed the tail-wheel was. British pilots were more meticulous, working out the manifest according to the book and ending the loading when maximum weight was reached.

The heavily laden planes rose up from the Brahmaputra Valley. Hugging the jungle-clad Naga Hills and flying low above the dense jungle covering the Patkai Range, the pilots headed for the drop zones. Sometimes, these were open paddy fields, sometimes a dry riverbed, or thin jungle where, if parachutes caught on trees, they could easily be recovered. Skilful pilots negotiated the tightest of spaces to circle for the drops. Sometimes, they delicately pivoted in river valleys so narrow they could have been manoeuvring inside the confines of a well. The aircraft flew low, so low the pilots and the men on the ground could exchange smiles.

Supply drop over Burma (IWM)

'A CORPORAL'S WAR'

The aircraft circled the drop zones, while we kickers sat opposite the doorway. With our backs against the fuselage, we pushed heavy bundles of supplies out of the plane with our feet. Parachutes billowed open as bales tumbled from the plane, carrying them gently to earth. Other items, such as bales of clothing, boots or fodder for the mules, were dropped without parachutes, a deadly business for anyone on the ground in the spot where they landed.

Mission accomplished, the planes, unarmed and defenceless, returned to base, if they were lucky.

Sunday, August 15th, one RAF plane did not return safely. On board as a kicker was Corporal 'Hinny' Henderson. The plane crashed somewhere in north Burma's jungle. It was a daylight flight. Attacks by Japanese Zeros were rare. Maybe the plane flew into a surprise monsoon squall. Nobody really knew what happened.

Distressed by the loss of my friend, I went to see Major Cave.

"Sir, I've heard about Corporal Henderson's plane going down. He's a good man, sir—a close friend. Permission to go out with the American Air and Rescue Service to search for him, sir."

"If the Americans allow you to go, I have no objections, Corporal Wickman. Good luck with your search."

I spent a whole week with the Air and Rescue Service, squeezed into the tail section of a small bomber, looking for signs of a downed plane and any survivors, but it was an impossible task trying to see any signs of life beneath the jungle's dense cover.

Numerous planes had been lost in that area. Most of the crews and passengers were never heard from again. With each day that passed, the likelihood of finding Hinny diminished. The jungle was a hostile place. Beneath the bright, green, jungle canopy, little sunlight penetrated to brighten the gloomy, jungle floor. Any survivors would have to contend with an enemy more deadly than the feared Japanese Army. Hostile natives, malaria, blood-sucking leeches, lethal scrub typhus, dysentery and hunger lurked along every stream. And then there was the possibility of stumbling into fanatical, thought to be invincible, Japanese soldiers. We'd heard enough

Flying over the jungle-covered hills that separate Assam and Burma (IWM)

stories of the difficulties the Chindits had endured in the Burmese jungle, and of atrocities committed by Japanese troops, to know survival in that environment required a miracle.

My imagination ran riot, picturing Hinny lying injured and starving to death, or wandering round in circles, lost and alone in the dense foliage, until he fell exhausted, waiting to die. I feared that he could have been found by natives and mistreated, murdered or even turned over to the Japanese.

After one week, with all hope gone of finding Hinny alive, Major Cave put an end to my searching. Not wanting to lose more men, he also banned us from volunteering as kickers. The British Army in India was developing a shortage of manpower with little hope of replacements arriving from Britain. There were hardly any men of fighting age left to be recruited into the armed services, and Europe had first call on those who were available.

I sat on my bed and looked at Hinny's empty bed in the corner. I couldn't believe there'd be no more long talks with him. It was so easy to share your worries with Hinny. He was a gentle, caring man concerned for others, and he enjoyed a joke too. Everyone felt it. We had often talked about how we belonged to a lucky company. Now, after more than four years together, Hinny was the first of our group to get it. We wondered if our luck was going to change. A grim pall hung over the *basha*.

We obeyed Major Cave's orders—for a while, but as we talked with one another in the canteen and spent evenings grumbling in the *basha*, a mood of rebellion developed.

"There's nothing in army regulations says I can't do what I like in my free time," said Mac.

"I miss being a kicker. I felt I was doing something useful," I said.

"You'd think they didn't want to end the war," said Tommy.

"If there's nothing in army regs says we can't continue being kickers, well then, let's go back to being kickers," I said.

"I'm for it. It's boring round here without going on the supply drops," said Darky.

"Me too."

"Count me in."

Feeling we were at liberty to be kickers in our free time if we so wished, we ignored Major Cave's disapproval and drifted back to the airfields.

◆ ◆ ◆

One of my duties was to lead patrols, consisting of three British privates and six Gurkhas from the Mahindra Dal Regiment stationed at the airfield, into the 9,000-foot high Naga Hills. The Gurkhas, seasoned jungle-fighters, were there to ensure my safety and the safety of any NCO leading the patrol. Danger threatened, not only from the perils to be found in the drenched rain forests of moss-covered oak, chestnut and rhododendron on the summits of the hills, but from the ferocious headhunters we were to meet. Patrols travelled by truck as far as the track allowed and then by foot to prearranged meeting places in the jungle near Laju, and Yediuk, only five miles from the Burmese border. Here, we met

1943

with Jing Phaw tribesmen. They had straight black hair, cut short above their ears. Most wore black loincloths and went barefoot. All wore necklaces with strands of brightly coloured beads, and some sported necklaces threaded through tigers' teeth. Those Jings who came from deeper in the jungle had tattooed faces and carried long spears with metal points, as well as heavy, two-foot long, wide-bladed knives.

A bush telegraph must have told the Jings that a patrol was on its way because it didn't take long for the tribesmen—some still headhunters, some never having seen Europeans before—to appear at the meeting places.

We were there on a mission and squatted down with the tribesmen to negotiate. The British Government paid one thousand silver rupees for each lost serviceman the Jings found and brought to the patrols. During the time I had been going on these patrols, the Jings had brought many servicemen's bodies out of the jungle. Carrying out this duty caused me much inner conflict. It was interesting meeting with these natural people unspoiled by civilization, but it was miserable work. No one ever seemed to be brought out alive. On one particular patrol, soon after Hinny had been lost, I found a Jing who spoke a little English.

"Don't they ever find any live soldiers in there?" I asked, nodding towards the forest.

The Jing conversed with his people. Whatever he said caused them to exchange glances, talk excitedly and then burst into merriment. He translated their reply.

"They did not realize the British Army wanted live men. If they found men alive, they killed them because it is easier to bring them out that way."

"Gordon Bennet! Gus . . . !" one British private cried out in horror.

"God, no! Tell them we want any soldiers found alive to come back alive," I cried, appalled. "Tell them to spread the word to all Jings. We want the men alive. Alive, not dead."

As the patrol carried the dead man back to the truck, I berated myself and cursed the world. How many lives were wasted because we didn't specify we wanted these men alive?

"Corporal Sahib, no your fault they no understand we want men alive," one of the Gurkhas tried to reassure me.

On returning to camp, I immediately went to Major Cave to inform him of my discovery. The army promptly doubled the reward to two thousand silver rupees for any live soldier the Jings rescued, and after that, it was no time at all before they were returning live men to the army and air force.

News from Assam, October 1943

"Darling Ivy,

We just got back from three days at Sadiya jungle camp. The 2nd Battalion Assam Rifles gave demonstrations and instructed us in jungle warfare and survival. I took snapshots of us all in our bush hats. We look quite the handsome adventurers. We were shown which fruits and plants we could eat and which were poisonous. We learned the easiest way to travel through the jungle without getting lost. We were also shown some of the Japs' dirty tricks such as making *pungyi* sticks from bamboo. They sharpen the ends into points, sometimes impregnating them with poison, and then plant them, pointed end up, in the foliage beside the jungle trails. Then, when you move down the trails, and they ambush you, of course, you dive off the trail to what you think is the safety of the forest, only to end up impaled on rows of these terrible *pungyis*. Jungle training was interesting. We had a lot of fun, and it was a nice change from the airfield. We were hoping we would soon be moving on the Japanese, but it looks like that's on hold for a while. Pity. The sooner we sort them out, the sooner we'll be home.

"Did Joan get the airgraph I sent for her birthday? She's six years old and hasn't seen me in one and a half years. Does she know who I am anymore? She'll be growing up so fast now, and I'm missing it all. It has been a long eighteen months without you. I worry about you all when I read of the air raids over England. Please stay safe. Don't worry about me. I know I'm coming back, but just in case anything does happen to me,

1943

I want to tell you about 'Crasher' Prail's widow. Remember I told you he died of typhoid a year ago, when we were at Deolali? Well, his widow wrote to Major Cave. She has not received an army pension yet. She hasn't even received the money from the collection we had for her. The men are up in arms about it. It's a shabby way for the British Army to care for the widows and dependents of its soldiers. So, if anything happens to me (and it won't because my mother always says only the good die young), but if it does, I don't want you to let the grass grow under your feet. Kick up a fuss and start screaming blue murder for your pension—you're entitled to it.

"I'm really missing Hinny. He was a good friend. I could talk to him about more personal things compared to the chitchat with the rest of the lads. When I hear about the fiasco with 'Crasher's' widow, it's a relief to know that Hinny wasn't married, but even that's sad too. Fancy dying without ever experiencing the kind of love that we share.

"Major Cave is doing what he can at this end. He's not saying much, but we can tell he's pretty well disgusted by the whole matter. He's a good commanding officer, doing a decent job in difficult conditions. Our rations are really pathetic, especially when we can see how well the Americans fare in relation to us. Sergeant Wellington told us that Major Cave even went so far as to buy vitamin C tablets from the Americans to try and keep us healthy. This is just another way the British Army is letting us down. They want us to fight a war, but by the time we go in, with the food we're getting, we won't be fit enough or strong enough to fight. But the C.O. isn't sitting on his backside. You'll never guess what he has us doing. Now that the monsoon is over, units at the airfields are planting vegetable seeds and raising ducks to help eke out the rations. So, now you know how I'm spending my spare time—fishing and gardening.

"We follow current affairs from news-sheets distributed to us. We're excited about what's happening on the Russian front and the latest Russian offensives, but we wonder what's going on in Italy with Badoglio's declaration of war against Germany. We can't understand why the Allies accepted this rather than unconditional surrender. Anyway, on to a subject that really gets us excited, and that is the Beveridge Plan. What a wonderful idea for employers and every worker to pay contributions from wages into a National Insurance Fund. At least no one need worry anymore about surviving if they lose their jobs, or become sick, disabled, or just too old to work. Most of us are all for it. Like us, the men here have memories of deprivations in the Depression and of widows struggling to raise families on next to nothing or ending up in the workhouse. Looks like we'll be returning home to a New Britain, if Beveridge's idea of instituting a welfare system is adopted.

"There's a terrible famine in Bengal. People are dying on the streets of Calcutta and all over the area. Our *coolies* working on the airfields and roads are all right because we sell them rice at a reasonable price. We've been asked to contribute money to a famine relief fund for the destitute in Bengal. We'd be all for it except the government of Bengal says there is no shortage of rice, and any shortages are due to transport difficulties. If this is right, it would seem that any money we give to charities to buy rice will go straight into the hands of profiteers charging exorbitant prices, so as yet we haven't had a collection.

"There was an earthquake the other night. I woke up needing a pee. Bleary-eyed, I stumbled to the back of the *basha* where I relieved my bursting bladder at the jungle's edge, (too much beer the evening before). I was standing next to my truck when I suddenly felt the ground trembling. Then it began heaving. Everything was rocking. As the ground pushed me upwards, my truck was moving downwards. It was a queer sensation, especially after a night's drinking. I called to the lads to come outside. They thought there was an air raid, till I told them it was an earthquake. It lasted about three minutes. I couldn't believe it. The next morning's news announced the earthquake had killed quite a few people at Quetta, 1,500 miles away. When we went to inspect the airfield, it was all ridged like the sand on Redcar beach after the tide's gone out. We had to set to work re-levelling it. It'll take several weeks to get it back into shape.

1943

"I went on leave before we went to jungle camp. I could have gone to Calcutta, but after hearing it's full of staggering skeletons because of the famine, I decided to spend my leave on a tea plantation instead. I wouldn't have enjoyed myself seeing all that tragedy in the streets and knowing there was nothing I could do to change things. Anyway, I enjoyed the company of the managers Mr. and Mrs. Melville, and I think they enjoyed mine. It was strange sleeping in a proper bed instead of a rope and wooden framed *charpoy*. I spent a lot of time on the veranda enjoying the roses, blue hydrangeas and carnations. I felt homesick because they reminded me of my mother's garden.

"The labourers work hard tending the tea bushes. The women (now don't be jealous) work bare-breasted. They're not in the least bit self-conscious about being naked above the waist.

"I read a couple of books from Mr. and Mrs. Melville's book shelves and had lots of interesting conversations at mealtimes. This was a bit disconcerting because while we talked a dozen pairs of glass eyes, from the stuffed antelope heads that adorned the dining room walls, were watching us. The highlight of my stay came one evening as we sat on the veranda. It overlooked a game trail on which I saw deer, wild boar, and a leopard. Mr. Melville told me that wild elephants sometimes came along, but I didn't see any during my stay. On the plantation, the atmosphere during the day was pleasant and industrious, but towards dusk, the dark forest, with its giant ferns and clumps of bamboo edging the plantation, became more sinister and dangerous. This particular night, we were sitting quietly when we heard a tiger growling. Mr. Melville silently left his chair, put his finger to his lips to signal me to keep quiet, and then flicked a switch to turn on a big spotlight that lit up the trail. Standing in the glare of the light, only about twenty yards away, was a huge tiger. I held my breath as it stopped, looked up at the light and then glanced around flicking its ears to catch any sounds. Satisfied there was nothing to worry about, or better still, that there was no hunting for him there, he just carried on his way, as if he was the king of the jungle strolling through his realm, which of course he was. My heart was pounding in my ears I was so excited.

"We have lots of soldiers at the base now—British, Chinese, Indian and more and more Americans arriving all the time. They're really livening up the place. I'll tell you more about them in my next letter. I love you with all my heart.

Always,
Norman"

Disgruntled Yanks

American fighter pilots, technicians, and gunners were posted to the airfields of north Assam. Their job was to keep supplies moving into China by flights over 'The Hump' and to keep General Stilwell's engineers supplied so they could complete the Ledo Road, winding from Assam through northern Burma to China.

While morale among the British soldiers was high, that among the American servicemen, especially ground personnel, was low. By American standards, living conditions were generally bad. We lived in tents or insect infested *bashas*. In this land of heat, humidity, sheeting rain, and cloying mud, we felt deprived and neglected. Amenities in the valley were few and far between. There were no dances or cinemas as in Bombay and Calcutta and little in the way of recreational facilities. The majority of Americans hated the place—the malaria, the dysentery, the lack of even the most basic items such as razor blades, toothbrushes or toilet paper. Assam was at the end of the line for supplies and equipment brought by rail and truck from Calcutta, a thousand miles away. Even then, monsoon rains, earthquakes, and 'Quit India' terrorists blowing up railway bridges, were apt to disrupt the supply line on a regular basis.

Life was monotonous. The food was monotonous. Canned fish, corned beef, dehydrated potatoes, and Spam, Spam, and more Spam till it came out of our ears. With no refrigeration

1943

cars on the railways, no fresh meat was shipped in. It was common to see off-duty American pilots and soldiers, scruffy and unshaven, sprawled around their *bashas* playing cards, flicking through well-worn, dog-eared magazines, or just sitting about bored to tears. They were angry, argumentative, belligerent and undisciplined.

We tended not to mix with the Americans. Although we got on well with most of the aircrew personnel, and we admired the American push and drive to get things done, we found the ground crews to be braggarts. Strutting about with pistols in their belts and mouths as big as the Grand Canyon, they boasted about how brave and tough they were. They frequently vented their anger and frustration at being stuck in Assam by taunting British servicemen, calling us cowards for letting the Nips run us out of Burma. They believed they wouldn't be in this God-forsaken-place if the Limeys had put up a fight and kept the Burma Road open.

◆ ◆ ◆

I became friendly with some American anti-aircraft gunners at Dinjan airfield, especially Leroy, who introduced me to the Post Exchange or PX. Leroy and I spent many an evening talking over a few beers in the PX or in my *basha*. Leroy, like most of the servicemen stationed at Dinjan, had not yet been involved in combat. He listened in awe to the stories we told about our experiences in France and at Dunkirk.

I was sitting in the PX one evening with Leroy, some of the other gunners and Blondie and Darky. We became targets for ridicule and insults, as an American ground crew, itching for excitement, anything to liven up the place, tried to provoke a fight. Energetically chewing gum, jaws pumping like pistons, three American ground crewmen sauntered into the canteen. Seeing us, they sauntered over and surrounded our table like hunters who've cornered their prey.

One man, tall with square shoulders and a short, bristling crew cut, spoke.

"Well, well, Leroy, what've we got here stinking up the place? Leroy's shooting the breeze with some yella-bellied

Limey bastards," he broadcast to anyone who would listen. "Tell me somethin' will ya?" he said, directing his question at me. "How come all you Limey's have a yella streak down your back?"

"Knock it off, Johnson," growled Leroy.

"What do you mean, yellow streak?" said Darky, his mouth tight and jaw set.

"Y'all ran away at Dunkirk, didn't ya? Didn't stay and face the Krauts and that's a fact," Johnson sneered, eyes glaring at Darky, challenging him to get up and fight.

I flashed a look at Darky and Blondie, warning them to stay calm and not antagonize the Americans. I could see the night turning into an ugly brawl, unless we showed some restraint.

"Yuh wanna be careful what yuh calling these guys with yuh big mouth, Johnson. These guys've been in action once. They're fighters. They're the men who had their backs to the wall at Dunkirk. They didn't run away. They had to fight their way to the beaches," warned an enraged Leroy.

Glowering, he stood up, pushing back his chair, daring Johnson to say more.

Still seated, looking unruffled and relaxed, I asked Johnson, "How much action have you seen?"

"He ain't seen nuthin," Leroy gloated, triumphantly.

"When I do," Johnson retaliated, his face flushed an angry red from Leroy's disclosure of his lack of combat experience, "when I do, the Nips won't see no yella streak down my back."

He turned and walked away.

I sighed.

"When we do see some action, we'll find out just how brave you are, chum. You'll find out what it's really like," I muttered after the departing soldier.

"Aw, Gus, fellas, I'm sorry they keep puttin' you guys down," Leroy apologized.

"One of these days, Leroy, I won't be able to help myself," said Darky, still steaming. "I'll clobber one of the cocky buggers, no matter how many warning looks Gus gives me."

"It's not your fault, Leroy. They think they're big men, strutting about with pistols in their belts. They don't know what it's all about yet," said Blondie.

"I don't know what it's like to be in action either, but I don't go takin' cheap shots at yuh," said Leroy.

"You're not as angry as they are, Leroy. This place isn't full of hula hula girls. It's not glamorous enough for them here. We're all forgotten, while everything's happening in Europe and the Pacific," I said.

"This ain't gonna stop you comin' over, is it?" asked one of the other gunners.

"No. It'll take more than that gorilla to stop us coming for some decent beer," said Darky, laughing.

Depot Raiding

A few days after the incident in the PX, I strode into the British canteen. I was furious. Looking round, I saw Tommy, Darky and Cliff sitting at a table. Blondie was returning from the counter, his hands full of beers. I made my way to the table, squeezing past lounging soldiers relaxing over a beer or cup of tea and a cigarette after a hot day's work.

"If looks could kill, Gus, somebody would be dead. What's the matter?" asked Cliff.

"I'm seething. It's those Yanks. The cheeky buggers have raided our supply depot. They're boasting about getting all the Limey squaddies' beer. They stole whisky and beer from three or four of the railway wagons."

I paused, took a *cheroot* out of my pocket and lit it, giving myself a moment to calm down and look round the indignant faces of my friends.

"I say we give them a taste of their own medicine."

The men perked up and grinned mischievously. Tommy was first to speak.

"Count me in."

"Me too. We can't let them get away with this," said Darky.

"I'm with you," said Blondie. "When do we do it?"

Hunched low over the table, heads huddled together, we made plans in hushed voices.

"I know when they change the guard," I told them. "We'll have half an hour after they dismount the guard and before the new guard arrives. When I'm at the siding tomorrow, I'll make a note of the numbers on the American supply wagons."

Sergeant Wellington spotted our group. He could tell we were up to something and came over.

"What are you lot scheming about?"

"Nothing, Sarge, nothing. Why don't you come by the *basha* tomorrow night to see us?"

He scrutinized us, looking for clues, but found none.

"I'll be by tomorrow night, then. Good night, lads."

"Who's free tomorrow afternoon?" I asked.

We looked round at one another and heaved sighs of relief. It was obvious from our beaming smiles that none of us was on duty. No one would miss the fun.

"I'll borrow a truck and pick you up at the *basha*, 1:30 sharp."

At the siding the next day, I enlisted the help of my foremen Sanjay, in finding the American supply wagons. Taking him along the track close to where the American wagons were standing, I told him to walk along and note the numbers of three American supply wagons. Sanjay strolled along the railway siding, blending in with the activity in the area. Returning to me, he reeled off the numbers, which I quickly scribbled down on a piece of paper.

"I'm going to fetch a truck. When I come back have half a dozen men by these wagons to help me do some loading."

At first, Sanjay stared blankly at me. Then, as understanding dawned, a wide smile embellished his face in anticipation of the rewards he and his men would receive for cooperating with the Corporal Sahib. Pressing his palms together as if in prayer, he repeatedly bowed and nodded his head.

"Yes, sahib. Thank you, sahib."

"Mum's the word," I said with chuckle, holding my finger to my lips. I was already enjoying the excitement.

1943

Leaving my crew of sappers to supervise the unloading of shale and gravel, I disappeared to collect my friends. Returning to the siding, we sat and waited for the Americans to change the guard. From a safe distance and growing hot and sticky with sweat, I watched from the cab of the truck. As soon as the guards left, I roared up to the wagons.

"Okay lads, we've only got half an hour. Let's go."

As the truck arrived, the foreman and six *coolies* stepped from between the wagons earmarked earlier that morning.

Soldiers and *coolies* alike began flinging the plunder into the truck as fast as we could—whisky, beer, large cans of fruit, vegetables, flour, whatever we could get our hands on. With only thirty minutes to fill the truck, there was no stopping to wipe brows dripping with sweat or eyes stinging from perspiration. *Coolies* working in that area of the siding were signalled to turn a blind eye to these shenanigans. In no time at all, they'd vanished from sight, leaving us up to our mischief.

After distributing some of the pillaged supplies to my Indian crew, I drove the groaning truck, chock full of loot, away from the area, my friends crammed in the back. Driving back to camp, I waved as we passed the American guards arriving for their stint of guard duty.

We were elated. Back at the *basha*, we took our pick of the plunder. Mac, resting on his bed after completing his shift, jumped up to see the spoils of war we were unloading.

"In God's name...! You've enough to feed an army," he said, gawking in admiration.

"Come on. Don't stand there yapping. Help us unload this stuff," yelled Tommy, red faced and wet with sweat in the afternoon's heat.

"How'd it go?" asked Mac, grabbing a heavy carton.

"Piece o' cake," said Darky, exhilarated.

"Wasn't it great?" I said. "I really enjoyed myself."

"I'd like to see their faces when they open those wagons," said Blondie, chortling.

We stacked cans of fruit, beer, and whisky under our *charpoys* and along the walls of the *basha*. The place looked more like an overstocked warehouse than an army camp.

"This should keep us happy for a few days. Now we know how it's done," I said, "we can go back again next week."

Everyone laughed. After a couple of beers to celebrate and cool down, Darky and I decided to distribute the remainder of the booty. First stop was the cookhouse. Then we visited the other British camps.

I drove to the Combined General Hospital at Dibrugarh where matron welcomed me with open arms.

"Don't I know you, Corporal?"

"I used to stop here with the mobile canteen a few months ago."

"Of course. Now, I understand you've brought something for us, is that right?"

"Yes, Matron. We thought you might be able to make good use of some extra supplies," I said, guiding her to the rear of the truck.

She looked at me, a puzzled expression on her face.

"Look inside. Is there anything there you'd like?"

She lifted the flap of the truck, stood on tiptoe and leaned forward, allowing her eyes to adjust to the dimness inside. Her face remained expressionless. Her bespectacled eyes darted here and there. Leaning back and lowering her heels, she turned to look at me.

"Corporal...?"

"Corporal Wickman, Matron."

Face suddenly beaming, she patted my arm.

"Corporal Wickman, you're an angel in disguise. Come and have a cup of tea, while I arrange for someone to unload the truck."

My visits to the hospital became a regular event after each of our forays into a redistribution of supplies—visits where I could look forward to enjoying a bit of female company and a cup of tea. During my chats with matron and the ward sisters, I learned some of the difficulties they faced. They worried about the men in their care, most of whom had nightmares and kept shouting out in their sleep about taking cover, warning of *pungyi* traps, machine guns, or Japanese approaching. During the monsoon season, they couldn't keep cows from wandering into the wards. At night, as they did their rounds, carrying a hurricane lamp, they would sometimes trip over a cow lying down between the beds. Other joys of jungle nursing involved dealing with unwelcome visitors such as snakes in the rafters or insects flying into their hair. They all agreed that life as a nurse in Assam was certainly different to life back home.

Presents of whisky were accepted by the officers without my being asked too many questions. Major Cave, wanting to confirm his own intelligence reports about the tit-for-tat raids going on at the sidings, tried questioning me one day.

"Corporal Wickman, dare I ask where you're getting all these provisions you're distributing round the camps?"

Shoving a bottle of whisky and some cans of fruit on the Major's desk, I smiled brightly. "Best you don't ask, sir. Got to run now. I still have a lot to do, sir."

"Very well, Corporal. Dismissed."

As I bolted out the door, I caught a glimpse of Major Cave, smiling and nodding his head in satisfaction as he examined the bottle of whisky in his hands.

"Good show, men. That's the spirit," I heard him mutter, as I passed his window.

We made no money from the raids. The adventure and excitement helped to pass the time. I enjoyed every minute of it. First pick of the spoils was all the reward we wanted. I got a kick out of inviting our American friends over to the *basha* for a game of cards and then offering them a drink of whisky or bourbon stolen from their own supply depot.

"Where the hell did you get this booze?" they asked in amazement.

"We're in the know," we told them, tapping the side of our noses with our index fingers, smug smiles on our faces. "Drink up, we've got plenty."

Our gang became the toast of the camp and our *basha* was the place to go for a social evening. Darky nailed up a sign on a veranda post that said, "Swingers Inn." The raids continued. The excitement lifted our spirits enough to overcome all the gibes we endured from some of the Americans.

Then one day, I was ordered to report to Major Cave.

"Blimey, Gus! Do you think he's going to put an end to our fun?" Darky asked.

"I don't know what he wants. I'll meet you in the canteen when I get back from Chabua."

I stood at attention in Major Cave's office.

"Stand at ease, Corporal."

Major Cave, still sitting behind his desk, his fingers twirling a pencil, looked across at me.

"You seem to be the man to talk to round here when things are needed, Corporal."

"Me, sir?"

"Yes, Corporal Wickman, you."

As the Major paused, I wondered what sort of punishment I was going to receive this time.

"We have a serious problem here."

I eyed the Major intently. He coughed to clear his throat, then smiled self-consciously.

"You may be aware we're having trouble getting all the supplies we need. We're desperately short of tea. Do you think you could find some for us?"

I blinked in shock. Realising I was holding my breath, I started to breath again.

"Yes, sir. No problem, sir. I'll take a thirty hundredweight truck, if that's all right, sir?"

"A thirty hundredweight? You're expecting to er . . . obtain such a large amount of tea, Corporal?"

"Yes, sir," I answered, grinning

Major Cave struggled and failed to control a smile of relief.

"Very well, Corporal. Do your best. Dismissed."

I stepped out of the office. A delighted smile spread across my face. *Authorized pilfering, eh? Whoever would have thought it?*

My friends looked up as I walked into the canteen.

"What happened, Gus? Did you lose a stripe?"

"No, not quite." I said. "Major Cave asked me to get some tea for the army."

"He what? Asked you to get some tea?" Darky shoved me playfully. "Pull the other one, Gus, it's got bells on."

"I'm dead serious. He wants me to scrounge some tea."

1943

"How did you wangle that?"

I shrugged, an innocent expression on my face.

"I guess we've got a bit of a reputation in high places."

Next day, I made the first call on my rounds of the various tea plantations. I stopped the truck and found the manager.

"Do you have any tea to spare for the British Army?"

"Who are you?"

"I'm Corporal Wickman, 62 Field Company, Royal Engineers. We're building airfields in the area, and we don't have any tea. Can you provide us with some tea?"

"I certainly can. It would be my pleasure. Our warehouses are piled to the rafters with chests of tea that we can't sell because of the war. I'll get my men to load your truck."

Plantation workers transferred the chests to the back of the truck. When it was so full that they were unable to squeeze in another chest, I returned to Chabua to report to Major Cave.

"Good grief! How did you manage to get all that tea—and so quickly, Corporal?" Major Cave asked, staring at the packed truck

"I just went to the tea plantations and asked for it. If there's anything else you want, sir, you only have to ask."

"Rest assured, Corporal, I won't hesitate to call on your services whenever I need them. In the meantime, you know we're short of everything. If you see anything lying about that we might be able to use—pieces of wood, building materials, paint, you have my permission to er...requisition it."

My first port of call was 62 Company cookhouse. When the cooks had taken all the tea they wanted, I delivered tea to the other units and, of course, Dibrugarh General Hospital, followed by a pleasant chat with matron over a cup of delicious Assamese brew.

The Gurkhas

"We're almost at Dinjan lads," the pilot called back to the battle-weary soldiers of the Gurkha Rifles he was bringing from the front line. They were small men with Mongolian features half-hidden beneath the Australian bush hats on their shaved heads. Gurkha soldiers were ferocious fighters from Nepal and greatly admired by British soldiers who had fought alongside them. Sixty years earlier, when the British found they could not beat the Gurkhas in battle, they enlisted them into the British Army. Since then, the Gurkhas had served king and country with unswerving loyalty.

The advance party of twenty Gurkha soldiers stepped out of the C47's doorway into the steamy heat of the Brahmaputra Valley and squinted in the bright sunlight. They were a sorry looking bunch. Scrawny and ragged from months of fighting behind enemy lines, they were more like survivors of a Japanese prisoner of war camp than legendary, fearless warriors of the British Army. The thirsty men congregated on the tarmac at Dinjan airfield in the scorching heat, wondering where to go and what to do next. No one thought to ask if they needed help.

The Gurkha sergeant or havildar decided to see if he could find where they were supposed to be going. They set off walking, eventually reaching the railway siding where I was supervising the unloading of gravel shipments. Seeing an Indian foreman, the Gurkha sergeant approached him.

"We're looking for the camp being built for the Gurkha battalions. Do you know where it is?"

"No, but the Corporal Sahib will help you. He will take you, if you wish."

I was busy conferring with one of my soldiers when I saw the Gurkhas talking to Sanjay out of the corner of my eye and walked over.

"Hello, Sergeant. Can I help you?"

"Excuse me, Corporal Sahib," said the havildar. "We're an advance party sent to prepare the camp being built for Gurkha units. Do you know where it is?"

"It's tucked away in the jungle somewhere. I've a vague idea where it is. Let's see if we can find it."

I called to Sanjay, "Go and find..." I stopped to estimate how many vehicles I needed. "Go and find an Indian driver with a truck. These men need a lift."

1943

We loaded the men into two trucks. I led the way in my truck with the havildar beside me, first onto Udalgari Road, then east on the Ledo road. At the first road barrier, I checked with the security police officer.

"Is the new Gurkha camp up on the left near Tinsukia?"

"Yes. About four miles ahead."

We found the camp a hive of activity with Indian *coolies* busy erecting *bashas* and putting on roofs.

"I don't envy you, Sergeant," I said, with a laugh. "It looks like you'll have your work cut out getting this place tidy before the regiment arrives."

"We'll soon have this building site put straight," the Gurkha told me with an impish grin. "Thank you for your help, Corporal sahib."

I drove back to the siding, thinking of the Gurkhas and all I'd heard about them. They had a reputation for bravery and savagery, and I'd heard tales of them having no compunction in slicing off an enemy's head with their razor sharp *kukris*. But I did like their mischievous sense of humour. I learned a lot by going on jungle patrols with them. Most British NCOs and officers thought they were superior to Gurkha and Indian soldiers and treated them with disdain, but that was their loss. One British officer, who served with a Gurkha regiment, was supposed to have said, "If a man tells me he's not afraid of dying, he's either a liar or a Gurkha."

Lost in my thoughts, I was unaware of the effect my small act of kindness would have. I found out a week later.

Going into Tinsukia, I had to pass the Gurkha camp. I had the shock of my life when they turned out the guard for me. This became routine. Every time I passed the entrance to the camp, I would slow down. The Gurkha soldiers would parade and give me a ceremonial salute, and I would salute them in return before driving on. I had no idea why they decided to honour me this way, but I thought it was wonderful to receive such special treatment and savoured every minute of it.

Major Cave was not so happy. He ordered me to report to his office.

"I understand the Gurkhas are turning out the guard for you. You're not entitled to that, Corporal."

"Yes, sir. I know that, sir. There's nothing I can do about it, sir."

"Is it correct that when the Gurkhas arrived, you left your duties to help them get settled in their camp?"

"Yes, sir. I thought it was something I should do, sir. The men had just arrived from fighting in Burma, and no one was helping them. Besides, they were cluttering up the work area, sir."

"They seem to think you're special."

"I've never claimed to be special, sir."

"Well they think you are. They turn out the guard for you. They don't even do that for me, or any other British officer. I'll put a stop to this nonsense."

The next day Major Cave complained to the Gurkhas' commanding officer, telling him to stop the Gurkhas from turning out the guard for me. I heard all about it later from the havildar.

The Gurkha colonel's response was, "Major Cave, if my Gurkhas hold Corporal Wickman in such high regard that they want to turn out the guard for him, there's nothing I can do about it. Orders or no orders, they'll turn out the guard."

Major Cave was infuriated. With an exasperated "hrrrumph", he turned on his heels and marched briskly away, his shoulders stiff with anger, but nothing more was done about it.

Another effect of my kindness to the Gurkhas, was an invitation to attend a nurses' party at Dibrugarh. I was delivering yet another truckload of booty to the hospital, filched from the American supply depot during our most recent raid.

Matron hurried outside to speak to me.

"Corporal, I want you to come to our party on Saturday night."

"Me? But I'm not supposed to. I'm not allowed to fraternize with the nurses. Only officers are allowed at your parties. I don't want to get into more trouble than I need to."

1943

"Nonsense, Corporal. If we want you there, we'll have you there. I won't take no for an answer. We'll look after you. You can sit between one of the sisters and me. The officers won't dare say a word."

On the night of the party, I arrived in my truck. My friends envied me, and all I could do was feel nervous about being there. I wondered what Major Cave would have to say about it—never mind him finding out I drove here in a 62 Company truck.

With a large smile, Matron came to welcome me.

"I'm so pleased you decided to come and to hell with the consequences," she teased. "Come and sit over here."

She led me to a chair at the head of the table and poured me a tot of rum. I saw the Gurkhas there and realized it was not just a party but a *ramsammy*. I'd heard about *ramsammys*, or Gurkha parties, and now I was attending one. I was looking forward to having a good time.

I didn't realize it, but I was the guest of honour. Relishing every moment, I ignored the looks of annoyance I could see on Major Cave's and some of the other officers' faces as they muttered to one another. I could tell by the disapproving looks being sent my way that they were wondering why on earth I should have the best seat at the head table.

The nursing sister sitting beside me asked, "Have you been to a ramsammy before, Corporal?"

"No. First time, but I hear they're great fun."

"You'll have a marvellous time. Let your hair down. You're in for a treat."

The drums rolled signalling the start of the entertainment. Conversation at the table faded away. Nurses, doctors and service men settled themselves to enjoy the show. Starting slowly and sensuously, the drummers' hands moved faster and faster, until they became a blur. Accompanied by the melodic tones of a flute, they created a throbbing, bawdy atmosphere. Some of the Gurkha soldiers were playing the women's parts, wearing long twirling skirts and shawls over their heads, while their partners wore male Nepalese costumes. Ankle bells tinkled as the dancers whirled round on bare feet. They

Men of the Gurkha Rifles dress as women to dance the "Dhan Ropne". (Imperial War Museum)

approached me and hauled me out of my seat. Everyone was laughing, stamping his feet and giving ear-shattering whistles. I was happy enough to join in, until they tried to put a shawl on me to make me look like a female.

"Not on your life," I cried. Laughing, I deftly avoided the shawl and made a run for my seat.

This brought forth more howls of laughter—and the Gurkhas danced on. The "female" dancers gracefully moved their arms. Flirting with the audience and each other with lust-filled eyes and ribald suggestive movements, they depicted, in the lewdest way possible, the story of a girl promising her lover an unforgettable night of passion. The dancers held their audience spellbound with their uproarious sexual innuendo. I laughed until my ribs ached and tears coursed down my cheeks.

At last, the dancing stopped. People caught their breath and wiped their eyes. Food was brought to the table. A battered, wind up gramophone played a scratchy record of Count Basie's *One o'clock Jump*. I downed my rum and ate heartily. Then Matron stood up and banged her knife on the table to attract everyone's attention.

"Ladies and gentlemen, it is my pleasure tonight to host a very special occasion. Tonight, by special invitation of the Gurkha Rifles, we have Corporal Wickman with us."

Woozy from the rum, I blinked in surprise and turned to look at Matron, wondering what she was up to. From the shadows, Captain Richardson of the Gurkha rifles stepped forward.

"Corporal Wickman, would you please come to the front?"

A Gurkha soldier sharpens his kukri (IWM)

I left my seat. I had no idea what was going on.

Another soldier, grinning broadly, moved forward. It was the Gurkha sergeant, the havildar I had helped at the airfield.

"My men want to present you with a gift, Corporal," Captain Richardson told me.

The Gurkha sergeant handed me a parcel. I tore it open and gasped in awe.

"What is it, Corporal?" Matron called.

I held up my gift for everyone to see. Two solid silver *Kukris* gleamed in the light shed by the hurricane lamps. I lowered my arms and read the inscription on the knives.

"They're engraved. The inscription reads: Presented by the Gurkha Rifle Regiment in Honour of Corporal Wickman of 62 Field Squadron R.E."

Matron clapped loudly, leading the applause, pleased with herself for engineering the whole affair for the Gurkhas.

I was thrilled.

"Thank you. Thank you. I don't know what I've done to deserve such an honour, but I'm over the moon. Thank you."

I walked over to Matron.

"I didn't know you were such a schemer, Matron"

"Oh you've seen nothing yet, Corporal. Now that you've broken the ice, we'll be seeing you at a lot more of our social evenings, never fear."

Surprises at the Airfield

Down at Dinjan airfield, birds could be a problem. For some reason, large flocks of kites congregated at the end of the runway, causing frequent accidents when aircraft took off. Detachments of American soldiers armed with shotguns were regularly sent to shoot at the birds, killing some and scaring the rest away, at least for a while.

I was never sure, but I heard that some wise crack from a British Tommy about the substandard quality of the Americans' marksmanship brought about the call for a shooting competition by top brass. Aware of the existence of

1943

some bad feeling between the different units based at the airfield, they hoped this competition would allow each unit to show what it could do. Teams of men competed in the heats. With each heat, the distance from the targets was increased. One by one the contestants fell out of the competition until, in the end, it boiled down to yours truly against a captain in the American Air Force.

Excited cries from my friends cheered me on.

"Go on, Gus! Give it stick! Give it stick!"

The American was confident. *Cocky too*, I thought, every bit as sure of my own abilities with a rifle.

"You're a good shot, soldier, but this is the end of the road for you."

"Your Garand's a good rifle. I've tried them out, but it'll never beat my 303."

"Wanna bet on that, soldier?"

I sure did. Confident of my abilities in marksmanship, I wagered ten shillings, a whole week's allowance.

"You're on."

The American fired first. All his shots hit the makeshift target close to the centre.

"Good shooting," I said. "Now watch this."

"This ain't no turkey shoot, Corporal. Make them all count if you want to collect your dough."

I grinned, waved at my friends, then settled my mind, until nothing else existed but the target. Squeezing the trigger, I fired off three rounds in quick succession. All the shots hit the target dead centre.

The British Tommies couldn't contain themselves. After months of insults and taunts from the Americans, I'd shown them.

"Champion, Gus! Champion! You showed them where to get off, Gus" they shouted, cheering jubilantly.

I was triumphant.

"Nice try, sir, but you lost your bet."

I couldn't help grinning at the American officer's surprise.

As I pocketed my winnings, Major Cave and Lieutenant Davies approached.

"Good show, Corporal Wickman. Damned good show," praised Major Cave, pride and pleasure at the British victory evident in his face.

We moved towards the refreshment tables.

"You're a good shot, Corporal. Where did you learn to shoot like that?" asked the American.

"The army taught me, but it might be in my blood. My father's a crack shot with a rifle."

"Your father is? How come?"

"One of my earliest memories is going to the fairground with my parents. The people in charge of the shooting gallery used to call to my father, 'Billy, Billy come and give us a show.' He'd go and do his tricks, which always attracted a large crowd and brought business to the gallery. Pop would fire over his shoulder at the targets with his back towards them using a mirror, or he would take aim holding the rifle under his legs. He always hit the targets. He told us he learned to shoot in order to get to school in one piece. Pop lived in northern Sweden in the Arctic Circle. When he skied to school in the middle of winter, he was sometimes chased by packs of wolves. He had to shoot at them to keep them away."

The American laughed, delighted with the story.

"No wonder he became such a good shot. I guess I would too if I had to face a pack of wolves on my way to school."

"No wonder he ended up running away to sea," I said, grinning.

◆ ◆ ◆

December 23rd, the Japanese Air Force visited Dinjan airfield to deliver some early Christmas presents. Their mission? To destroy the only airfield in north Assam capable of accommodating B25 bombers.

I was in the *basha* with Tommy, Darky and Mac, busy writing yet another airgraph to Ivy. Mac was reading titbits to us from the South East Asia Command newspaper.

"Hey, look at this! This'll get you drooling," said Mac, holding out the paper so we could see the picture of Betty Grable showing off her long legs.

1943

"She's a beauty all right," said Tommy, wistfully.

"Never mind the pin-ups," scoffed Darky. "Tell us the football results. How's Sunderland doing?"

As Mac rustled the paper, looking for the football results, the sirens sounded. Startled, we looked at one another for several seconds before rallying for the emergency.

"Come on, lads!" I shouted. "In the truck! Let's see what we can do."

We grabbed helmets, rifles and gas masks before running out of the *basha* to the truck. I revved the engine. Mac barely had time to scramble aboard before the truck pulled sharply away, heading for Udalgari Road. Helmets were placed on heads, straps pulled tight. Adrenaline gushed. Mouths dried. We were excited, bodies covered in goose bumps and ready for the skirmish.

At the airfield, twenty Japanese bombers, accompanied by twenty-five Zeros, were roaring down one after another like shrieking banshees. Cannon and machine guns clattered, frenziedly spewing out bullets. Bombs dropped on planes and installations. On the ground, men scurried about. Gunners were in the gun pits. Fire-fighters were ready with their hoses. Ground crews and support personnel hid and prayed in the slit trenches, until the raid ended. From the trenches, Indian and Gurkha soldiers opened fire at the Zeros. A few brave American pilots from 529th Fighter-Bomber Squadron climbed aboard their fighter planes, trying to get off the ground. Relentless Zeros, undaunted by the rat-tat tatting of the ack-ack guns, zoomed in to shoot and bomb the fighters. Loud explosions, flashes and flames smashed the taxiing aircraft, leaving them crashing one into the other unable to become airborne. For those that did manage to lift off, enemy fire knocked them down from the skies as easily as hailstones smashing down a butterfly. The sound of screeching metal hurt the ears as burning planes scraped along the tarmac. The air filled with acrid black smoke. Soon, no one was trying to do anything but stay safe.

In this chaos, I spied Lieutenant Davies shouting orders to British troops and raced over. Leaning out of the cab, I yelled, "What do you want us to do, sir?"

"Pick up any wounded you can find and take them to the hospital."

In the thick of the bombing, seasoned as we were by the Dunkirk experience, the men of 62 Company were the only personnel out on the runways of Dinjan. When bombs were falling, we dived onto the ground, lying flat on our bellies, being showered with flying asphalt, shards of wood and shrapnel. When each wave passed, we jumped into our trucks and drove round the airfield, looking for injured men. Mac, Darky and Tommy were kept busy. Leaping in and out of the truck, they picked up the wounded and placed them in the vehicle.

Then they found one man, his stomach muscles ripped by shrapnel, intestines bulging from his body. Mac ran to the cab. "We've got a bad 'un, Gus. Get us to the hospital. Quick!"

Darky took his shirt off and pressed it hard against the wounded man's stomach. I raced to Panitola hospital, a short distance away, while Darky comforted the moaning man.

"You'll be all right, mate. We'll soon have you at the hospital. You're going to be all right. Hang on."

We shouted warnings to people in the trenches to stay well down, as bombs rained from above. With bullets whizzing by and bombs exploding all around us, creating shock waves which nearly knocked us off our feet, we British soldiers saved many lives with our prompt actions. For one hour, the enemy ruled the skies over Dinjan. Little damage seemed to be inflicted on the Japanese planes despite the work of the anti-aircraft gunners. Then, as suddenly as they appeared, they were gone.

For a few seconds, there was deafening silence. Then the all clear was given. Men started running. Pilots raced to find an undamaged machine and hurried into the air, trying to catch the Japanese attackers before they disappeared into the skies over Burma. Shaky men came out of hiding places, looking around at the damage caused to the airfield.

1943

"That was some raid," said one stunned American ground crewman. "It scared the bejeesus out of me."

"Well at least you cut your teeth on a light one," I said.

"Light air raid? Are you kidding? You call this a light air raid?"

At that, an American officer approached our group.

"I saw you on the airfield. You were driving round as if you were on a Sunday outing instead of in the middle of an air raid."

"They were all at Dunkirk, sir," said Lieutenant Davies, coming up behind him and overhearing his comments. "Some of your men think this was a bad air raid, but these men experienced much worse in France, isn't that so, Corporal?"

"Yes, sir. This was a tea party in comparison, sir."

The American officer looked us over appreciatively. A serviceman approached to tell him, "Excuse me, sir. Major Haas wants you on the phone, sir."

The officer looked back at us.

"You did well today, men. I'd be proud to have you under my command."

An unexpected by-product of the raid was a complete turn about in Anglo/American relations on the airfield. The following day, Christmas Eve, we were celebrating Christmas in the PX with Leroy and the other gunners. We were talking about the air raid and the repairs already being carried out.

"Good job they moved the gasoline that was bein' stored next to the shells before the Nips paid us a visit. The whole airfield could've been blown to kingdom come," said Leroy.

We gasped; heads turned sharply to look at Leroy.

"What did you say? They were storing fuel next to the ammo?" Darky asked, not believing his ears.

"They sure were. I told Sarge more than once that we were too close to it, that one of these days we'd get it 'cos some stupid, empty headed joker . . ."

Leroy's voice trailed off as he watched Johnson weaving his way across the room towards them. All eyes turned to see what he was looking at.

A CORPORAL'S WAR'

"Hey up. Here's trouble," said Cliff, resigned to more unpleasantness.

We eyed Johnson warily. It was Christmas. We didn't want a confrontation, at least not tonight.

Johnson was swaying slightly; his breath smelled heavily of beer. Clumsily, he pulled a chair from the next table. Placing it so that he was sitting with his arms folded across the back, his long muscular legs straddled the seat as he faced the men at the table, who waited, wondering what was coming next. Darky was tense, ready to pounce if this ape started anything. Darky was not going to let him spoil their Christmas.

"I wanna buy you guys a drink," Johnson announced, his voice loud in drink.

Our eyebrows lifted to our hairlines.

He looked at us with unfocused, earnest eyes.

"I saw what y'all did out there, durin' the raid." He burped softly. "I take back everythin' I ever said about y'all. You're a brave bunch of guys."

That's a turn up for the book I thought.

"Sure, we'd be happy to have a drink and, what is it you Americans say, bury the hatchet? Merry Christmas, Johnson."

1944

The Ledo Road

With the change of year came a change of employment. To the east, General Stilwell and his American engineers were slowly moving forward over the challenging terrain of the Patkai Mountains as they extended the Ledo Road from Assam through North Burma to China. They could advance only as fast as supplies and equipment reached them and as fast as Stilwell's Chinese troops drove back the resisting Japanese Army from the road's projected path.

My unit was assigned to the Assam Trunk Road project, that part of the Ledo Road between Makum and Digboi, where I supervised the widening and resurfacing of the road, ready for the day when convoys of trucks would carry supplies from India to China.

Road construction labourer in 1944 Assam

A CORPORAL'S WAR

Building roads in Assam is labour intensive in 1944

One of my jobs was to hire and pay the daily labourers who worked on this section of the road. I would arrive at the site early in the morning and set up a trestle table in preparation for taking the names of the assembled workers. Every man, woman and child who worked on the road earned one silver rupee a day. Bare-foot *coolies* clamoured for work. Bare-breasted women teased and flirted with me in order to be employed. I always had a twinkle in my eye and a grin on my face as the women jostled to give their names. Never having forgotten the horrors I'd seen at the military hospital in Deolali, I refused to employ anyone with sores, rashes, grey skin patches or any other symptom of highly infectious syphilis.

Work was labour intensive as there was little in the way of machinery to build the road apart from the occasional steamroller and bitumen sprayer. Because of the depth of the subsoil, ninety feet in most areas, thousands of 9x4 inch bricks were made and hammered by hand into the ground one on top of the other to a depth of twenty feet, or at least until they stopped sinking. They often needed re-packing after a convoy of trucks, travelling along the road, caused it to subside.

1944

At the end of each hot, sticky day, workers gathered at the trestle table to collect their pay. The system required them to place a thumbprint on a sheet of paper beside their name in order to receive the rupee they had earned. Some of the paymasters took a cut of the workers' wages, only paying seventy-five percent, or twelve annas, and pocketing the difference. It was a way of life in India. I always paid the full amount, but occasionally, to deter cheating, I picked one or two of the *coolies* at random and refused to pay them, insisting they were trying to trick me into paying them twice.

One relatively cool January night, we were relaxing in the *basha* over a game of cards and a few beers.

"We had a bit of fun at the road today," I said. "Those American drivers take the biscuit. They think they own the place. One of them was right up behind the steamroller, threatening to push it off the road with his truck. When he wouldn't take any notice of my orders to back off, I went to the truck for my rifle, strolled back as casually as you like and aimed it at his truck. Told him I'd shoot his tyres if he didn't back off. Well, he began swearing, every other word beginning with "f". Still he didn't budge." I chuckled. "He threatened to stick my rifle up you know where."

"We heard him," Mac butted in, "so we decided to join in."

"I had to laugh," I said. "The Yank suddenly stopped swearing. I glanced out the corner of my eye to where he was looking, and there was Mac and the rest of the crew, standing in a row with their rifles aimed at his tyres and ready to shoot. 'Now, back off,' I ordered him. Cursing up a storm, he eventually moved back. The poor steamroller driver looked very relieved. We had a good laugh about it, didn't we?"

"Yeah, today was a good day," Mac gloated.

Darky picked up his cards and glanced at his hand in disgust.

"Those damned American engineers," he growled. "Someone needs to teach them a lesson. They don't treat Indian women well at all. I've stopped them a couple of times from snatching women off the tea plantations to force them to go with them."

"Me too," I said. "They don't see anything wrong with it. I bet they don't treat American women like that."

"Hey, Darky, have you seen the effect Gus has on the Indian women?" Tommy asked.

"What do you mean?" Darky and I blurted out in unison.

"You know the Indian women from the tea plantations are naked from the waist up? Well, they're all over him, giggling and swarming round his table so he'll employ them."

"Give over," I said, red-faced.

"Hey, look. He's blushing,"

"I said give over," I repeated, breaking into an embarrassed grin. "They just like to work for me because I pay the full rupee a day. I don't take a cut like some of the other supervisors do."

"Ssssh," said Blondie. "I heard something."

We fell silent and listened.

"What's that kitten hissing at?" asked Blondie.

"Let's take a look."

Carefully, we checked the inside of the *basha*. Nothing.

"It must be outside. There's something rustling in the bushes."

Mac and Darky each took hold of a hurricane lamp. Blondie, Tommy and I picked up our bayonets. Cautiously, we moved outside. In the light of the lanterns, we could see the young cat, hair standing on end, back arched, ears back, mouth wide open hissing defiantly at a large cobra, its hooded head raised and swaying back and forth. Instinctively, I lashed out with the bayonet. The cat leapt a mile into the air then bolted for the bushes. The cobra collapsed in a writhing heap, its severed head falling with a thud onto the ground.

Darky took hold of the cobra by its tail and dangled it in front of him. We watched fascinated as the snake continued to writhe and thrash about for several more minutes.

"You got a big 'un, Gus. Must be seven-foot long. Wouldn't have liked to find that in my bed."

We re-entered the *basha* and carefully pulled back our bedcovers to check our beds.

"You can't be too careful, can you?" said Mac.

1944

Battleground

In 1944, Assam was abuzz with more activity than a nest of angry hornets as a result of the Quebec Conference, August 1943, where Winston Churchill, President Roosevelt and the Chiefs of Staff began to give serious consideration to the invasion of Burma.

They decided Lieutenant General Slim would lead the regular British forces, and Major General Orde Wingate would lead the British long-range penetration units known as the Chindits. These soldiers, trained in jungle warfare, were first used to infiltrate behind enemy lines in early 1943. Although the first Chindit operation was not a great success, its exploits boosted morale in the British lines. British soldiers were at last meeting the Japanese on their own terms and starting to turn the tide. Finally, General Stilwell would command a 3,000 strong American volunteer long-range penetration unit in north Burma, dubbed Merrill's Marauders by a war correspondent, after their commander, General Frank Merrill. General Stilwell would also command the Chinese Divisions, which would move on Myitkyina and Mogaung with the assistance of the Marauders. A new organisation, the South East Asia Command (SEAC), would conduct the campaign with Lord Louis Mountbatten as its Allied Supreme Commander.

War in Burma was a daunting prospect. Soldiers battled as much against the elements and the terrain as against the enemy. Wide, fast-flowing rivers presented formidable barriers. The men had to hack their way through dense, disease-ridden jungles, struggle through steamy swamps, survive 130° F temperatures, and torrential monsoon rains.

In November 1943, as soon as the dry season began, the British 14th Army went on the offensive in the Arakan in some of the worst terrain in Burma with its steep hills, dense jungle, and innumerable *chaungs*. It advanced southwards along the Mayu peninsula with the aim of capturing Akyab and its airfields. This would reduce the Japanese air threat to Calcutta and industries in that vicinity. It would also provide an air base to cover the planned offensive in Burma.

At the beginning of 1944, Merrill's Marauders began their long march along the Ledo Road into north Burma. Their task was the same as the Chindits, to operate in scattered groups, in the rear of the enemy forces, using guerrilla tactics to destroy railways, bridges, fuel and supply dumps. One of the Chindit units, Sixteenth Brigade, followed on February 4th to start its 450 mile trek into Burma.

As early as January, intelligence sources and air reconnaissance reported Japanese units were strengthening along the India-Burma border. Indications were that Lieutenant General Renya Mutaguchi intended to pre-empt General Slim's offensive by invading India to capture the small hill stations of Imphal and Kohima before moving on to seize the massive supply dump at Dimapur.

Mutaguchi sent his 55th Division to attack the British forces in the Arakan on February 4th. He expected this development to force the British to divert troops from Imphal to Arakan to rescue XV Corps, which would leave the way open for him to invade India. At the very least, it would deprive General Slim of reserves from the Imphal plain.

The Japanese attack caught the British by surprise, but instead of retreating, soldiers held firm and formed what became known as the "Admin Box". Surrounded by Japanese troops, the British went on air supply, 714 sorties flown in five weeks. The new tactic was successful. The Japanese Army lost 5,000 of its 8,000 men and gave up the assault on the "Admin Box". This victory was the turning point of the war in Burma.

The remaining 10,000 Chindits, with all their equipment and 700 mules, were flown into Burma aboard gliders and transport planes by the First Air Commando of the American Air Force on the nights of March 5th and 6th to begin their campaign of attacking the Japanese from the rear.

On March 6th, General Mutaguchi began the "U-GO" offensive to capture both Imphal and Kohima in what Tokyo radio heralded the "March on Delhi". Mutaguchi's forces thrust through the Chin Hills into Manipur State, surprising the British by their swift advance through the difficult terrain. They surrounded the British IV Corps in Imphal and the British garrison in Kohima, then moved on to try to cut the railway at Dimapur, 70 miles inside India's border, in order to sever supply lines to Stilwell's troops who were driving back the Japanese in north Burma.

Knowing how aggressive, almost foolhardy, the Japanese could be, General Slim intended to allow Mutaguchi to cross the Chindwin, which would dangerously over-extend his line of supply. By falling back, the British Army would draw the Japanese into the Imphal plain. When the Japanese Army ran into serious trouble through lack of supplies, Slim knew from past dealings with the Japanese that they would press the offensive all the harder, making it easy for the British forces to destroy them.

The Japanese started their campaign with supplies for only twenty days, which meant they needed to capture Imphal and the supplies there by the end of March. Despite suicidal charges in which units of company size were annihilated, they failed to achieve their objective. Yet even without adequate supplies of food, ammunition, and medical facilities, the Japanese continued to fight.

In April, the situation at the garrison town of Kohima, seventy miles north of Imphal, was desperate as 20,000 Japanese attacked the town containing only 7,000 troops. Some of the war's fiercest fighting, much of it hand-to-hand, was taking place here when troops at the airfields received a visit from the Supreme Allied Commander.

Lord Louis Mountbatten

When Lord Louis Mountbatten became Supreme Allied Commander of SEAC, he visited the troops based in India and on the front line in an effort to boost morale and to bolster the fighting spirit of the soldiers. He was the perfect man for the job; no one could fail to respond to his charm. He had a sharp mind, a remarkable memory, and tireless energy. He soon blew the cobwebs off the British Army's bureaucracy in India and instigated changes to improve efficiency and conditions for the troops, including the SEAC newspaper to lift the men's spirits and keep them informed. When he met with ordinary soldiers, he talked with an irresistible frankness and charm.

At 0805 hours on April 4th, Mountbatten's large transport aircraft landed at Chabua airfield. Among the regiments lined up on parade for his visit was 62 Company. I watched as Mountbatten, a tall, handsome man in his forties, stepped down from the plane. Stopping half way down the steps, he called to the waiting soldiers.

"Never mind standing over there. Gather round, men." Mountbatten looked round the assembled men. "I'm going to tell you now," he said, "I'm not here to praise you. I'm here to tell you it looks like we're going to have the Japanese storming over the top of us. They're going to try and infiltrate behind you and cut you off. All we want you to do is stay put and keep fighting. We will supply you by air with all the ammunition, weapons, and food you will need. That's my job as Supreme Commander of the Allies in South East Asia. Also, we are not going to quit fighting when the monsoon comes like drawing stumps at a cricket match when it rains. If we only fight for six months of the year, the war will take twice as long. The Japs don't expect us to fight on; they will be surprised and caught on the wrong foot.

"Who started this story about the Jap superman? I have seen the Japs in Japan. Millions of them are unintelligent slum-dwellers with no factory laws, no trade unions, no freedom of speech, nothing except an ignorant fanatical idea that their Emperor is God. Intelligent, free men can whip them every time."

We cheered, heartened by his speech. The commander of 62 Company called out the names of an officer, a sergeant, and then I heard my name called as the corporal chosen to have a private conversation and a cup of tea with Lord Mountbatten. In all, eight men were chosen from the various units on the airfield. When it was my turn to speak with him, I stood smartly to attention. An army photographer busily took photographs.

"Stand at ease, Corporal. Stand at ease. Don't stand there like a soldier."

"But I am a soldier, sir."

Lord Louis Mountbatten with Corporal Wickman (left)
April 1944

"And that's what we want you to be. You're the sort of person I want to meet. Are you married, Corporal?"

"Yes, sir. With one daughter, sir."

"When did you get married?"

"July 17th 1937, sir. I'm twenty-five, sir."

"Oh, you married early then?"

"Yes, sir. I did"

"You've already seen action. You were at Dunkirk, weren't you?"

"Yes, sir."

"So we have no need to worry about you when the Japs arrive. You know what's expected of you."

"I just want us to get on with it, sir. Beat the Japs and end the war so I can go home to my wife, sir."

"We are getting on with it, Corporal," Mountbatten said as he shook my hand, "and I intend for us to win. Now, let's see if we can find another cup of tea."

With the speech over and Mountbatten flying off to another venue to make yet another rallying speech, we walked towards the trucks taking us back to the airfields. Darky marched next to me. "Well, go on then. What did he have to say?"

"He's a great chap. Seemed to know a lot about me. Asked how long I've been married. He knew I was at Dunkirk. With him in charge, I'd say we're going to win this war and soon."

Patrol

Relaxing over a few beers in the canteen, conversation focused on atrocities committed by Japanese soldiers.

"I was talking to some soldiers the other day," I said. "They were telling me about 58 Company's cooks. Did you hear about it?"

"No," said Darky. "What about them?"

"Back in February, the cooks were up most of the night cooking for 58 Company, which was going out on early morning patrol down at Palel near the Burma border. After the

1944

patrols left camp, the cooks went to bed to catch up on their sleep. A Jap patrol found them. Killed the lot as they slept."

"The savages!" Mac exploded. "I've heard about their dirty tricks. I know how they treat prisoners and wounded British soldiers."

Blondie joined in. "There's all those stories about the Chindit wounded who were left hidden in the jungle while the column engaged a Jap unit. When the column came back for them, they found the Japs had got there first and slit their throats, or bayoneted them to death as they lay on their stretchers."

"I'm never going to let myself be taken prisoner," said Darky. "We know they tie prisoners to trees and use them for bayonet practice. That's a cruel way to die. I'd rather go down fighting."

Murmurs of agreement floated round the table.

"You on patrol in the morning, Gus?"

"Yes. I'll be turning in shortly. Got to be up early."

"Hear you found a dead sergeant on your last patrol."

"Poor bugger. He must have had a skinful and fallen in the ditch, too drunk to climb out," I told them. "He was covered in leeches and the animals had had a go at him too. We alerted the nearest army camp to go and get him." I stood up to leave. "So, now you know. Don't get too drunk to make your way safely back to the *basha*. And don't make a racket when you come in, I'll be fast asleep."

I left camp early next morning with eight men in the truck, heading for the area around Rangagora village. Leaving the truck, the patrol picked its way through jungle, splodged through calf-deep water, and struggled over muddy, waterlogged ground. We were vigilant even though there was little Japanese activity in this area of Assam. With no contact made with Japanese patrols that first day, we spread our ground sheets and settled down for the night. After a meal, a change of socks, and a session removing swollen blood-filled leeches, we soon fell asleep.

Before daybreak, we were driving to Dibrugarh to check the installations there. We arrived at the hospital at sunup.

A CORPORAL'S WAR

Jumping down from the truck, we looked around. It was quiet—too quiet. A shot rang out. The bullet whizzed by my head. In an instant, we were on our bellies in the dirt, cheeks pressed to the ground, hands cocking weapons. Alert eyes scrutinized buildings and rooftops.

I ordered four men to run behind one of the buildings, while the rest of us covered them. It remained silent. Cautiously creeping forward from building to building, we came upon a scene straight from hell. A Japanese patrol had paid a visit to the hospital.

At the gruesome sight, the men cried out, "Oh, my God!" "Christ all bloody mighty!"

Unable to speak, I signalled five of the soldiers to scout around while I and the other three ran over to trees at the edge of the hospital compound. Four dead nurses, completely naked, had been pinned to the trees by Japanese bayonets. Their upper bodies were hanging down like floppy rag dolls.

I took hold of one of the dead women.

"When I lift her up, pull the bayonet out."

With the bayonet removed, I gently laid the nurse on the ground. She had been raped and mutilated, her breasts sliced off. It was the same for all the victims.

A wave of nausea engulfed me. Saliva gushed into my mouth. One soldier moved away to vomit.

"Check the patients," I ordered, my voice thick with horror.

Alone with the nurses, I knelt beside one of the dead women and took her hand. Scrutinizing her disfigured body, I trembled with murderous rage towards the barbaric perpetrators. Then suddenly, sadness overwhelmed me as I thought of her terror before she was killed. My eyes filled with tears, and I stroked her hand.

"I promise you this, love, I'll take no prisoners. I'll kill every Jap bastard I come across. After what they've done to you, they'll get no mercy from me."

I turned my ashen face towards the sound of the returning soldiers' footsteps. With disbelief etched on their stunned faces, the men stared at the mutilated bodies, unable to turn their eyes away.

1944

"What's it like in there?" I asked.

"None of the patients have been hurt, Gus. Looks like we got here before they could do more damage." The man's voice was subdued.

"They've done enough, haven't they!" one man spat out.

The five soldiers returned, bringing two nurses with them. Seeing the bodies of their friends lying on the ground, the nurses let out moans and cries that made our blood curdle. They rushed to the disfigured forms, knelt beside the bodies and rocked backwards and forwards. Tears streamed down their faces, dripping onto white, unflinching skin. Gently, the nurses touched arms, faces, closed eyes. Wailing, they pulled the lifeless women to their breasts, held them tight and rocked them as if they were distressed children. It was a heartbreaking sight.

"We didn't catch sight of the Nips, Gus, but we found these two survivors."

I knelt beside one of the swaying nurses and gently took the corpse from her. She turned to me with glazed, unseeing eyes. Gently, I asked, "What happened?"

Between ragged sobbing, the nurse managed to tell me, "Japanese soldiers cr-crept into the h-hospital before daybreak . . . they s-started to round up the nurses near the central office . . . s-some of us managed to slip away into the jungle . . . w-when we realized . . . when we could hear . . . w-what was happening." Still on her knees, she started rocking again and wrapped her arms round herself.

"Look what they've done! Look what they've done!"

I put my arms round the distraught woman's shoulders and patted her arm.

"Shush, shush, shush," I comforted. "It's all right, pet. We're here now."

One of the soldiers lifted the other nurse to her feet. "Come on love. Let's get you inside."

"We'll take your friends into the hospital, nurse. Show us the best place to put them," I said.

We picked up the dead women and followed the nurses into a storeroom out of sight of the patients. We laid the bodies on the floor, found sheets, and covered them. The nurses stood dully, looking down at the forms.

"Oh my God!" one of them suddenly blurted out. She spun round, her eyes wide with alarm. "The patients! The patients!"

"It's all right," I said. "We checked the wards. They've not been harmed." I looked at one of the soldiers, who had checked the wards, seeking confirmation.

"They're all safe," the soldier told her. "Sleeping like babies when we looked round."

She nodded her head in silent response, a deep shuddering sigh escaping from her lips.

"We have to go after that patrol," I told her. "We'll send help for you, but we have to go now. Will you be all right?"

"Yes. Yes, Corporal. What time is it?"

"Quarter past seven."

The nurses wiped their faces dry with the palms of their hands and smoothed their hair and became the professionals they were.

"Day Sister will be here in a few minutes. Get on, Corporal. We'll manage here."

Subdued and quiet until approaching the truck, one soldier suddenly found his voice.

"Let's get the bastards and kill 'em!"

It was the Japanese patrol's lucky day. No one ever saw them again.

Bombay Explosion.

On February 24th, 1944, an ammunition ship, the *S.S. Fort Stikine*, set sail from Birkenhead, England bound for Bombay, India. In her hold, she carried 1,395 tons of explosives. Calling at Karachi, the ship added a cargo of raw cotton to her load. Unknown to the captain, this was a volatile substance, which could burst into flames through spontaneous combustion. The ship proceeded to Bombay. When she berthed at Victoria Dock on April 14th, the crew discovered smoke coming from the hold.

1944

The fire spread, refusing to be contained. No one thought to hoist the red flag to warn that the burning ship was carrying a dangerous cargo. Unaware of the catastrophe about to befall them, the dock area was filled with people hard at work when the ship finally exploded. The force of the blast was so powerful, it was captured on a seismograph at Simla's meteorological station, 1,000 miles away in the foothills of the Himalayas.

Smoke from the explosion and fire in Bombay harbour could be seen for miles.

In Bombay, buildings shuddered, windows shattered. A colossus of black smoke surged upwards from the docks, spreading wide until it dominated the skies. Of the one hundred and fifty-six brave firemen battling the blaze aboard the *Fort Stikine*, sixty-five were killed instantly in the explosion, and eighty were seriously injured. From out of the flames and belching smoke of the ruined docks, survivors emerged, shocked, dazed, bloodied and burned. Just in time, for only thirty minutes after the first explosion, there was a second, far more devastating blast as the *Fort Stikine* exploded again. Hot, molten debris, flung far and wide by the blast, started fires in the docks, residential areas, railway depots, and warehouses full of grain and ammunition. The *Fort Stikine* disintegrated completely. The explosion hurled her anti-submarine gun and mounting, weighing thirty tons, 500 feet onto the dock road. Berthed to the stern of the *Fort Stikine* was the 4,000 ton *Jalapadma*, which was spectacularly swept up out of the dock in the tidal wave caused by the explosion. She was twirled around at right angles and dumped on top of a thirty-foot high shed. When the water receded, the ship's stern was perched on the crushed building, the bow left hanging off the edge of the dock over the water. Twelve other ships in the Victoria Dock caught fire and ended up drifting around the port. During the following days, their magazines continued to explode, flinging debris over a wide area.

No emergency plan of action was in place to deal with an event of such catastrophic proportions. Thousands of servicemen rushed from local barracks to work alongside fire fighters, and heroic individuals, working on their own initiative, fought the fires and rescued the injured. Army officers ventured into the decimated docks to assess the situation and report to their superiors.

Only a small part of the docks was still available to shipping—a serious matter, as the port of Bombay was indispensable for meeting the needs of the armed forces in India. It was crucial that it be rebuilt as quickly as possible, and so the task of clearing and reconstructing the docks was given to the British Army.

Troops were dispatched to Bombay from all parts of India, including me and half the section, left kicking our heels in Assam. We had recently completed six weeks training in parachute jumping for going into Burma to build airfields behind the Japanese lines for the Chindits' 'Operation Thursday', which began March 5th. However, Colonel John Alison, of the American Army Air Force, whose planes were being used to fly troops and supplies into Burma, decided he wanted American engineers, not British, to build the required airfields.

1944

Frustrated and indignant, we cursed the Americans for wanting all the glory, but the army soon had another job for us. Deprived of the task for which we had been trained, we were available to go to Bombay when the call came.

Damaged ships and debris litter Bombay docks after the explosion (IWM)

Taking trucks, equipment and my water tanker, we entrained for the tedious 2,000 mile journey. Not for us the comfort of a carriage, but eight days sitting in trucks, transported on flat cars. Our involvement was to be in the clearing up operation. Other units would be brought in for the reconstruction of the docks.

That first day, driving towards the docks, I looked about in horrified disbelief, gawking at blackened, burned-out ruins, collapsed buildings, a scene of total desolation. Homes and shops gone. Everything so different from the last time I was here. When we left Assam, we were told only that there had been a bad accident in Bombay, and our help was needed. Taking in the devastation, I was shaken and sickened. What sort of accident caused this? The decomposing carcass of a horse lay in the street. I could see the remains of a human leg, lying lost at the side of the road. What happened to the man it belonged to? Did he survive? Like bones picked clean by vultures, the stark frames of razed trams remained as tribute to a cataclysm beyond comprehension. A large object in the road ahead caught my attention. I drew closer and couldn't believe my eyes. It was a ship's heavy gun embedded in the asphalt, waiting to be removed by a bulldozer.

Railroad cars loaded with ammunition blew wide open as a result of the explosion in Bombay docks. 1944

When I arrived at the dock gates, my gaze lingered on the clock tower, its hands frozen at six minutes past four—the time of the first explosion, I later discovered. I turned into the docks with my supply of water. Driving carefully round the rubble and wreckage, I had difficulty keeping my eyes on where I was going as I peered about with morbid reverence at this display of a powerful, destructive force. A great sadness overwhelmed me and nausea churned my innards. The place was a shambles. Under the railway tracks, wooden sleepers were now piles of ash. In the dock basins, bodies, wooden debris and bales of cotton created a thick carpet floating on the water's surface. I saw a ship's anchor enmeshed in the rigging of a ship. I was too stunned to ask myself how it got there. Among all the destruction, I felt puny and uncomfortable in this crematorium. I was just a speck of dust on the planet that could be obliterated without anyone noticing. Twisted, blackened framework was all that remained of the cargo sheds. Dockside cranes tilted and turned at crazy angles. Moving further into the dock, I gasped in horrified fascination at the sight of a crippled ship, the *Jalapadma*, resting atop the wreckage of a shed.

These bodies of native workers were found on the devastated docks among the wreckage and debris after the Bombay explosion. April 1944

Gazing at the devastation all around me, my thoughts turned to my friends. I didn't envy them the difficult, unpleasant job of clearing up. My duties were going to be easy in comparison. As well as being responsible for ensuring the trucks were kept roadworthy, I was the company water man, collecting water from wells in the vicinity, purifying it with chemicals, and supplying any army group or mobile canteen that needed water. The service I provided was invaluable. With the high humidity and temperatures hovering above 90°F, the men working in these conditions needed fluids, lots of fluids.

With bulldozers, cranes, mechanical shovels, and their bare hands, soldiers worked long hours to clear the docks and surrounding areas. In the evenings, they relaxed in their barracks—talking, playing cards and drinking a welcome glass of beer available from a mobile canteen manned by volunteers. Talk was mainly about how disagreeable the job was.

"Aw, it's a fair stinker. The rubble's still on fire. The sun's hot enough without shifting all that hot stuff. Phew! I sweat buckets today."

"It stinks down there too. I moved in with the bulldozer, and when I shoved all that rubble to one side, the smell just about knocked me over. There were piles of rotting food underneath and rotting bits of God knows what else. It was horrible."

"We're working on Victoria dock. When the ship exploded, it made huge craters in the dockside. We, er . . . we, er . . . ," the soldier's voice faltered. Clearing his throat, he continued in a quiet voice. "We found some charred boots and blackened bits of bone. I think they were the remains of the firemen."

We fell silent and looked down into our beers as we thought of the poor men blown to smithereens with barely a trace of them left to receive a decent burial.

All sorts of debris and burnt ships litter the docks after an ammunition ship explodes at Bombay. 1944

1944

Steering the conversation to a lighter vein, I joked, "Just think, we could be having an easy time of it in Burma, building airfields behind enemy lines."

Sardonic laughter rippled through the group. Most of us would have preferred fighting an enemy we could see and understand rather than struggling to come to terms with the strong emotions sweeping over us here in Bombay. Cleaning up the aftermath of the explosion, we felt small, insignificant, mortal.

Someone asked, "Have you heard the rumours? They say the Japs blew up the ship."

Crewmen work to recover what they can from their ship damaged in the Bombay explosion. 1944

"It wasn't the Japs," I said. "I talked with an army captain who was about at the time of the explosion. There was a fire in the hold of an ammunition ship. He said the explosion sent rockets and shells streaking across the sky like roman candles on bonfire night. Ammo was flying all over the place like tracer bullets."

"It must have packed some clout. Did you see the anchor—and that gun? Did you see it stuck in the road?"

227

"They're getting on with clearing the docks of all that floating debris, using tugs with nets and booms between them to sweep all the rubbish out to sea. Once they've got rid of that lot, they're going to drain the docks."

My movements through the docks brought me close to the *Jalapadma*, where I caught glimpses of the progress the men were making in removing her. I saw the engineers using flame cutters to carve the ship into movable sections, even though she still had 500 tons of coal burning away in her bunkers.

Although 62 Company thought the work was unpleasant, at least we weren't up to our necks in oily ooze. Soldiers clearing the 15,000 tons of debris from the dock bottom were called the "Mudlarks". Walking through the mud shoulder to shoulder, they probed the sludge with bamboo poles. As chunks of wreckage were located, the soldiers hauled them out with ropes and winches.

Days were filled using acetylene torches to cut through mangled metal. Bulldozers cleared rubble. Some 350 trucks a day travelled back and forth, taking the debris, 800,000 tons of it, to Sewree where four dumps stretched for two miles along the roadsides. At a later date, much of this material would be carried back to the dock area to be used in the reconstruction segment of the project.

Before we returned to Assam, 300 acres of devastation had been cleared in the area outside the docks. Altogether, 9,800 people were involved in the clearing and rebuilding of the docks. Indian, British, and West African troops worked side by side with skilled civilians and men of the Royal Indian Navy. Within seven months, the docks were back in operation, leaving no signs that this was the site of a major tragedy where well over 500 people had died and 1,376 were wounded.

Return to Assam

I pulled up beside the *basha*. I'd been travelling for days and felt weary after the long journey from Bombay. Darky stepped onto the veranda. "Gus, you're back. How was it?"

1944

"Long trip. Any beer inside?"

Between large gulps of the thirst-quenching liquid, I told Darky about my disquieting experiences in Bombay and the terrible the things I saw.

"We all felt so small, just piddling little people when we looked at the damage caused by the blast."

"I was annoyed I couldn't go with you, but now you've told me about it, maybe I was better off here, although we've not had much excitement. We've been told we'll be in Dinjan for at least another six months, but no hints as to what they've got in store for us after that. The siege at Kohima was broken April 18th. The Japs had lost thousands by the time they pulled out. The SEAC newspaper says the Jap soldiers are in a terrible condition—exhausted and hungry, with their lines of communication incapable of supporting them."

"What about Imphal?"

"The lads are still battling it out, but everyone's confident we're going to chase the Japs back to Burma even though the monsoon's started. Let's go down to the shower block. I only finished work minutes before you got back, and you're looking dusty. After that, it'll be time to eat."

Tommy and Mac joined us in the canteen.

"I was just about to tell Gus he had a lucky escape," said Darky.

"Escape from what?" I asked.

"You know all that parachute training we did, so we could go and build airfields in Burma, and then the Yanks decided their engineers could do it better than us? Well, they were all wiped out as soon as they went in, the whole lot of them, mowed down by Jap machine-gunners."

"Poor devils," I said. "We were lucky they didn't want us after all."

We quietly pondered the quirks of fate.

Mac broke the silence. "Did you hear the announcement on All India Radio while you were travelling back from Bombay, Gus? The Allies landed in Normandy June 6th."

"Yes, we're kicking Hitler's backside," said Tommy, chuckling with delight.

A CORPORAL'S WAR

This good news provided the excuse we needed to enjoy a booze-filled, laughter-packed night of celebration.

◆ ◆ ◆

Soon after my return, a brigadier came to see me.

"I've come to talk to you, Corporal, because you have the experience necessary to lead an Indian company. I'm offering you a captaincy to take charge of an Indian Engineer unit going into Burma."

I was stunned, then my mind raced with questions.

"If I do decide to accept your offer, what happens when the war's over?"

The Brigadier's tone was confident, sure he'd found his man.

"You'll be expected to stay on in India and serve as captain for at least three years."

I stared at the brigadier for only a moment before replying.

"Then I can't accept, sir. I've been away from home over two years already. When my time comes for repatriation, I want to go home to my wife and daughter."

The brigadier's face flushed. Through narrowed eyes, he gave me a withering glare. He reeled off all the benefits that came with being a captain in the British Army, omitting to say that officers were the first soldiers the Japs shot at.

However, my mind was made up.

"Sorry, sir, but when 62 Company goes home, I go home. I've no wish to leave the company, not even for this promotion."

The brigadier was astounded.

"I don't understand you, Corporal. I thought you would have jumped at the chance to become captain. I'm very disappointed, very disappointed. Have you anything else to say on the matter?"

"No, sir."

"Very well. Dismissed."

The brigadier made the same offer to other NCOs in 62 Company, but not one man accepted a captaincy. They were all northern lads who had been together for five years in what they considered to be a lucky company. No one wanted to risk breaking the spell, which so far had kept most of us safe.

Foray into Burma

June 22nd, two weeks before I left Assam for Burma, the siege at Imphal was broken, the enemy offensive smashed. On July 8th, the Japanese decided to withdraw. Of the 84,000 enemy soldiers who had swarmed into Assam, more than 60,000 became casualties, over half of them fatal. The remaining

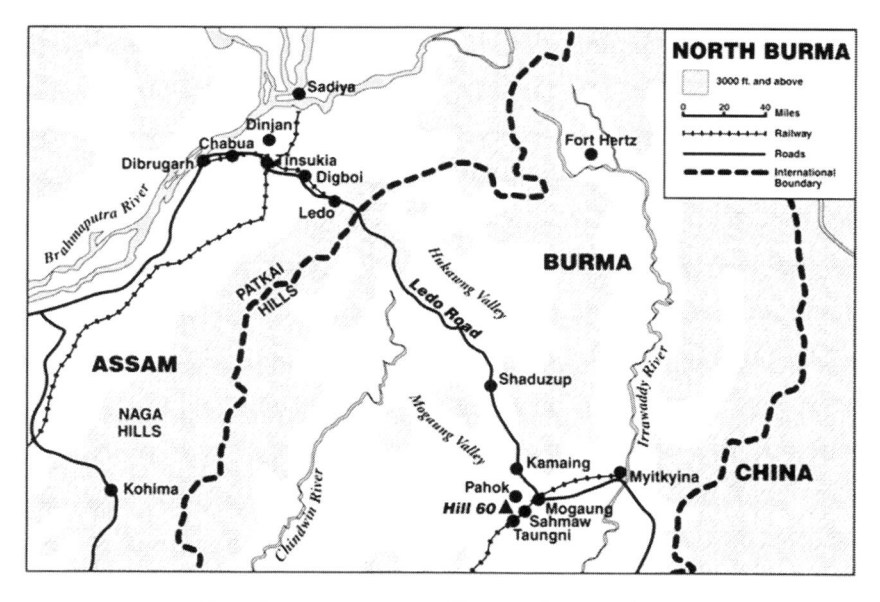

24,000 were, for the most part, diseased, starving, and walking wounded. Lieutenant-General Stopford's XXXIII Corps pushed steadily forward, harrying the exhausted Japanese, giving them no opportunity to consolidate as they stumbled through drenching rains and liquid mud towards the Burmese border.

In north Burma, the task of General Stilwell's Northern Combat Area Command was to capture Kamaing, Mogaung and Myitkyina to ensure completion of the Ledo Road. For this purpose, he had under his command 3,000 American soldiers of Merrill's Marauders, three Chinese Divisions comprising 50,000 men and 12,000 British Chindits. Opposing them in the jungles of upper Burma were between 40,000-60,000 well-trained Japanese troops.

Merrill's Marauders and the Chinese 150th Regiment captured Myitkyina airfield on May 17th, but failed to capture the town, and the battle for Myitkyina deteriorated into a seventy-eight day siege.

On June 16th, the 149th Chinese Regiment occupied Kamaing, forcing the Japanese Army to withdraw to Sahmaw to regroup.

After fierce fighting, "Mad Mike" Calvert's 77 Indian Infantry Chindit Brigade, despite being decimated by malaria and dysentery, entered Mogaung on the morning of June 26th soon after the Chinese arrived from Kamaing. So worn and battle-soiled were the uniforms of the armies fighting in these jungles that the Chinese and Chindits tied orange strips to their hats and arms to distinguish themselves from the Japanese. With the capture of Kamaing and Mogaung, Stilwell's land communications were cleared, allowing the forces attacking Myitkyina to be reinforced.

Meanwhile, Stilwell ordered the Chindits' "Morris Force" to capture Maingna, east of Myitkyina, a task ill-suited to a Long Range Penetration battalion which lacked the necessary heavy artillery. "Morris Force" attacked the village, but the soldiers, suffering from malnutrition, exhaustion, sickness and battle casualties after four months of jungle warfare, were unable to hold the town against ferocious Japanese counter-attacks. The men were so exhausted that they fell asleep under fire, yet they were allotted the task of offensive patrolling in the area to prevent Japanese reinforcements from entering Myitkyina and to keep the Myitkyina Task Force informed of all Japanese movement east of the Irrawaddy River.

◆ ◆ ◆

1944

This was the state of affairs as I left Assam for Burma. My place was behind Blondie's truck, part of a convoy carrying supplies into north Burma for 36th British Division's advance party. Leaving the jungle-clad roads of the Brahmaputra Valley, the vehicles ascended into the wilder country of the Patkai Range. Along the Ledo Road, the convoy folded itself round bend after hairpin bend as the road climbed and descended the steep slopes. Leaving Ledo behind, rain sheeted down. It was difficult to see the truck ahead as we slid and slithered on the newly built road, which the monsoon downpours turned into a sea of mud. Frequent landslides held us up until bulldozers appeared to clear the way. The trucks ground in low gear, struggling up steep inclines and swinging round sharp bends with stomach-jarring sheer drops on one side. With heavy, bloodshot eyes, we slowly coaxed the trucks along the soggy road enclosed by sodden jungles, dark heavy skies, and monsoon mist.

Driving conditions during the monsoon, and this was a "good" road. (Imperial War Museum)

One hundred and fifty miles into the journey, we reached Shaduzup, where we found the American engineers with their bulldozers, power shovels, caterpillars, steamrollers, and hundreds of labourers hacking a way through swamp and forest, toiling to construct the road towards Myitkyina. During the next leg of the journey, we drove along a rough track, skidding and lurching and repeatedly getting stuck in the mud, until we finally reached Myitkyina airfield.

At the edge of the airfield, early in the morning, we drew to a halt, descended from the trucks and stretched our legs. Lieutenant Rowse went to the command post. I joined Blondie, lining up for refreshments. We were handed mugs of hot, sweet liquid.

"What's this muck?" said Blondie, pulling a face after his first taste.

"It's muck being passed off as tea," I answered with a chuckle. "Get it down your neck because it's all we're going to get."

The torrential rain had stopped. The sun was beating down. Steam rose from the earth and the atmosphere was unbearably clammy. Beads of sweat trickled down my face. I looked around and nudged Blondie with my elbow.

"Hey, look at this lot."

We watched as an American combat patrol returned to the airfield. They were exhausted, dirty and caked in mud, the strain of the fighting reflected in hollow-eyed, gaunt faces.

Overhead, the drone of a C47 could be heard now that the rain had stopped and overcast skies had cleared. As it came in to land, ground fire erupted.

"Where's that coming from?" I asked one of the catering corps.

"It's the Nips in 'Mitch.' They're only a mile from the strip. When the planes come in to land or try to take off, the Nips fire on them. It's a risky business for pilots using this landing strip. It's in crappy condition, and we can't maintain it properly because of the monsoon rains and enemy activity. Take a good look. It's a graveyard of downed planes and gliders. This week alone, two C47's veered off the runway into flooded ditches. Yeah, those pilots sure have guts. If you want some excitement, be around at 0700 hours."

"Why? What happens then?"

"It's chow time. We'll be dishing out the food while the Nips drop a few rounds on us. Happens all the time. Killed one Chinese and wounded two others yesterday."

1944

Blondie and I exchanged glances.

"You take me to all the best places," I joked.

Lieutenant Rowse returned.

"Tonight we'll dig in on the northwest edge of the airfield. Get as much rest as you can because tomorrow we're to attack and capture the village of Namkwi. We'll be helping an advance party of 72nd Brigade, the 6 South Wales Borderers, flying in this afternoon."

The weather was kind to us that evening as we sat in soggy trenches, snatching what sleep we could. No rain fell, but the rumble of artillery fire and the crunch of incoming rounds landing nearby kept us awake. Blondie and I smoked cigarettes and watched artillery fire light up the sky.

"Looks like the battle for Myitkyina's in full swing judging from that lot," I said.

"We'll be up against the Japs in a few hours," said Blondie.

My jaw stiffened, set in hate.

"I'll be taking no prisoners."

In the early afternoon, with only a few hours of sleep to fortify us, we set off towards Namkwi. With us were two hundred and fifty men of the advance party of 6 South Wales Borderers and a unit of five hundred Merrill's Marauders, now mainly made up of raw recruits fresh from the troop ship. These men, now part of "Mars Force", had replaced the original Marauders most of whom had been evacuated to Assam because of disease and exhaustion after their long jungle campaign. We made our way down a narrow jungle trail, ankle deep in mud and flanked by six-foot high elephant grass. It was impossible to see anywhere but straight ahead. We were edgy and tense, straining all six senses for signs of danger.

Eventually, we arrived at the waterlogged paddy fields that surrounded the village on three sides. The western boundary of the village backed onto the Namkwi Hka River, which was in full spate. We had to cross nearly three miles of open fields, dotted here and there with banana groves and clumps of trees. It gave the Japanese a good field of fire. But we waited for nightfall, and the night was kind, the moon in hiding, as we silently inched forward into thigh high muddy water. My column moved towards the eastern flank of the village. The remainder cautiously moved straight ahead to approach from the south.

After an hour of stealthily crossing paddy fields, I heard machine gun and mortar fire south of the town. The officer sprang to his feet, waved an arm, and crouching low, we ran forward to be greeted by grenade and mortar fire. I watched a British soldier struggling to get his machine gun into action at point-blank range. *Come on mate. Come on. You can do it*, I silently urged him. I flooded with relief as the soldier began firing at the enemy posts, which soon fell silent.

"He's one brave lucky blighter," I called to Blondie. Then another burst of bullets flew around us as we ran for shelter behind the nearest group of buildings.

We watched and waited, looking for the source of gunfire. It came from an enemy bunker nearby. We fired rifles and machine guns at it with no effect. Flame-throwers were called up and put to use. It was an impressive spectacle in the pitch-black night. From inside the bunker, Japanese soldiers began screaming in agony, and the only thing I felt was hate-filled indifference. Not one Japanese soldier attempted to escape the fiery grave, where they all perished consumed by the flames.

We moved into the village among *bashas* and corrugated iron structures, shooting at targets hidden in the shadows. Then it was hand-to-hand with bayonets as, with wild cries, the Japs spewed from hiding places to face off their attackers. Merciless use of flame-throwers dealt with well-dug-in enemy soldiers.

I lost my footing in the slick mud. My tumble into the mire saved me from a Japanese bullet, which whizzed by my ear. I heard Blondie gasp and cry out, "Gus! Gus! Oh God, he's been shot!"

A Japanese soldier rushed from the shadows to stab me with his bayonet. I rolled to one side, as Blondie rapidly fired several rounds. The enemy soldier collapsed onto my prostrate body, spraying me with warm blood.

"Get this bugger off me," I yelled.

1944

Blondie kicked the Jap off, bayoneted him to make sure he was dead, then hauled me to my feet. Together we stumbled to the safety of a dark corner.

"Thanks, Blondie. I owe you one."

The clearing of the town continued, until we heard one long blast of the officer's whistle signalling "Stand Down".

We checked buildings and thrust bayonets into Japanese corpses to be sure they were dead. We'd heard stories of wounded Japanese, thought to be dead, shooting British soldiers in the back. It wasn't going to happen to us.

No prisoners were taken. The Japanese soldiers had fought to the death, or leapt into the swollen waters of the river to drown.

After clearing the village of enemy dead and taking wounded comrades to the airfield hospital, the village was placed in the hands of the Marauders.

The following day, Lieutenant Rowse gathered the drivers together.

"Tomorrow, we march along the Mogaung Valley," he informed us. "We are to relieve the Chindit Special Force mopping up in the Pahok area. The Sergeant here will give you instructions. Carry on, Sergeant."

"Listen well. I want your full attention. Rifle Companies will move up daily—Advanced Guard becoming Rear Guard. Now that we have taken over Morris Force's mules for carrying our equipment, the Rear Guard will have the task of protecting the mule echelon. Normal marching hours will be 0400 to 1000 hours. Companies will observe a twenty minute halt at ten minutes to every clock hour. No man may leave the ranks without the permission of the officer. Strict water discipline will be observed. Water bottles will be filled before each march and used as ordered. All water, each and every drop, will be chlorinated or boiled. You will receive a salt supply daily. In case you hadn't noticed lads, you're sweating buckets. Slit trenches will be dug at every *laager* area. Passwords are in use. You'll be told what it is tomorrow as we move out. That's all men. Get what rest you can."

The march started next morning. It was a nightmare. The sluice gates of the heavens opened wide. Rain fell without mercy. Water flowed like waterfalls from brims of bush hats pulled low over faces. The rain was so heavy I almost lost sight of the man ahead, yet I could easily have reached out and touched him. The march took us across fast-flowing, chest-deep rivers. Clothes were soaked. Feet were wet. I was jaundiced and feverish, my temperature hovering around 101°F, as I struggled through sloshy mud. When the rain stopped, the sun appeared as if someone had opened a blast-furnace door. Sizzling steam enveloped men and mules in misty sauna vapours. I wished I'd opened my mouth more to the saturating rain now that dehydration was desiccating my body.

After the second day's march, we were sitting on our backpacks, resting. Lieutenant Rowse assembled the men.

"The Japs have reoccupied Namkwi, and we've been ordered retake it. Tomorrow we'll be retracing our steps."

Blondie groaned.

"Trust the Yanks. We hand it to them on a plate, and they go and lose it."

"I feel like the Grand Old Duke of York," I said and began to sing the nursery rhyme, "He had ten thousand men." Blondie joined in.

"He marched them up to the top of the hill and he marched them down again."

The men around us began to sing.

"And when they were up they were up, and when they were down they were down, and when they were only half way up they were neither up nor down."

"A cheer for the Yanks!" I shouted.

Mild boos and hisses spread through the bivouac area.

"Trust the Yanks to keep us busy."

"Can't bear to lose us, that's what it is."

During the next two days, the column, sweaty and bad tempered in the 125°F heat, retraced its steps. At the airfield, we ragged the Marauders.

"What's wrong with you, lads. Need us to hold your hand?"

1944

"They're a right shower. Fresh off the ship."

"Knock it off!" growled a scowling American soldier.

"Or what?" challenged a wiry private of the 6 South Wales Borderers.

"Or I'll make yuh swallow yer teeth, yuh Limey bastard."

The private raised his fists like the army boxing champion he was. Men stepped back to clear a space.

"Come on, blossom. I'm ready for you."

A British sergeant stepped between them.

"Let's be having yer! Come on! Break it up!" "Save your energy for fighting the Japs."

"Don't reckon yuh going to get off so easy, jughead!" the American threatened, raising his arm over the sergeant's head, repeatedly thrusting his pointed finger at the Welsh man.

"I'll be waiting for you, boyo!"

"I said knock it off!" shouted the sergeant.

Grumbling loudly, we all dispersed.

That night, the Advance Party of 36th British Division concentrated on the southern outskirts of Namkwi. Lieutenant Rowse walked among the men.

"We're going to give them what for this time, men. Can't have them thinking they can retake our positions whenever they feel like it. They're on their last gasp. Let's take their breath away."

We moved forward through mud and pouring rain. Talk about déjà vu. To the east of the village, one hundred and fifty Marauders created a diversion for the main force to the south. The enemy was ready for us, but after hours of fierce fighting, we finally recaptured the village, thus cutting off the Japanese garrison in Myitkyina by depriving it of the last remaining road approach to the town.

Over the next few days, the village was prepared for the arrival of 36th Division's 72nd Brigade. Transport planes deposited the regiments onto Myitkyina's airfield—10 Gloucesters, 9 Royal Sussex, further companies of 6 South Wales Borderers and 62 Company R.E. It was an unnerving welcome, deplaning and running for cover if arriving in the middle of a Japanese bombardment of shellfire.

July 17th, my seventh wedding anniversary, was spent on route march from Namkwi to the concentration area at Pidaung on the Rangoon-Myitkyina railway. I walked along lost in thought, reflecting on what I would write to Ivy about how I'd spent this special day. *Darling, you know how mudpacks are supposed to be good for the complexion, well, I must have the best complexion you've ever seen.* I felt a wry smile forming. *Or how about . . . had a lovely day today, playing mud pies.*

British soldiers wade through a Burmese chaung. (Imperial War Museum)

Reveries went flying as I skidded in the mud. Darky grabbed my pack to stop me from falling.

"You were miles away, Gus. Concentrate on what you're doing."

"I was composing a letter to Ivy. It's our wedding anniversary today. Just thinking about what I'll be telling her about today."

"You can tell her you're on Shank's pony, walking through a bog in scorching heat and pouring rain, while the equipment's being carried very comfortably on Jeep trains. Or better still, tell her to send you a boat, so you can keep your feet dry in the trenches."

A further fourteen-mile march the next day brought the Brigade to the village of Mayan. Moving on, we passed through the devastated remains of Mogaung.

"I thought Mogaung was a town," said Blondie, surveying the trees without branches and buildings rendered uninhabitable by Allied air attacks.

"We should find the cinema. James Cagney's on tonight," I joked.

"Nah, too tame. We need the dance hall and some good looking girls," said Darky.

"I could murder a pint," said Mac. "I hear the 'Mucky Duck' has the best beer in town."

The men around us joined in the joke.

"Where's the chippy?"

"Mine's cod and chips, lots of vinegar."

"I want to find the swimming baths and cool off."

"What's wrong wi' yer? Aren't yer wet enough?"

Laughter rippled through the ranks.

We passed sappers salvaging pieces of galvanized iron sheeting and timber from the ruins in order to build shelters. Jeep trains, consisting of Jeeps fitted with specially adapted wheels and pulling three trucks, arrived at a bridge near Mogaung twice daily, bringing in supplies and evacuating the sick and wounded to Myitkyina airfield thirty-seven miles away.

Unable to believe our eyes, 72nd Brigade looked at the battle weary Chindits waiting for the train. Filthy muddy rags covered their emaciated bodies; bushy beards adorned their haggard faces. Many of the men had developed painful eruptions of boils and carbuncles.

"Hey, look at this lot with their rosy cheeks," said one Chindit in greeting.

The men with him grinned, relieved to see the arrival of some of 36th Division at last.

"Hiya lads. Time to get some well earned rest?" I called to them.

"No, not yet. The bright lights of Calcutta are calling," some bright spark answered.

"Give the Japs what for lads," another yelled.

With waves of hands and friendly banter our two groups passed—one at breaking point both mentally and physically, the other fresh for the fighting ahead.

By the end of July, all the regiments had reached the Brigade concentration area at Pahok. Since leaving Namkwi, we had not had any contact with the enemy. A situation that was about to change.

At Pahok, we lived under tarpaulins before airstrip fatigues were found to improve living quarters. The few remaining Chindit Brigades were to be relieved by 72nd Brigade, which was then to attack the Japanese, dug in around Sahmaw and Taungni in an attempt to block further moves south by 36th Division.

Only two Chindit Brigades remained in the area—14th Brigade, which was to reoccupy Point 2171, lost during the relief of the Chindit Forces, and 3rd West African Brigade, which was to gain control of the hills west of the railway. For three weeks, the weakened 3rd West African Brigade and three Nigerian Regiments had been unsuccessfully attacking a key position dominating the only road to Sahmaw. This key position, known as Hill 60, was situated ten miles south of Pahok and three miles from the village of Sahmaw.

As 72nd Brigade planned the attack on Hill 60, the Myitkyina Task Force finally took the town of Myitkyina on August 3rd, clearing the way for the completion of the Ledo Road as soon as the monsoon rain stopped.

Hill 60 was not much of a hill, but the Japanese were organized and determined. They had built cleverly positioned bunkers to give support to one another, so that it was

1944

impossible for assaulting troops to reach a bunker without coming under fire from at least two others. The bunkers were strong points usually made of heavy logs and covered with about five feet of earth. They held from half a dozen to as many as twenty men well supplied with machine guns. They were so well constructed that field guns and medium bombs rarely caused damage.

As well as the bunkers, the Japanese had dug connected foxholes deep enough for them to stand on bamboo platforms to stay dry. With no barbed wire available, they surrounded their trenches with palisades of sharp, pointed bamboo stakes and built observation posts and snipers' nests in trees.

The Chindits' constant mortar and artillery fire and bombing by the air force had stripped Hill 60 of all foliage, so there was no concealment for the troops on either side. The only possible lines of approach for 72nd Brigade were across open country in full view of the strong enemy force. The Hill would be tough to capture.

I was reunited with 62 Company R.E, which was attached to 6 South Wales Borderers. At 1930 hours on August 3rd, the battalion began the arduous march to the assembly area. In the moonlight, we struggled knee-deep through slippery mud the consistency of thick, tomato sauce. Seven miles later, having made no contact with the enemy, we arrived at the assembly area where the battalion had to lie up in thick scrub for thirty-six hours without being seen or heard by Japanese patrols.

Sheltering underneath ground sheets from the pelting rain, we cleaned our rifles to be ready for the action that lay ahead and complained about being wet all the time if not from the rain then from sweat. With fires banned, there were no hot meals or mugs of tea, and with no let up in the weather, we'd be going in without air support.

On August 5th, at 0230 hours, the battalion formed three columns. 62 Company formed the right column with 'A' and 'B' Companies, 'C' and 'D' Companies formed the left, with Battalion HQ and HQ Company in the centre. It was a brilliant moonlight and the columns were some distance apart. An hour later, the start line was crossed and the advance began with the

A CORPORAL'S WAR

Gurkha Rifle Platoon well out in front as a screen. The country was wide open. The ground, covered with short grass, offered no protective cover except for occasional trees and bomb craters.

At 0405 hours, we heard the centre column come under heavy machine gunfire. A tense feeling of nervous expectancy swept over me. A few minutes later, heavy automatic fire was raking the column. Everyone belly-flopped into the muddy grass and fired back at the well-prepared bunker position. 'B' Company and 62 Company R.E. was ordered to right flank. Major Jones was shot in the neck and killed while giving orders to 'A' Company to attack the bunker position. Major Vivian took over command and 'A' Company's attack on the bunker went in. 'B' Company moved round the flank and came under fire from another bunker position.

The sergeant rounded up twenty Royal Engineers, me included, and took us to the Lieutenant, who ordered, "Get these forty-gallon petrol drums up the hill while 'A' Company is keeping the other bunkers occupied. We'll burn the buggers out."

While the remainder of the column engaged the bunker, we struggled up the slope, pushing the forty-gallon drums ahead of us as silently as we could. It was a sweaty, muscle-straining effort as we slipped and slithered in the slick mud. At the top, we punctured the drums with pickaxes then rolled them down onto the bunker. Gurkha machine-gunners fired at the petrol, setting it alight.

A ball of flames erupted in and around the bunker. Inside, Japanese soldiers were screaming. Two soldiers, enveloped in flames, bolted into the open and fell to the ground, screaming in pain, frenziedly rolling round in the mud in an attempt to put out the flames. Ear-splitting explosions shook the bunker when the ammunition ignited. Darky and I raised our rifles to shoot the burning men, but while Darky immediately fired to end one man's agony, I hesitated. A picture of the murdered nurses filled my mind. Filled with hate, I eyed the shrieking, writhing, enemy soldier.

1944

"For God's sake, Gus! Shoot him! Shoot him! Now!" Darky shouted.

I roused myself and squeezed the trigger.

"What the hell . . . Gus?"

"The nurses . . ."

Darky stared at me incensed then nodded abruptly in understanding.

I looked at the charred, smoking bodies on the ground and felt a grim satisfaction and an inner emptiness.

With this position cleared, the company made another advance, clearing a second enemy machine gun position in the same way, but this time, snipers' bullets thudded into the ground around us. One man was hit in the thigh. I caught the flash of rifle fire, took careful aim and fired at a distant tree. The Japanese sniper tumbled from his hidden perch and fell into view, his lifeless body swinging upside down by the rope that fastened him to the branches.

By 0715 hours, 'B' Company had reached its objective and consolidated. An hour later, 'A' Company joined us. We dug in and began patrolling forward.

◆ ◆ ◆

While the left and right flanks were clearing bunker positions, the centre column was suffering severe casualties. Heavy machine gunfire had them pinned to the ground in an area completely lacking in cover. After an hour of stomach crawling, the commanding officer and most of his Tactical HQ reformed in a dyke only thirty yards from the enemy post.

For the men still trapped in the open, the heat of the sun was becoming more dangerous than enemy bullets. A heavy rainstorm saved them just before noon, bringing relief from the effects of sunstroke and dehydration. Under cover of mortars and smoke put down by artillery, a difficult withdrawal began. The men crawled on their stomachs back to their lines, dragging with them what wounded men they could. It took several hours before safety was reached. By 1730 hours, nearly all the casualties had been evacuated, but this late in the day, with nightfall fast approaching, it was decided to postpone shelling of enemy positions until the next morning.

At 1800 hours, the battalion, less 'A' and 'B' Companies, was ordered to withdraw to Hill 60 and guard the left flank of the West Africans. While withdrawal was being carried out, the battalion came under attack from snipers and bursts of machine gunfire, suffering two casualties.

◆ ◆ ◆

Next day, August 6th, was grey and overcast. Today's attack would once again have to go ahead without air support. From 0900 hours, the remaining Japanese positions were shelled for one hour. The Japanese inside the bunkers were deafened by the thunderous noise. Some were shell-shocked and dazed, but all were fanatical about not surrendering.

Patrols from 'A' and 'B' Companies silently inched forward. I felt a touch on my arm and was told by hand signals to use more petrol drums on the bunker. Again, there was the laborious job of pushing the drums up a muddy incline, as slippery as an icy ski slope, while trying to make as little noise as possible; the swing of pick axes; the strong odour of petrol as fuel spilled from the rolling drums; the burst of automatic fire and more enemy deaths by incineration. The men inside this bunker did not try to escape the flames, preferring a fiery death with honour than life and a shameful surrender.

It was all over well before midday. 3rd West African Brigade relieved 'A' and 'B' Companies, which moved forward to join the battalion on Hill 60.

That afternoon, a party of one hundred strong went out to recover kit and arms and to trace men missing from the battlefield. Losses to 36th Division were twenty-two killed and fifty wounded. Forty Japanese dead were counted.

After relieving 9 Royal Sussex Regiment, which continued the advance on Taungni, the Battalion spent an uncomfortable night in the soggy sludge which passed for ground in the area around the hill.

With the fall of Hill 60, 72nd Brigade quickly followed up their advantage. We soon succeeded in ousting the Japanese from Sahmaw. Like everywhere else, the town was a quagmire. Only two houses and a brick chimney-stack were left standing. On the outskirts of the town, my patrol checked out the ruins of the sugar factory, destroyed by American bombs. Nearby, we discovered a large Buddhist shrine hidden in the jungle. The shady glade was peaceful, clean, and unspoiled by the turmoil of war. The tall statue of Buddha wearing a serene smile fascinated me. "Look at his smile," I said to Darky. "It warms the cockles of your heart to see it, especially in our situation."

"I'd smile too if I could have that corrugated iron sheeting over my head in this rain."

Moving on Taungni, the Battalion advanced through 9 Royal Sussex Regiment. Battalion headquarters, with 'A' and 'C' Companies, established themselves at Kyungon, while 'B' and 'D' Companies continued the advance, mopping up small parties of Japanese rearguards.

Several wild rifle shots were fired at the advancing men from a nearby copse—then silence. Crawling through creepers and mud, we found five severely wounded Japanese soldiers lying on the ground, close to death. One soldier was propped against a tree, his rifle across his lap. A black and red stain from slowly oozing blood marred the front of his uniform. He struggled to lift his rifle to shoot again, but lacked the strength. We cautiously approached. Gasping his last breath, the Japanese soldier's head sagged and fell to one side, eyes staring at eternity.

'D' Company fanned out through the brush and discovered a hamlet of three *bashas*. The soldiers inched forward, until they were so close they could hear the murmur of Japanese voices inside the huts.

With 'B' Company, we headed for the stream where we spotted Japanese soldiers on the bank behind dense bushes, resting and filling their water bottles. Suddenly, one enemy soldier shouted a warning to his comrades. Grabbing their weapons, they dived for cover, but I already had one in my sights. A single shot got him in the throat.

"Take that, you yellow-bellied heap o' shite."

A burst of machine gunfire raked the bushes above my head, splintering tree bark and showering us with green-leaf confetti. Ducking my head, I caught Darky's eye.

"Close shave."

Darky grinned and nodded. More firing, Japanese and 'B' Company's, and then gradually, enemy fire petered out, until there were only the sounds of 'B' Company's weapons. Crouching low, we moved towards the enemy group and found them lying spread-eagled in the grass, eyes open, heads tilted back, mouths gaping, grimaces of painful deaths frozen on faces, while blood seeped from fresh bullet wounds. We kicked and bayoneted the bodies to ensure lifelessness.

Hearing the noise of fighting from the direction of the *chaung*, 'D' Company attacked the three *bashas*. Exploding grenades, machine gun and rifle-fire blitzed the buildings. Screams and shouts erupted inside, as enemy bodies shredded under the onslaught. British soldiers were jubilant. We were beating back the Japanese and proud of it.

"Good work, men," praised the captain. "We'll soon have them pushed all the way back to Rangoon. Take a twenty-minute rest. We need to find materials to build a bridge over this *chaung* in order to move on Taungni."

"There was a stack of big bags of sugar in the factory at Sahmaw, sir," I told him. "They might do the trick."

The captain sent a team of muleteers and ten engineers to see what they could find at the factory. Several hours later, they were back, the mules laden with bags of sugar and pipes to act as culverts.

We set to work, standing chest deep in the muddy water, to construct a bridge sturdy enough for artillery and trucks to use. It took some time and energy, battling the fast flowing water and handling the heavy bags of sugar, but at last, it was completed, and we clambered onto the bank. Then it was time for de-leeching.

"Look at this big bugger," said Darky. "It's the size of a sausage."

"I've got some in my boots," I said, looking at blood seeping through the eyelets. I sat down to remove my boots.

1944

We cleansed ourselves and one another of the engorged parasites and moved on to the next village on the map.

After the excitement of the mopping up, the capture of Taungni was an anti-climax. Enemy troops were retreating rapidly after the pounding they'd received at Hill 60. At 1310 hours, August 8th, 'B' and 'D' Companies walked into Taungni alert for signs of danger.

Taungni in peacetime was little more than a railway station. Now it was little more than a communal burial ground. The sickly stench of death assailed our nostrils when we arrived. While some men hurried away from the smell as fast as they could, I, and others who were just as curious, walked in the direction of the stench and made a gruesome discovery. Several hundred dead Japanese, in various stages of decay, had been dumped in a bomb crater. Swarms of black flies filled the air; maggots crawled among the rotting flesh and bleached bare bones. Rib cages and skulls stood out amongst the filth where vultures had scavenged their fill.

"We must be really pushing them back. They've made no effort to bury their dead properly, or even cover them with lime," I said, backing hastily away. I'd seen and smelt enough. This was not a place to linger.

Intent on reclaiming Burma, 36th Division continued its advance. This was the parting of the ways for 72nd Brigade and 62 Company R.E. Turning north, we retraced our steps to Myitkyina. Everyone but the drivers boarded transport planes to return to Dinjan. Blondie and I, with the rest of the convoy, began the tortuous drive to Assam through the deep mud of the Ledo Road.

Safe and Sound

On my return to Assam, I started a letter to Ivy.

"Well, Darling,

I'm safely back at Dinjan after a hellish drive along the Ledo Road. It wasn't any better coming back than it was going into north Burma. Of course, once they got us there, they involved us in the fighting. Now I've got the mildew off my boots, and my filthy mud-caked uniform is in the wash, and I'm all bright and shiny after the most wonderful shower I've ever had in my life, I finally feel clean of all the musty, dank smells of the Burmese jungle."

I chewed my pen, wondering how much to tell Ivy, wanting to bare my soul, but not wanting to cause her concern. I sighed and lay back on my bed. I wished Hinny was around to talk to, but he wasn't. His bone were lying somewhere in Burma, picked clean by ants. My emotions were bubbling. I'd experienced a side of my nature I'd never felt before—pure hate and the heartlessness that came with it. Calming myself, I continued writing.

"They had us mopping up small pockets of resisting Japanese, so we were involved in one or two skirmishes. No one from the company was lost or injured during our escapades, and now we're back on road works for our sins. The monsoon rains keep washing them away, and heavy traffic, trying to keep supplies moving, causes them to collapse and sink, so we're being kept busy.

"They're sending small parties of us for training in mechanical equipment to be ready for whatever they have in store for us when we leave here—and who knows when that will be. The rumour is we're leaving in November, but you never can tell.

"There's so much going on right now. We've got the Japs on the run. We're chasing them out of Assam back to Burma, and they can't run away fast enough from our advance in north Burma. Even though the monsoon has turned the land into the biggest bog on earth, we're keeping after them, not giving them a chance to regroup. There's a great feeling of hope and optimism in camp, despite the mud and gloomy wet days.

"Write soon, darling. You have no idea how much I look forward to news from home. Send some photos. I miss you all so much my heart could burst,

Yours always,
Norman"

1944

◆   ◆   ◆

I was sent with the next group of eight men to the quarries at Namrup to receive training in mechanical equipment. While there, I bumped into Bill McMahon of 58 Company. We'd first become friends when we shared the same lodgings in Ilfracombe and had travelled together on the *Cape Town Castle* to India. Since then, we'd seen little of each other as Bill's company had been involved in a lot more of the fighting and riot control than mine.

Bill spotted me sitting in the NAAFI with my friends and strolled over. "How's it going, Gus? Long time no see."

Irene McMahon (left) and Ivy Wickman (right) with their daughters

"Well, look what the cat's brought in. Fancy seeing you here."

Bill pulled out a chair and sat down. He fished about inside his pocket for a photograph. "Thought you'd like to see our Joan."

"Look at the sparkle in her eyes. She looks full of mischief. I bet she's a holy terror."

"That's what Irene says. She named her after your Joan 'cos she thinks your Joan's an angel, but our Joan's a real handful even though she's only three. Irene's got to have eyes in the back of her head where our Joan is."

"Ivy tells me she's been to visit Irene in Blackburn several times. They've become good friends. It's good that they have one another to talk to. I hear you had a rough time of it in Kohima."

"It wasn't Kohima. When we pulled back from Palel onto the Imphal Plain, we took up position in a defensive box north of Imphal at Kanglatongbi. Those Japs take the biscuit. We were manning the perimeter and the roadblock when they started their night-time tricks. They were in the jungle opposite our position, rustling bushes, clicking rifle bolts, talking and throwing thunder flashes, trying to draw our fire, so they could see where we were, but of course, no one fired a shot. Well into the night—we could see as clear as day in the moonlight—we watched a Jap patrol, about ten strong, walking along the middle of the road towards the roadblock. Then eight of the buggers disappeared into the jungle, and the other two carried on strolling down the road as bold as you like. I shot one at five yards. The other one got away into the jungle. Then the others opened fire on us, but a burst from a Bren gun soon shut them up."

I was amazed. "I can't believe those Japs, just walking up like that."

"The real fun began two nights later. The Japs broke through the perimeter fence. We had a right old skirmish. One of their snipers polished off six of our men with shots to the head. We lobbed grenades and fired like hell and prayed for the tanks and infantry to arrive. Eventually, we beat them back, but soon after that, we moved to another box closer to Imphal. Those defensive boxes, that's a good way to fight. Better than falling back all the time. How about you, Gus?"

"We had a few skirmishes in north Burma," I said, nodding to my friends sitting at the table, "But nothing like you. We were never cut off by the Japs for, how long, four months? They were on the run by the time we got there. We only had one tough fight and that was at Hill 60. The rest of the time, we were just mopping up."

"It was rough in the box. I was glad to get out of it. I can't tell you how happy I was to see 2nd Division's tanks coming down the road, firing at the Japs in the hills. We'd been cut off for three months. They sent us to Shillong for a rest. Now they're getting us ready to do something other than fighting by the looks of it."

"Yes, it makes you wonder, doesn't it?" I said.

I didn't have to wonder for long.

River Rescues

Back at Dinjan, I barely had time to unpack my kit bag, before I was packing it again after being ordered to supervise a unit of Indian soldiers constructing a pontoon bridge across the half-mile wide Burhi Dihing River. The men toiled in the clammy heat to build the bridge by coupling together rafts that rested on pontoons for support. The bridge became an important thoroughfare for the Military Police and the transportation of supplies.

I never wore a shirt while working. Officers wanting to cross the river would approach me, unaware that I was a mere corporal. With a salute, they'd ask, "Permission to cross the bridge, sir." I played along, getting a kick out of acting the part of an officer. "Of course, Captain. Permission granted," I'd reply, returning the salute before organizing rafts for the trucks and a launch to tow them to the far bank.

The monsoon brought heavy rains and the river's swollen waters became a force to be reckoned with. One night, a little after midnight, an Indian soldier rushed into my tent and shook me awake.

"Corporal Sahib," he called. "There are men in the water, sahib. A boatman lost control of his large bamboo raft in the fierce current. It smashed into the bridge and the bridge broke apart. Nineteen soldiers have been swept away. Some managed to cling to one of the rafts; others fell into the river. They've all disappeared into the night, sahib."

I rubbed my eyes and reached for my boots. "Tell me again. What happened?"

As I grabbed my shirt and a flashlight and ran towards the river, the Indian soldier ran alongside, describing the situation. The river was swollen and dangerous, and I knew I had no time to lose. I jumped into one of the skiffs, furiously jerking the outboard motor to life.

"Corporal Sahib, not that boat. The motor is not working well on that boat, sahib."

The torrent's roar drowned out his words, and I was already well out onto the river. Spray from the churning waves soaked me to the skin. I raced downstream in the surging waters, calling to the lost men.

"Where are you? Answer me."

"Corporal Sahib," men called.

Aiming my flashlight towards their voices, I saw them clinging to bushes on almost submerged islets.

"Here, Corporal Sahib, here," came shouts from the far bank.

"Hang on. I'll be back for you after I pick up the men in the water," I shouted.

By the light of the flashlight I counted thirteen men on land. *That leaves six men in the river* I calculated.

Battling the heaving tide of currents, I struggled to manoeuvre the boat alongside the men I found in the water. Three times I hauled men into the boat which almost capsized when a tree trunk, bobbing crazily in the water, caught the skiff and spun it round. With three men aboard, I searched for the other soldiers swept away in the water, but without success. The small boat was pushed to its limit as I forced my way upstream against the current. Finding a sheltered spot on the south bank, I put the men ashore and allowed the overheated motor to cool down.

1944

"It's a long way, but after you've rested you'll be able to walk back to camp from here. I've got to go and find the others."

Returning to the foray, I was just in time to save a man clinging to an overhanging branch. As I struggled to manoeuvre the boat alongside him, he lost his grip. I grabbed his shirt and yanked him into the skiff. The boat tilted and rocked in the wild current. Thinking the boat would capsize, I held my breath. But we stayed afloat, and I made my way back upriver.

Guided by men shouting, I collected more survivors from islets and sandbars, making several trips to deposit them on the south bank. I was frustrated by the need to rest in sheltered shoals and calm pools by the riverbanks to allow the overheating motor to cool down. The urgency of the situation drove me to plunge back into the turbulent torrent before it was wise to do so. With my last load of rescued men, and only three hundred more yards to navigate, I managed to reach the edge of a sheltered bay, before the motor burned out.

"Hurry," I shouted. "Jump out and pull us to shore before we're swept back into the current."

The weary men responded. Jumping into the water, they pulled the boat to shore and hauled it onto the bank.

Now it was time to walk. In the jet-black night, with only a small beam from the flashlight to guide us, the exhausted men—clothes dripping, hair plastered to foreheads, turbans lost—stumbled along occasionally tripping over roots and skinning their knees. One soldier had an injured leg and needed to be supported by two of his companions. Five hours after the accident at the bridge, our group, the first to return, walked into camp. Our arrival almost went unnoticed by the men in camp, who were engrossed in praying for our safe return. Suddenly, one man called out, "Look! Corporal Sahib is back! With the men! He's rescued the men!"

Cries of joy echoed all round the camp with congratulations and celebrations filling the air. As more of the survivors trickled into camp, cooks hurried forward with hot warming tea. Medical orderlies wrapped them in blankets and ushered them to the medical office. The Indian officer in charge approached me.

"You've shown exceptional bravery tonight, Corporal. I am going to commend you for a medal."

"Thank you, sir. But anyone would have done the same."

"You think so? Come with me. You should see the river now that dawn is breaking."

At the riverside, my face turned ashen and my blood ran cold. I stared at the roaring fury of the silt-stained water fighting savagely like a wild animal to free itself from the containment of the river's banks.

"It's a good job I couldn't see what I was launching myself into. I might have had second thoughts," I said, when I was finally able to speak.

"I'm amazed you came back alive, Corporal. The Gods were with you."

Leaving the riverbank, I glanced back for one last look, thinking I must have been stark raving mad, unable to believe I'd gone out into that wild water in a small skiff and survived. Someone was looking after me. I felt an intense gratitude.

I had barely recovered from my first river adventure when I was called upon to perform yet another daring feat. Salvage parties had been sent downstream to find and repair the lost pontoons and rafts in order to rebuild the mangled bridge.

Less than a week later, word reached camp that four soldiers were in danger, cornered in a village seven miles downstream. The Indian sergeant had shot and killed a villager, who had attacked the soldiers with a machete after one of them raped his wife. The commanding officer sent for me.

"I take it you've heard of the situation we have downstream, Corporal?"

"Yes, sir."

"I want you to go and bring all four men back safely. Do whatever it takes."

"Yes, sir."

I put on my best uniform, pressed until it was in pristine condition, then set off in a launch to find the village, accompanied by two Indian sergeants and two British privates. As we made our way downstream, I racked my brains. How was I going to tackle this situation? How would I get them away from the village in one piece? How could I make sure *we* didn't end up getting hurt or even killed in the attempt?

My stomach churned.

Hearing a hullabaloo coming from round a bend in the river, I warned the soldiers, "Stay alert. Be ready to shoot if you have to."

As we neared the beach, clamouring villagers rushed to the river's edge, angrily waving their machetes.

"Looks like they're pleased to see us, Gus," one private noted dryly.

"This is going to be tough. Don't show any nervousness or fear. I want you two to stay with the boat," I told the Indian sergeants, "and you two come with me into the village."

Hoping I looked poised and dignified, I stepped out of the launch. *Laurence Olivier couldn't act better at this moment*, I thought. The yelling crowd clustered round, menacing us with their knives. Mangy, yapping dogs nipped at our heels. Standing tall, a stern expression on my face, I mustered an air of authority. Taking control of the situation, I demanded, "Where is the headman?"

A thin, wiry man, a scowl on his wrinkled face, burst from the crowd. He began shouting and waving his arms.

"Indian soldiers kill man here. We kill them. Not let get away."

I fixed the man with a steely gaze.

"I have come to take these soldiers back, to be punished by the army."

Looking towards the cluster of huts that made up the village, I saw the four culprits squatting back to back under a bamboo shelter surrounded by hostile men. Every once in a while, a villager would take a swing at them with his machete, which the soldiers warded off with rifles and bayonets. It looked like they'd been holed up there for some time. I could see blood stains on two of the men's uniforms.

A CORPORAL'S WAR

The villagers were in an uproar. Becoming more aggressive, they began yelling, "Not leave village. We keep till police come."

"I am here on the King's business," I proclaimed. "It is my duty to arrest these men and take them before the magistrate. It would not be wise to interfere with the King's business. You say they have killed a man. Let me see him."

The headman beckoned me into the village and led me to the victim. The villagers had built a bamboo shelter over the corpse to keep the sun off him, but he was already starting to smell, and flies were buzzing around. A bullet hole stained the centre of his forehead. It was an impressive shot. With an angry man running at him with a machete, the havildar couldn't have had much time to take aim.

"I can see these men have caused harm to your village. I will make sure they will receive the punishment they deserve. Now, we will escort them to the boat."

The pugnacious headman blocked my path.

"What happen to woman now husband dead, sahib?" he insisted, a cunning expression on his face.

He wasn't going to let us get away so easily.

"I am sure the army will pay compensation for her loss." A sly smile spread across the headman's face, revealing the few betel-stained teeth remaining in his mouth.

"That is very good, sahib. It is only right."

I wonder how many rupees will end up in your pockets before the widow receives her share.

The headman waved the villagers back.

"Let them through."

"Bring the men to the boat," I ordered the British soldiers.

"Get back. Make way," they ordered, pushing their way through the sullen crowd with the prisoners.

Reluctantly, the crowd parted. At the beach, I stripped the rescued Indian sergeant of his rifle and bayonet. To make the arrest look real, I slapped him across the face, roughly shoved him towards the launch and growled under my breath, "You'd better get in pronto, if you know what's good for you."

1944

I could feel resentment building in the villagers' malevolent murmuring, as I deprived them of their chance for revenge. Murmurs were swelling into a commotion. I quickly manhandled the others into the boat.

"Let's go," I urged, climbing into the launch and heaving a sigh of relief, as the boat moved off without incident.

"Blimey, Gus, you pulled it off. I never thought we'd come out of there in one piece. I've got to hand it to you. You certainly have a way with the natives."

◆ ◆ ◆

"Good show, Corporal! Against all odds you've done it again," the delighted commanding officer praised, after hearing my tale. "I'm impressed by your ingenuity, your style, and let's not forget your bravery. Well done! The best thing I can do now is transfer these men to other units as quickly as possible and find some money to compensate the widow."

I walked out of the office, strolled to the riverbank, and stared at its muddy waters, while I smoked a cigarette and calmed myself. *Bloody army! Its soldiers rape and murder civilians and all they receive is a slap on the wrist and a transfer. And what compensation will the woman receive? A thousand rupees, or should I say whatever's left after the village headman and council take their cut. Where's the justice in that? No wonder they want us out of India. I'm giving you fair warning, river. I've had enough excitement in the three weeks I've been here. There's only one week to go before I return to my unit, and I'd like a quiet time from now on, thank you very much.*

Goodbye to Assam

"The camp looks busy. What's up?" I asked, entering the *basha* on my return to Dinjan.

"You got back just in time, Gus. We're moving off to Dhanbad, to a large open-cast coal mine," said Darky.

"You'll feel right at home then, won't you, with your dad being a miner?"

Darky pulled a face.

"That's why I became a painter and decorator. Couldn't face going down the pit. Still, open-cast mining's a bit different from that."

"Lieutenant Ellis says we're going to be reorganized and join with 58 Field Company," said Blondie.

"Keep your fingers crossed that we can all stay together," I said.

The Royal Engineer Companies in Assam were part of General Reserve Engineer Force. Owing to General Slim's successful advance towards Burma, G.R.E.F. as a separate engineer force was no longer suitable for work in the forward area. With the change in fortune of the British Army in Burma, the higher command on the Burma front was reorganized. A new headquarters, Allied Land Forces South East Asia (A.L.F.S.E.A.), was set up under the command of Lieutenant-General Sir Oliver Leese.

Major Cave received a memo from Colonel Pearce, HQ Detachment, G.R.E.F., Dibrugarh, which was posted in the canteen. It read:

> 1. With your departure from this theatre and from Detachment G.R.E.F., I wish to thank all officers and men for the splendid support you have given us.
>
> 2. Since your arrival in N.E. Assam, a great amount of work has been done, not by you alone, but by all in Detachment G.R.E.F., as a team. You have all and everyone played a very important part in that team.
>
> 3. The U.S.A.A.F. have achieved here in Assam one of the world's greatest air transport feats in history. Their success is in no small measure due to your achievements.
>
> 4. I am proud to have had the privilege of commanding Detachment G.R.E.F. whose

1944

backbone has been in the sterling quality of companies of men like you.

5. You have before you new fields to conquer. I know you will be a credit and a great success. Good luck to all and every one of you.

We stood round the notice board reading the memo. "Well, isn't it nice to be appreciated," said Tommy.

"What's these new fields we've got to conquer? That's what I want to know," demanded Darky.

"They're not going to be green, that's for sure," I said, "not where there's open-cast mining."

"They're going to have us chasing Tojo all the way to Singapore," said Blondie. "That's what our new fields are going to be."

I moved out with the motor transport party November 2nd. The rest of the company had left by train during the previous four days. The seven trucks, carrying thirteen drivers and Lieutenant Lind, were driven to Siliguri where we entrained for Calcutta.

On our arrival, we were allowed one and a half days rest before commencing the 240 mile drive to Dhanbad. We drove from the camp at Barrackpore into Calcutta, filled with excitement at being in a big city after eighteen months in the back of beyond of Assam.

The crowds, the noise, the smells at first stimulated the senses then overwhelmed us. Exploring the city, we found soldiers—American, British, Indian, African—lining up at brothels, not caring if they became infected with disease and some even hoping for it in order to avoid fighting in the jungles of Burma and Malaya.

The effects of the famine were still visible in the weak, skeletal people lying and dying in the streets or foraging through rubbish for food. One man clutched at my arm.

"Sahib, sahib."

His gestures indicated his desperation and willingness to sell his young daughter, possibly only eleven years old, to me and my friends.

"No! No!" Horrified, I shook my arm free of the man's grasp. "I can't take any more of this," I said, waving my arm at the beggars and a woman lying on the ground, waiting for death, with her baby clasped to her chest. "Let's go back to camp."

The next day, we decided to go swimming in the Sundarbans, a huge area of thousands of square miles of tropical marsh with hundreds of small watercourses. After refreshing ourselves with a swim in the cooling water, we sat on the riverbanks, which provided the only firm ground. We were surrounded by mangoes, palms, bamboo, and swamp. Fifty feet away, naked children from a nearby village were sliding down the slick black mud on a steep riverbank. It warmed our hearts to see their carefree play and hear their shrieks of laughter when they landed with a splash in the water. The war seemed a million miles away.

◆ ◆ ◆

After a long dusty drive, the trucks pulled into 62 Company headquarters at Kanrra on the Grand Trunk Road. The camp was in a pleasant open area with tented accommodations. 58 Company had arrived five weeks earlier. Some men were still receiving training in mechanical equipment. My job was to supervise the transportation of coal from the stockpiles and its loading into railway wagons that carried the fuel to the steelworks at Calcutta.

November 14th was a sad day. Major Cave was reassigned after more than four years with the unit, and company quartermaster Sergeant Wellington was posted as lieutenant-quartermaster to an Indian Engineer company.

1945

25th Stores and Ports Section R.E.

With the Christmas and New Year celebrations over, I was transferred, along with Mac and thirteen other men, to 25th Stores and Ports Section R.E. under the command of Captain Perry. Before joining our new unit at Chittagong on January 11th, I enjoyed a final, subdued night together with my friends.

"So, we're getting split up after all," said Blondie. "We had a good run while it lasted."

Mac nodded. "Yes, pity it couldn't go on. At least Gus will be with me. We can keep each other out of trouble."

"We've had a great five and a half years together," I said. "Heck, I've spent more time with you than I have with Ivy."

"Yes, Gus, but do you love us as much?" quipped Darky.

I burst out laughing.

"Almost, especially after I've had a few beers."

We strolled back to the tent. At 1:00 a.m., it was time for Mac and me to leave. It was an emotional farewell, starting with handshakes and ending with hugs and much backslapping.

"Take care of yourselves, Gus, Mac," said Darky.

"See you back in England, if not before," said Blondie.

"Hey," said Tommy, "now that we get repatriated after only four years, we've only got eighteen more months before we go home. Let's just keep ourselves safe till then."

"You're a great bunch of friends. Couldn't wish for better," said Mac.

"We've had a great time together," I said, "and we'll have them again. This war won't last forever, even if it seems like it sometimes. Bye, lads."

Mac and I moved quickly away, the lumps in our throats keeping us silent as we walked to the train. Mac entrained for Chittagong at 0200 hours. I was to leave with the transport party five hours later. On reaching Calcutta, we were informed of a change in plan and redirected to Pandu, Assam. Ten days and 800 miles after leaving Dhanbad, I arrived at Pandu.

No arrangements had been made for a campsite for the unit, so we were put to work building accommodations. Two weeks after they were completed, Captain Perry received a letter explaining the future role of the unit. Its job would be the transhipment of bulk stores. In the meantime, we were placed under the command of 8 Engineer Supply Depot to receive training in the recording and shipment of supplies.

No bulk engineer stores materialized before March 19th when the unit received orders to proceed to Maungdaw in the Arakan.

The next day, at 1700 hours, lack of accommodation forced the fifteen of us to make ourselves as comfortable as we could in freight wagons. We spent the night in Pandu station before the train finally pulled out at midday. After five days of travelling in the freight cars, we arrived at Chittagong.

Captain Perry reported to the movement control officer.

"Ah, yes," said the officer. "Well, you see, there's no sea passage to Maungdaw. You'll have to proceed to Dohazari by rail and from there by road to Maungdaw."

Ten hours later, we arrived at Dohazari where Perry reported to the administration commandant.

"Maungdaw, you say? Let's see. It's 2000 hours, and I don't have accommodation for you here. Might be best if you spent the night on the train. Meanwhile, I'll arrange transport to take the men and baggage to 60 Indian Reinforcement Camp in the morning."

Captain Perry returned.

1945

"I'm sorry, men, but we're going to have to spend the night on the train. They can't organize trucks to take us to the reinforcement camp till morning."

Groans and muffled swearing met his announcement.

"Here we are then. Been stuck on this train for bloody hours, and now we're left here like fried eggs stuck in fat that's gone cold 'cos nobody wants us," said Mac, in disgust.

"We'd be better off in the front line," I said. "At least they'd know what to do with us."

"All right, men, settle down and get some sleep," said Perry. "I know this isn't great, but the army's focused on getting things right at the front. That's where it counts at the moment. When we reach Maungdaw, we'll be fine."

"What's at Maungdaw?" I asked.

"It's a small port in Burma on the estuary of the Naaf River. It took a beating during the fighting because of its position at the head of the only road in the Arakan that goes from the coast to the interior. It's changed hands a few times—been occupied by the Japs, then us, then the Japs and now we've got it again. We don't have to worry about the Japs coming back. We've just about pushed them completely out of the Arakan peninsula, and this time they won't be returning."

After two days at 60 Reinforcement Camp and ten hours driving in trucks provided by West African General Transport Company, we arrived at our destination at one o' clock in the morning. The next day, we began taking over the stores from 11 Field Park Company (West African). Then a case of smallpox was discovered in the district, and we were lined up for vaccinations.

Welcome to Maungdaw!

Teknaf

"I'm being sent where?" I asked.

"Teknaf," said Captain Perry who had sent for me. "It's the southernmost village of Chittagong district in East Bengal, across the estuary from Maungdaw. You and your men are to maintain and protect the water supply for the Royal Navy's ships in the area."

I began my seven-week posting in Teknaf along with Jock, the cook, and Sandy and Mac. "It looks like it'll be a cushy duty," I told the men. "All we have to do is climb up the hill to the reservoir each day and check that the water is flowing along the pipeline to the barge being used as a water tanker. We've to keep the water tanker full at all times. Simple!"

We moved into a large wooden bungalow perched on the hillside. The windows were boarded up as protection against the approaching monsoon season. Just as well. It wasn't long before the area was hit by a cyclone. Howling winds rattled the shaky structure. Fierce gusts threatened to remove the roof. Heavy rain lashed the building. The water surge was sixteen feet, so high it lapped against the doorstep. We sat up all night long, listening to the building groaning and creaking under the onslaught. Hurricane lamps lit the scene in the living room where, with knotted stomachs, we sat anxiously on metal trunks, holding our rifles across our knees. The winds intensified.

Mac, biting his lips and frowning as he struggled to keep fear at bay, shouted above the roar of the wind, "What if the wind gusts are powerful enough to destroy the bungalow?"

"We'll all be blown away like dandelion clocks," Sandy tried to joke, but we were so scared no one cracked a smile. The thought of the bungalow disintegrating under the pulverizing power of the wind was too terrifying to contemplate.

"The bungalow must have been through storms like this before," I tried to reassure the men, including myself, "and it's still standing. We just have to sit tight till it blows itself out."

"How long's it going to last?" Jock murmured. I knew he was wondering if his nerve would give out before the storm did.

It was a long, tense night. Then like a knight in shining armour, the morning sun arrived, bringing with it a softening of the winds. From out of the nightmare's chaos, order was restored. Four shaken but relieved men ventured outside to survey the flooded landscape.

"That was a hell of a night. I've never experienced anything like it," I said, "and to think this is the sheltered side of the peninsula."

"If this is the sheltered side, I'm glad I wasn't on the other coast," said Sandy, voice soft in awe of the powerful force we had somehow managed to survive.

"I'm just grateful we came through it safely. Who'd have thought this bungalow would have stood up to those winds?" muttered Jock, shaking his head in disbelief.

We'd survived our close encounter with a cyclone. After that, the miseries and hardships of monsoon rains were child's play.

We got on with the tasks required of our posting. As part of our duties, we regularly patrolled the wide, wooden deck, wrapped round the exterior of the bungalow. Although the Japanese Army had retreated towards Rangoon, there was always the risk of stragglers appearing to cause havoc in the area. Edged with mangroves that led into dense jungle, the *chaungs* and inlets off the channel were ideal places for stray Japanese soldiers to hide.

During an early morning deck patrol, I rounded the corner and froze in mid-stride, stunned to find myself face to face with an aggressive, rogue elephant. Fear hit me like a sledgehammer. I felt the colour drain from my face. It was a strange feeling, as if someone had pulled the plug in the sink for the water to flow away. Villagers from the nearby hamlet had warned me about the elephant, which had been on the rampage, destroying crops and knocking down houses and even killing some people. The gargantuan beast was magnificent, terrifying, and dangerous. Catching my scent, the elephant lifted its trunk. It flapped its ears, kicked up dust and trumpeted, challenging this puny human across the twelve-foot gap that separated us. The sound shook me out of my paralysis, and I quickly backed away. Once round the corner, I ran to fetch my rifle from inside the bungalow. I didn't think the 303 was powerful enough to kill the elephant, but maybe I could scare it away.

Rushing back, I fired several shots over its head. The elephant turned away, giving one last loud trumpet. Ears flapping, it lumbered down the hill, the earth vibrating beneath its less than majestic departure. I let out a sigh of relief. Knees suddenly weak, I leaned against the veranda railing for support. I sent up a silent prayer,. *Thank you, God.* The clatter of army boots running along the veranda announced the arrival of my companions, rifles at the ready, to see what all the commotion was about.

"Stone the crows! It's not only Japs we have to watch out for, it's bloody elephants as well," Mac spluttered, dressed only in his underpants.

"Do you think he'll be back?" asked Sandy, half his face still covered with shaving soap.

"Let's hope not. We'll just have to keep our eyes open," I said, before bursting into laughter at the sight of these would be heroes.

Fortunately, the elephant never bothered us again, although it still made the occasional destructive foray into the villagers' fields.

The village of Teknaf was half a mile away from the reservoir over steep, hilly terrain. Hoping to placate us so we would not cause problems for their village, the people of Teknaf sent a number of young teenage girls to the bungalow. Accompanying them was an English-speaking villager.

"The village elders send these girls to work for you. Keep house, cook, clean, and satisfy your needs," he informed me.

I also wanted no trouble, especially from involvement with females. I still remembered touring the service hospitals and seeing the terrible effects of syphilis on the infected soldiers there. These young, pregnant girls had already been raped and used by the Japanese troops who had occupied Teknaf prior to the British offensive in the Arakan. I was determined they would not be used by the British.

I shook my head.

1945

"We thank you for thinking of our comfort and welfare, but we don't need any girls round here. Please send some boys to work for us instead. We're British soldiers. We won't harm your people."

Next day, a group of boys arrived. When I saw them I thought my heart would break. Sandy, Mac and Jock gathered round, staring in disbelief and horror at the sight of these youngsters, all of them missing a right hand. My eyes moist, a lump the size of a golf ball in my throat, I gently took hold of one boy's stump. My voice was a choked whisper as I struggled to control my emotions.

"What happened?" I asked the English-speaking villager.

"Japanese soldiers cut off right hands of all males over thirteen so we cannot take up arms against their army."

Clearing my throat, I announced, "We have work for all these young men. I'm sure they'll be a big help to us."

I ruffled one boy's hair, smiling encouragement before turning away. I sniffed hard, shook my head in disbelief and sorrow. I would never get used to the barbarity of Japanese soldiers. My mind flashed back to the gruesome discovery of the butchered nurses in Dibrugarh. Then, I had felt an intense, slow burning anger. Now, I could barely contain my dismay and despair at man's inhumanity to man.

The boys brightened our lives. They smiled impishly. They teased mischievously. They worked willingly. Their spirits remained high despite their disabilities and hardships. In quiet moments, they told us how the Japanese had behaved toward their village and about how happy they were to have the British back again.

Posted to Teknaf, we were mainly left to fend for ourselves and organize our own routine. Captain Perry paid us a visit every eight to ten days. He travelled by sampan down the coast of Bengal to bring our pay, supplies and mail. He arrived in the morning and left late in the afternoon after feasting on a lobster lunch and checking that everything was going well. Apart from his visits, we were on our own with no contact with the outside world. When the villagers realized we meant them no harm, they talked with us and welcomed us into the village store. Pleasant though this was, the villagers' friendliness did not alleviate the feelings of loneliness and isolation we experienced by being sequestered at Teknaf. There was no wireless and no entertainment in the area apart from playing cards and talking together.

I frequently passed the time fishing for lobster from the wooden jetty. The village shop sold the fishing hooks I needed and for bait, I used small fish called mud flappers. At first, I wasn't successful in landing my catch. When I brought the lobsters to the water's surface, they would let go of the mud flappers and sink back into the water. So I devised a technique involving two hooks. The second hook, placed in the mud flapper's tail, snagged the lobster's mouth making it impossible for the lobster to escape. I'd always been a popular man because of my knack for providing extra supplies to the army camps and hospital in Assam. Now my continuing popularity was assured. The lobsters made a welcome change to the usual bully beef stew and rice, or scrawny chickens bought in the village. I became so adept at catching these crustaceans, I kept the village well-supplied too.

Late one afternoon, a motor launch inched cautiously along the channel. We were sitting on the wooden jetty, legs dangling over the edge, shirts off, talking, laughing and enjoying the sun's warmth on our skin, while I fished for our supper. Sandy caught sight of the approaching boat. Tapping me on the shoulder, he nodded in its direction.

"Hey up, we've got company."

We fell silent. Tossing partly smoked cigarettes into the water, we grabbed our rifles and rose to our feet, on guard and ready for action. The men aboard the boat stood alert by the launch's gun. The bright, glaring sunlight, reflecting off the water, made it difficult to see clearly. We were unable to determine if the launch was an enemy craft. Like us, the men in the launch were watchful, on the alert for any movement, which would indicate they were in peril—and still the launch drew closer.

When it came within hailing distance, I raised my rifle and shouted, "Halt! Who goes there? Friend or foe?"

1945

There were hearty sighs of relief when a voice came back through the loudhailer, "We're British. We've come for water."

The Royal Navy launch moored alongside the jetty. "We've been searching for you in order to take on water. Good job you didn't shoot. We'd have blasted you with gunfire first and asked questions later," one of the sailors told us.

The arrival of eight new faces brought good news as well as welcome company. Germany had surrendered May 8th. The war in Europe was over, and we took Rangoon on May 3rd.

"That's ruddy marvellous!" I gasped.

"This calls for a celebration," said Jock. "How do you like your lobster?"

"We'll have a beano while we're at it. We've plenty to drink and a good selection to choose from," offered the Lieutenant.

Celebrate we did. Full glasses clinked together; bottles quickly emptied. It was a pleasant change from our quiet existence of the past few weeks. Full of lobster and booze, we swapped stories, told jokes and exercised our vocal chords with a good singsong well into the early hours. Having over indulged on the sailors' liquor, we found bunks to fall into for the night. It would have been too much to expect four drunken men to climb the hill to the bungalow.

Next morning, when I began to stir, I thought I was still drunk. I felt sore and uncomfortable. My body was twisted; my chin was forced down onto my chest; my neck had a crick in it. I lay still for a few minutes, trying to understand why I was scrunched up along the inside wall of the cabin instead of lying comfortably in the bunk. Hung over, my mind dull and head aching, I couldn't figure out at first what was happening. Then rousing myself, I called to the others. "Wake up! Wake up, you lot! Something's wrong!"

I crawled through the launch to the deck where I realized what had happened. During the night, when the tide went out, the water level had fallen ten feet. The launch was tilted on its side, hanging from the mooring ropes above the water's surface.

"Come on, we've got to right this launch."

Blurry-eyed, with heads aching, tongues parched, and mouths tasting foul, we managed to pull ourselves together enough to climb up onto the jetty. The lieutenant assessed the situation.

"We should be able to lower the launch all right if we use ratchets. We've got some on board. Let's give it a try. No time to wait for the tide to turn."

We fitted the ratchets, and after releasing the mooring ropes, we carefully lowered the seventy-foot launch into the water without causing any damage. Problem solved, we broke into relieved laughter.

"I could think of a better way to start the day when I'm hung over," I said.

Cox's Bazar

The end of May brought another move for 25th Stores and Port Section R.E., this time to Cox's Bazar, a town on the Bay of Bengal. The seedy port with its mouldy buildings was surrounded by rice fields, flooded from the monsoon rains. We travelled in trucks. Despite melting in the heat, I looked about with interest, watching women beating clothes clean in the river, while children swam and splashed in the waters. A man stood in a flooded field in thigh deep water, placidly washing his cow.

I was soon employed loading coal, equipment, and supplies onto barges, which an Indian coxswain and I ferried to large ships anchored offshore. When the barges pulled alongside, derricks on the ships hoisted the cargoes from the barges into the holds.

One day, the barge was being loaded with bulldozers. As the crane lowered the third bulldozer onto the barge, I was dismayed to see it placed on the forward deck.

"I don't like the look of that. It looks too far forward to me," I remarked to the coxswain. "What do you think?"

"It is not good, sahib. It will make the barge bow heavy, and we could sink."

1945

I sought out the officer in charge of loading.

"Excuse me, sir, my barge has been overloaded with bulldozers, and the one at the bow is making the barge bow heavy. If we hit heavy seas, we'll sink."

The frazzled officer, busy checking his clipboard and papers had no time to listen to my problems. He was under intense pressure to load and ship the equipment to the forward lines as fast as he could.

"Just get on with it, Corporal. Those bulldozers have to be loaded on the ship. They're needed in Rangoon. Don't worry, the stevedores know what they're doing, and if you do get into difficulties, we've lookouts ashore on high pilings, keeping watch with binoculars. They'll alert a speedboat, and you'll be picked up in no time at all."

Well-trained British soldier that I was, I did as I was told, but I was not a happy man. The possibility of ending up in the waters of the Bay of Bengal was a frightening prospect. I'd seen numerous sharks while ferrying supplies to the ships and had no wish to be in close contact with the razor-toothed fish.

Returning to the barge, I told the coxswain to set sail.

"Corporal Sahib, this is not good."

"I know. I know. I don't like it any more than you do, but we've been ordered to take these bulldozers to the ship, so we'd better get on with it."

The barge pulled away from the quayside. We were in the wheelhouse, the coxswain at the wheel. As we sailed away from land, the barge moved into heavy swells. It struggled to plough its course to the ship up and down one deep wave after another. At the crest of the largest wave yet, the barge paused, teetering on the brink of a deep, deep trough. Then it slipped down. Instantly, the coxswain and I realized that this time the barge would not come out of it. Our eyes met, my consternation mirrored in the coxswain's face.

"It's not going to make it! Jump for it!" I yelled.

As bow and bulldozer disappeared from view under a large wave, we leapt from the barge, me to starboard, coxswain to port. We kicked and fought our way to the surface, coughing and gulping greedily for air, while, in ghostly silence, the barge continued its headlong plunge to the sea floor with its valuable cargo.

At the mercy of towering seas and voracious sharks, we anxiously cast about us. We treaded water and struggled to keep our heads above the surface, expecting at any minute to see menacing grey dorsal fins slicing through the aquamarine waves towards us.

"There are sharks in these waters, sahib," the Indian cried, his voice high-pitched from fear.

"I know," I said, eyes darting here and there, searching for dangerous dark shadows in the water. "Where the hell are those speedboats?"

"Did the look-outs see what happened, sahib?"

"I hope so!"

It was a tense thirty minutes before the roar of an outboard motor announced the arrival of a speedboat. We waved and shouted, "Here! Here we are!" The boat turned in our direction. Dazzling smiles of relief greeted the crew. We were hauled aboard by a cheerful corporal.

"Here we are, me hearties. We got you before the sharks did, lads. Aren't you the lucky ones?"

◆ ◆ ◆

On July 6th, the unit moved to Cox's Bazar airfield to assist in maintenance and salvage. Three days later, we were chattering and playing cards in the barracks when a new period for overseas tour of duty was announced on the radio. The period of service in the East was reduced to three years and four months, and the men affected were to be sent home as soon as possible without waiting for their replacements. A sudden silence descended on the room as the meaning of this announcement hit home, and we each became engrossed in calculating the length of our tour of duty.

Calculations over, I said, "Hey, how about that, Mac! We can go home next month."

"Too true!"

It turned out that all the men in the section were due for repatriation on August 14th. The atmosphere was relaxed with

1945

much laughter and smiling and joking about the long sea journey home. Then, as night was falling, we heard an aircraft's engine sputtering and coughing as the plane tried to land.

"That plane's in trouble," I said, jumping up and running out of the barracks just in time to see a Sea Otter falling from the sky and disappearing from view to the north east of the camp.

We raced towards the downed plane, which had made a forced landing in a stream. Mac and I waded into the water and tugged the airplane's doors open. The three dazed occupants were bruised and bloody from a few cuts to their faces, but otherwise unharmed.

"Sorry to drop in on you like this, chaps," said the pilot, managing an apologetic smile.

I pulled the pilot from the plane.

"Think nothing of it, sir," I said, with a grin.

"How's the old kite?" asked the airman, gingerly feeling the bump on his forehead.

"A bit dented and battered, same as you, sir. Let's get you to the Medical Orderly."

We helped the airmen to the first aid station. While their minor wounds were treated and nerves soothed by hot tea and sandwiches, overnight accommodations were found for the three aviators.

Next morning, we set about salvaging the Sea Otter. Using a small bulldozer, we towed the aircraft to flat ground near the jetty, while the pilot hovered anxiously.

"Take care with the old girl. Watch it! Careful!"

As we laid a Summerfield track road, I reassured the pilot. "Don't worry. We'll be as gentle as if she were a baby."

The plane was winched and towed to the airstrip for repairs. Four days later, it was as good as new. The airmen took off. They circled the airfield, tilting the wings in thanks to us below, standing on the tarmac, waving farewell.

A week later, on my eighth wedding anniversary, we received good news. The first two release groups received their stand by orders. Soon it would be my turn; then I'd be on my

A CORPORAL'S WAR

way home. By July 24th, the unit had finished its work at Cox's Bazar and was ready to move. Next posting was to Dohazari airfield for more salvage and maintenance work.

◆ ◆ ◆

At daybreak on August 6th, an American B29 bomber, the *Enola Gay*, carried a deadly new weapon to the Japanese city of Hiroshima. The instant the bomb reached its target altitude, 80,000 men, women and children died in the eclipsing, blinding flash of nuclear efficiency. Three days later, a second atomic bomb was dropped on Nagasaki with equally devastating effect. August 14th, the Japanese government accepted unconditional surrender.

◆ ◆ ◆

To the four of us left in 25th Stores and Port section R.E., the news of the Japanese surrender came as a shock, even though rumours had been flying for days that the Japanese were going to surrender.

"That's it then," said Mac. "We'll definitely be going home now."

"I can't believe it," I said, sitting on the edge of my bed. "I never thought the Japs would give up."

"I'll be glad to be out of it," said another man. 'I'm sick of India and sick of Burma. I just want to get back to England and see my mam and dad. It's been too long already."

Mac and I exchanged glances.

"It'll be nice to get back, won't it?" I said quietly, my thoughts on my wife and daughter.

"I'm just glad to be getting out of it, Gus. I've had enough."

It was a sentiment shared by all.

October 15th, those of us awaiting repatriation were sent to Calcutta. We thought we would be flying back to England, and then we were told we would be sailing from Bombay.

I boarded the train with mixed feelings. I was happy and eager to be returning home to my family. It had been a long time since I'd seen them; a reunion was long overdue. But now that I was leaving India, I felt a great sadness. I loved this country and the wonderful experiences it had given me. Even the graffiti scrawled on walls exhorting the British to "Quit India", and students waving green and gold banners of the National Congress Party and shouting "Freedom forever", did not diminish my affection. It was obvious there were going to be massive changes in India. I hoped freedom would be accomplished without too much bloodshed.

The Homecoming

Bombay was bustling. Every other day, ships were leaving the port, which was filled with thousands of servicemen eager to return home.

Mac and I marched along with soldiers from the train, heading for the *Duchess of Bedford* berthed at Victoria Docks. We filed up the gangway and went to find our berths on 'D' deck. Entering the room, we burst out laughing.

"This is a nice change," I said, "wall-to-wall hammocks."

"It's no better than when we left England," Mac grumbled.

"Guess our homeward journey isn't going to be any more comfortable than our outward one," I said with a laugh. Taking my treasured parcel from my kit bag, I told Mac, "I'm going to the purser's office. I want to hand my *kukris* in for safe keeping."

"I'll come with you. Then we can go on deck."

We joined servicemen gathered at the ship's rail, animated men, men excited to be going home. Tonight was to be our last night in India. No one was sorry that tomorrow we would be leaving for England, unlikely ever to return.

I watched the activity on the quays. It was frantic as if someone had stirred up an anthill. Docked behind us, I could see the *Arundel Castle*, a continuous stream of men filing up the gangway. Looking round the port, I saw nothing to indicate that only eighteen months before, this had been the site of a devastating explosion. Shivers ran along my spine as I remembered my own disturbed feelings when I'd driven among the ravaged remains of the docks. Now the docks were back to normal and running smoothly. I felt a proud satisfaction. We'd done a good job.

The ship set sail. It was November 5th, Guy Fawkes Day, but there were no celebratory firework displays as tugs towed the *Duchess* out of the harbour, closely followed by the *Arundel Castle*. The ships headed for the Suez Canal. This time there would be no long voyage round the Cape of Good Hope.

"It's great to be able to sail with the lights on and not be in blackout conditions," I said to Mac and our new shipboard friends. We were sitting round the card table with Bill McMahon, who was also on board.

"I haven't seen such happy smiling faces for a long time," said Bill.

"Well, the war's over. We came through it, and we've got the rest of our lives to look forward to," said Sandy, one of the other men in the game.

"Roll on Newcastle. It'll be a treat to get some decent northern ale down my throat," said Mac.

The men around us were laughing and joking, full of light-hearted bantering. The atmosphere on board was cheerful and relaxed. The frequent sing alongs were no longer arranged as a means to lift morale, but instead were a concerted expression of happiness.

In no time at all, the ship was sailing into the Gulf of Suez. I stood by the rail with my friends, scanning the banks of the canal for interesting sights to tell Ivy about, but apart from a few ports, all I saw were golden sands and other merchant shipping. When the ship stopped at Port Said to take on supplies, we wanted to go exploring, but were forbidden to leave the ship. Our small group stared longingly at the town instead.

"Well, I think they're a lot of rotten spoilsports not to let us out on the town," said a soldier called Tommo.

"It sure would be nice to find a bar or two," Mac drooled.

"A bar, yes, but he wants to go looking for a harem, don't you, Tommo?"

1945

"You want to go looking for a harem? Who do you think you are? The Sheik of Araby?" I said.

"There'll be plenty of girls waiting for you back in Blighty," said Bill.

"Yes, but remember, they've all been in love with the Yanks. He doesn't stand a chance, does he?" said Mac.

"Guess not. Better jump ship and go looking for that harem," I joked.

The *Duchess* sailed into the Mediterranean Sea. I loved to spend the evenings watching other ships passing in the dark. With no blackout required, their lights glowed as bright as candles on a birthday cake. It was a heartwarming sight. Whenever another ship was sighted, foghorns sounded greetings to celebrate safe travel now that the war was over.

On the evening the ship squeezed through the Straits of Gibraltar, Mac and I contentedly watched the pale full moon, floating above the hills of Tangier.

"We'll be home soon, Gus."

"Yes. It's a grand feeling, isn't it? Like Christmas Day when you've opened all the presents and eaten your fill of goose and plum pudding. Life doesn't get any better than times like this."

"Won't be long before we'll be feeling the cold again, once we pass the Bay of Biscay."

Mac was right. As we travelled into the Atlantic, the grey seas were heavy with white-crested waves. There was much moaning and groaning as seasickness felled the men. Looking at my comrades, I was thankful I wasn't afflicted. I spent many hours on deck in my great coat, collar turned up against the squalls. The air was fresh and bracing after the fetid humidity of Assam and Bombay. I felt alive, excited and eager to be home.

Ploughing through the whitecaps, the *Duchess of Bedford* headed north towards St. George's Channel and the Irish Sea. We'd been at sea for almost three weeks when word spread that the British coast would soon be sighted. We crowded the decks, straining to catch our first glimpse of Blighty for several years. A sailor shoved his way among us and searched the horizon. He pointed to a dark blue line where sky and sea met.

"There you are, lads. Watch that area. That's the Isles of Scilly. As we get closer, you'll see Bishop Rock lighthouse. You're home, lads. You're home. In a couple of days you'll be on dry land."

I pulled Mac forward. "You're taller than me. Can you see anything?"

"I think so. I'm not sure."

We clung to the rail for two more hours watching and waiting, searching for proof that we really were back in British waters. With the lighthouse clearly sighted, we went inside to warm up, playfully punching and shoving one another as we joked about which one of us would be off the ship the fastest.

It was a crisp November day when the ship arrived in Mersey Bay. While we waited for a berth to be allocated and for the tide to turn, the *Arundel Castle* arrived and anchored nearby. Tugboats approached to guide the ships into port. I joined the cheering soldiers on deck to celebrate our arrival.

"I've got to send Ivy a telegram to tell her I'm back on English soil, and I've got to go to the purser's office to get my *kukris*," I told Mac.

Soldiers jostled and struggled in the scramble to get off the ship. I queued up at the purser's office. Men impatiently demanded the items they had left for safekeeping. When I reached the front of the line, I handed in my ticket.

"We can't find it," the purser told me on returning to the counter.

"What do you mean you can't find it? I put my parcel in here for safe-keeping, and now you say you lost it?" I was boiling.

"I've searched high and low, but if you want to wait, we'll make some enquiries."

"Wait? Wait? You must be mad! I've been away almost four years, and some bugger on this ship's robbed me, and you want me to wait? Bugger off! I'm not waiting. I'm going home to see my wife and child." I turned angrily away.

"What's up, Gus?" Mac asked.

1945

"What's up? Someone's stolen my *kukris*, and they're trying to say they've misplaced them. Said I could wait till nearly everyone's gone, and then they'll see what they can do. They must be mad. To hell with them!"

"What a dirty trick! Fancy taking something from a soldier who's been away fighting all these years."

"Come on. Let's get out of here, before I do something I'll regret."

On the quayside, a continuous stream of army trucks was pulling in, filling up, and driving off, ferrying men to Lime Street station a short distance away. Troops packed the trains to be whisked off to various army camps. For me, Bill and Mac, the destination was Halifax. The train puffed eastwards across the moors and Pennines, at this time of year lightly dusted with snow. The winter sunlight was harsh and bright to my eyes.

"Wonder how long it'll take the army to finish all their bull so we can get on home?"

"I can't wait to see my mam's face. Won't she be surprised," said one soldier.

"Didn't you send her a telegram?"

"No, thought I'd surprise her."

"Hey, maybe she'll surprise you. Maybe she's moved," some smart Aleck joked.

Everyone laughed.

"Oh, don't be daft," said the young man, uncertainty in his voice.

More laughter rippled through the group.

"Don't take any notice," I said. "We're in for a great time. We're going to see more celebrating and family get-togethers in the next week than we've ever seen in our lives."

"Yes, and with decent beer for a change," said Mac.

British Army efficiency was at its best at Halifax camp. Men lined up everywhere to be inventoried, accommodated, travel-warranted, and fed. It was late afternoon the following day before we received our travel warrants. We went to the mess hall to grab a meal before catching the train. Meal finished, I sat enjoying a mug of tea and scanned the crowded room. Men were still coming in to be fed.

"I wonder when we'll meet up with the rest of the lads," I said.

"Talk of the devil," said Mac, nodding towards the door.

I stood up.

"I'll go to hell! Darky! Blondie! Tommy! Here!" I yelled loudly.

Mac winced and covered his ringing ears.

The three men's eyes searched the room. Smiles lit their faces as they caught sight of us waving in the corner.

"Fancy seeing you here," said Darky, grinning delightedly. He put his mess tin down. We playfully poked each other's ribs and punched each other's shoulders.

"Long time no see," I said, "almost a year."

"Aye, and now we're all back together again," said Blondie, looking satisfied. "Cliff's around here somewhere."

"We came in on the *Arundel Castle*. Where were you?" asked Darky.

"We were on the *Duchess of Bedford*."

"Come on, eat up. Let's catch our trains. We've a month's leave waiting for us. Let's get on with it," said Mac.

In the crisp, evening air, we waited only ten minutes on the platform before the train arrived. We were relieved to find it was warm on board.

"So, what did you get up to this year?" Darky asked.

"Oh, we were lucky, weren't we, Mac? We didn't get involved in any action. It was a cushy number really."

"Neither did we," said Darky. "After going into 58 Company, we were busy on Ramree Island. In the first couple of months we were there, we moved over 100,000 tons of earth at the site of the old runway."

"I couldn't believe it when the Japs surrendered. I never thought they'd do that," I said.

"It was those atomic bombs the Yanks dropped. That's what did it," said Tommy.

"I'm sure it was. God bless the Americans. They probably saved our bacon. I thought we'd have to chase the Japs all the

1945

way to Singapore. I was beginning to think we'd never get back to England alive."

"Well, we did, and here we are," said Darky.

"Yes, Christmas at home. It's wonderful. First one in four years," said Blondie.

We changed trains at York.

"Hey, Gus, look at that," said Darky, pointing to an advertisement at the station showing three energetic girls playing hockey. Below them were the words 'Ovaltine Fitness wins'. "That's why we didn't win the hockey match against those Indian Army nurses. We didn't drink our Ovaltine."

I laughed.

"Now come on, Darky. Admit it. They were better and tougher than we were."

"Never," said Darky, indignantly. "They were just having a good day."

I laughed even harder.

"They sure were. Almost made mincemeat out of us."

The Newcastle train arrived. Although it was getting late, and it had been a long day, the excitement of coming home kept weariness at bay. Joking and laughing, we arrived at Darlington where I, Tommy, Cliff and other soldiers from Middlesbrough, changed trains.

"See you all back at Halifax on New Year's Day."

"What train will you be catching?'

"The 1800 from Newcastle."

"We'll see you on it."

"'Night, lads. Have a great Christmas."

"Hey, Gus," Mac shouted. He was leaning out the window. "I hope Ivy's bought a soft rug."

"A soft rug?" I repeated, puzzled.

"Yes, a soft rug, 'cos you'll never make it to the bedroom, or even the stairs after all these years away."

Everyone laughed.

"Get away with you. Goodnight, lads," I called, still laughing.

The Middlesbrough train was waiting at the platform. We settled into one of the compartments.

283

"We'll be in Middlesbrough in half-an-hour, Gus," said Tommy.

"Yes. Can't wait."

"Do you think you've changed?" Cliff asked.

"Well, I'm four years older than when we left England and six-and-a-half years older than when I enlisted, so I'm more mature, I hope. And I've fulfilled a lifetime's ambition to travel. The sad thing is . . . I learned to hate like I've never hated before in my whole life. I guess the good news is that I've developed a philosophy on life that's going to guide me through the rest of it."

"Like what, Gus?"

"Oh, it's similar to something I read in the Bible years ago. I've learned there's a time to laugh and a time to cry; a time to live and a time to die; a time to love and a time to hate. Time heals everything. I was devastated when Hinny was lost, but I'm over that now, although I still miss him. He was a good man. Right now, I still hate the Japs for what they've done. I hope I can learn to let it go in the years ahead. So, what else? There's a time to keep and a time to let things go; a time for war, and now it's time for peace. I've learned the most important thing in my life is to be home with Ivy and Joan. That's how I want to spend the rest of my life. How about you?"

Cliff took a deep breath.

"By gum, Gus, that was deep. My thoughts are more basic than that."

"Like what?"

"I never want to eat bully beef or a grain of rice again as long as I live," said Cliff.

"I'll go along with that," Tommy chimed in, as we all nodded our heads in agreement.

"I wonder if I've changed too much. Will Ivy still know me? Will Joan remember me?"

"Don't worry, Gus. You'll pick up the pieces as if you've only been away a couple of weeks," said Tommy.

A few minutes before midnight, the train pulled into Middlesbrough station.

1945

"Goodnight, lads, see you New Year's Day, 1830 train," I said, as we stepped onto the street.

"Goodnight, Gus. Enjoy yourself."

I set off walking east on Marton Road, while the others headed south along Albert Road. The town was quiet. Most people were in bed at this late hour. The gas lamps threw out splashes of light, casting shadows in the darkness. My footsteps echoed in the empty streets. At first, I took my time, savouring the familiar sights and the smell of smoke floating down from the chimneys. I felt an intense gratitude to be returning home safely, all in one piece.

As I passed North Ormesby railway crossing, my footsteps quickened. Soon I was running. I turned the corner into Thorrold Terrace and hurried to number nineteen. I'd barely finished knocking before the door flew open.

"Norman," gasped Ivy. Then she was in my arms. My kit bag fell to the floor as we hugged each other tight, kissed passionately, felt faces, hair, and rocked from side to side, eyes squeezed shut.

We moved into the house and closed the door against the chilly night air. Arms wrapped round each other, we moved into the kitchen, pausing in the doorway for a lingering, tender kiss. Ivy snuggled her head into my chest. Stroking my chin against her soft, lavender scented hair, I became misty-eyed with overwhelming joy and tenderness.

Pulling slowly away from my arms, Ivy moved to the sink and filled the kettle with water. She chatted nervously.

"We were staying at my mother's when the telegram arrived. Mrs. Morley took it and came running round with it. Joan and I hurried back here. We've been waiting for you for hours."

She put the kettle on the gas stove and reached for the box of matches. I took hold of her hand and gave a gentle squeeze.

"Here, I'll do this," I said, taking the matches.

We were grinning at each other like Cheshire cats and couldn't stop. It was a long business taking the cups and saucers from the cupboard. Every move was followed by a kiss, a hug, a touch, a caress.

With the tea made, we sat at the kitchen table, holding hands, drinking tea, and talking.

"Is Joan asleep?"

"Yes. She fell asleep about ten."

"How's Mam and Pop? What's Eric doing? How are your sisters?"

We were laughing and giggling like lovesick teenagers when we heard a stair creak. Looking towards the stairs, we saw a dark head of tousled hair, half a face and one eye peeping at us from behind the wall.

"Hello, sweetheart. Come and see your dad," I called to Joan, holding out my arms.

The head pulled back for a minute before peeping out again.

"Come on, Joan. Let's have a cuddle."

Joan ran from the stairs to her mother and shyly buried her head in Ivy's breast. Cautiously, she turned to look at me and quickly turned away again.

I lifted her up and sat her on my knee.

"My goodness, you've grown a lot since I last saw you. Have you forgotten me?" I stroked her hair. She looked down and then sideways at Ivy. "I've got something for you in my kit bag. Have a look inside. See if you can find it."

Sliding off my lap, Joan picked up my bush hat from the table.

"Here. You can put it on," I said and quickly plopped it on her head.

She giggled as the hat fell over her eyes; then she moved to the kit bag and began to feel inside.

"Keep looking. It's in there somewhere."

She pulled out a jar of sweets.

"Ooh, Joan, that's a nice treat, isn't it?" said Ivy.

Joan climbed back onto my lap and gave me the jar to open. With a sweet in her bulging cheek and a contented smile on her face, she leaned back against me.

I looked over her head to Ivy and reached for Ivy's hand and held it, all the while rubbing the back of her hand with my

1945

thumb. My voice caught as I told her, "I've missed you both so much."

The minutes ticked by as we explored each other's faces. Ivy took in my suntanned features. The lines around my eyes and mouth had not been there when she'd last seen me almost four years ago.

"You suit a suntan," she said.

"Yes? But it's only on my face and neck. We're called the 'V' neck brigade," I told her, pulling my shirt open to reveal the lighter skin on my chest beneath the tan line on my neck.

I saw longing and tenderness in Ivy's eyes as she gazed at my smooth, bare chest.

"I think it's time this young lady was in bed, don't you?" said Ivy.

"I'll take her." I said.

With Joan in my arms, I climbed the stairs.

"I haven't done this in a long time," I said, as I pulled Joan's bedcovers up to her chin and kissed her forehead. "It's good to be back. You're going to see a lot more of your dad from now on. Night, night, sweetheart."

Joan kissed me on the cheek and spoke her first words to me since my return.

"Night, night, dad."

I picked up my bush hat. Quick as a flash, Joan's hand latched onto the brim.

"I want to keep it here."

"All right, pet. You can have it."

I turned away from the bed to find Ivy watching from the doorway. Her eyes were moist as she witnessed the scene.

"Time for bed, love," I murmured, bending my head to kiss her.

Ivy took my hand and led me into the bedroom. She turned to face me. I pulled her close. My lips brushed against her hair, her eyes, her lips. I spoke softly, breathlessly.

"Ivy, once I get out of the army, I'll never let anything separate us again—ever. I promise."

I reached out with my foot and pushed the bedroom door. It closed with a gentle click.

EPILOGUE

After demobilization in May 1946, I picked up the pieces of my life with Ivy and Joan. A second daughter Pauline was born in December 1946.

Like many returning soldiers, I experienced difficulty finding employment. I applied for work on Middlesbrough docks, but was told I had to have a union card before I could be hired. It was a "Catch 22" situation because when I went to the union office, I found I could not have a card unless I had a job. I was dejected but determined. I hung around the dock union office waiting for my opportunity. It came when I saw the union officer leave. I nipped into the office and informed the girl I had been sent to pick up my union card as I had a job and could not start without it. She unwittingly provided me with the precious card, and I worked at Middlesbrough docks and then at Teesport as a charge checker for over thirty years.

When I was in the army, I discovered that working conditions and the lifestyle of ordinary working people in the south of England were tons better than those of northern workers. After the war, I became a shop steward representing the dockers (longshoremen) in the Transport and General Workers Union in order to redress these inequities.

The interest I developed in fishing while in Assam became a lifelong passion. I founded Preston Park Angling Club with some friends and worked as club secretary for thirty years, dedicating myself to introducing young people to the sport.

In 2003, Ivy and I moved to Naples Florida to live with our daughter Pauline, the author of this book, and her husband Peter. My daughter Joan lives with her husband near Perth, Western Australia.

Glossary for Poems

Basha	bamboo hut
Bloke	a man, a chap
B.O.R.	British other rank
Burrah Sahib	Sahib a form of address in India to people of rank; Burrah is a play on Boro, the shortened form of Middlesbrough town
C.R.E.	Commander of the Royal Engineers
Dorman's buzzer	Dorman Long steel foundry; a loud buzzer signalled the end of the shift
Duffer	a fogy, useless old fellow
Gharri	a wheeled vehicle for hire
Lapper upper	drinker
M.O.	medical officer
Mossies	mosquitoes
O.C.	Officer commanding
Pukha	thorough, complete
R.S.J.	rolled steel joist
"The Smoke"	slang for London
Tyne	river in NE England
Wallah	Someone concerned with a particular type of work

These poems were written by the men of 62 Company R.E. for their commemorative magazine, except for Acksa Bridge, which was written by Captain Sheldon R.A.M.C. during his "holiday" at Juhu, when he was Medical Officer to the very few sick there. Note that it is written in a Yorkshire dialect where t' means 'the.'

ACKSA BRIDGE

There's a famous seaside place called Juhu
That is noted for t'fresh air and t'breeze.
Where the coconuts grow in the palm-groves
And goings-on at weekends in t'trees.

Now Six Two C.W. Company
Was up at Deolali on t'range,
While t'Colonel was all over India
Like—seeking a bit of a change.

One day he came back to Deolali
And read out a bit from a note:
"We're having a camp down at Juhu
And Six Two has got to build t'road."

The note it was all signed by t'general
So they packed all their trucks right away,
And sent for the M.O. from Poona—
He swore, but he had to obey!

They quite liked it down there at Juhu
As they bathed in the sea every day:
For there's plenty of nuts in the palm trees
And chi-chi girls down in Bombay!

But they didn't think nowt to road making
For when they'd been on it a day
They found that without a steamroller
The coolies did better than they.

So they went down to t'C.R.E.s office
And said—"We're browned-off on t'range
And now we're browned-off down at Juhu.
How about a fresh job for a change?"

The C.R.E. gave his opinion:
"I've got a job here you can do,
It's a bridge I've to build down at Acksa;
But I don't know if that'd suit you?"

"I'm sure we can do it," said t'O.C.,
And all the chaps shouted: "Yes! Yes!"
In spite of the fact that's the one thing
We've never been taught at 'B.S.'"

They managed to get a pile-driver,
And then Captain Cave had his say:
"Now, look here, you men, just get cracking
Working twenty-four hours a day!"

The office staff stayed back at Juhu
Busy bathing and fishing and all,
But the chaps out at Acksa thought nothing
Of working at night-time at all.

So every day about tea time
A note would come back to Juhu:
"Dear Frank, we have broken t'pile-driver,
Come and mend it, Love (signed) Martin Glew."

The O.C. ran round in a flat spin
And came out to t'site every day,
But things seemed to be going so slowly
They'd never get finished that way.

One day Mr. Glew came to t'office
And waving a note, he says—"Bill!
T'O.C.'s gone and gotten malaria,
We can finish the bridge while he's ill!"

And so they all worked to a schedule
For finishing t'job in ten days,
And t'chaps said: "We think we can do it
Provided we get t'R.S.J.'s."

So Captain Cave said to his Driver:
"Get haversack rations for t'week
We'll never come back till we get them,
It's these B.R.S.J.'s we've to seek."

It worked out all right in the long run,
T'job were done, and they left without sighs
"We don't mind leaving Acksa and Juhu,
If we see no more eggs, fish and flies!"

"Doc Sheldon."

A Guide to Three

There's a bamboo-covered basha to the west of "Swingers Inn"
There's a bloke there, and we call him "Peachy" Fields.
He's the biggest "lapper upper"
From Wake Island to Calcutta,
And his voice, like Dorman's buzzer, never yields.

There's a little bamboo basha to the rear of "Moaners' Inn"
It's as famous as the "Chequers" for its beer
If a booze you wish to dodge
Keep away from "Grousers' Lodge"
Or you'll rue the day you met the Muskateers.

There's another bamboo basha by the Yankee Doodle's guns,
It's the country home of Wally, Bill and Tom.
They call it "Sleepy Valley"
'Cos they never hear Reveille,
And you couldn't waken Wally with a bomb!

In the midst of all these bashas stands the home of one who's crackers,
It has "Krazy Kottage" painted on the sign.
If you're feeling quite contrary
Spend ten minutes with Alf Airey
And he'll tell you why Newcastle's on the Tyne.

Now the last of all the bashas is the one that I live in,
And its name (unjustly given) celebrated "Swingers' Inn"
Guys are known to call us dappy
'Cos we always look so happy—
Well, we look at life, and meet it with a grin.

BURRAH SAHIB

SUBJECT—Normal

We sat in our canteen tonight, a meeting quite informal,
We sat around and talked and talked—the subject? Well, 'twas normal.

We talked of happy, bygone days, of dames both dark and fair,
We talked still more of dames and dames, and wished we had our share.

Some talked of lovely dames they'd met, of love and all its glories—
I wish I could believe them all, these guys, and all their stories.

These guys have loved and loved and loved, the dames they've met and won
Are far too numerous to count—I can't see how it's done.

Of course, they may have hidden charms, something we cannot see,
But how they picked up all these dames is a mystery to me.

Still, their stories may be true, although they sound abnormal,
We talk again tomorrow night. The subject? Well, It's normal!

ARTUS

THEN

In the jungles of Assam
Where a man must be a man
And a woman's just a memory near forgot,
Where men's hearts are oft embittered
And the jungle paths are littered
With the bodies of good Britishers who've died from Assam Rot.

If you search among the greenness
With a Sherlock Holmes-like keenness,
You will find a little band of Engineers,
They've been gathered from the "Smoke"
From Newcastle and from Stoke
To drop their sweat on Assam for innumerable years.

Through a pukha Delhi bungle
They were landed in this jungle
Split in four, and promptly told to get to work.
Came a mutter from the mob:
"'Tis the first real useful job
Since we bunged projector barrels in the phani at Dunkirk.

Through the trying monsoon weather
"Six-Two" wallahs strained together,
To aerodromes and roadways giving birth.
Though not normally prolific
The results were just terrific
And the Company most surely proved its worth.

NOW

On the road to Mohanbari
Stands a derelict "Six by" gharri,
It has been there since Whist Watson tried to drive.
'Tween Dinjan and Sookerating
Never stirs a living thing
Since the "62" ceased to keep the place alive.

On Chabua's holy ground

Jungle grows in from around
Eating up the bashas—raiding our canteen.
Should you search among the greenness
With penetrating keenness
Would you find a relic there of days once seen?

In the jungles of Assam
Where a man must be a man
And a woman's just a memory near forgot,
There are silent bamboo huts
Where no B.O.R. now struts
And his works, and not his wounds, are left to rot.

                                                                H. S.

That Letter Home

It seems that almost every night
There's a letter I must write,
I sit me down, like one inspired
Meaning to write until I'm tired—
The pen is filled, paper I borrow,
I'll get the darned thing off tomorrow.
"My darling, thought I'd drop a line
To let you know I'm feeling fine,
The weather's damp, my throat is not!
The mossies bother me a lot.
My prickly heat is now much better—
At least it was until this letter.
"What's happened to the local rag—
Gone into the salvage bag?
The way we get our blinking mail
It might be brought here by a snail."
What else is there to write about?
If I say too much, they'll cut it out!
"Please, my dear, when writing me
Don't use such terms as 'son-of-a-B'
For although we know the Yanks are there
And we'd like to swop them jobs—Oh Yeah!
What a shock when home we come
To see our women chewing gum!"
Always when this much is written
And handle of pen is badly bitten
I find I've nothing more to say,
So I think I'll hit the hay,
Murmuring to myself in sorrow—
"I'll finish the dashed thing off tomorrow."
Young and old alike they suffer,
The lover, and the married duffer.
Even those with flowery phrases
Whose flow of love talk folk amazes
Find themselves as badly smitten
When the first few lines are written.
Sergeants, too, famed for invective,
Find it for letters most ineffective.

Officers, also, on lectures verbose,
Lose all incentive reading our daily dose.
All of us wait that day—next year?
When we can only say: "Yes, dear!"

LOFTUS

Matches

The usual way in India to light a cigarette
Is by using Indian matches, 'cos a lighter's hard to get,
For one anna you can buy a box, with "Tea Girl" on the cover,
Though which plantation she is on, I never did discover.
I've searched the country everywhere, to me it simply seems
She is only in an advertising agent's vivid dreams.
You could strike a match; it splutters, and a cloud of smoke appears
You grimly try another, despite the ribald cheers.
Then someone says: "Light two at once," result, a dismal flicker
Which only goes to prove that you can waste the darn things quicker.
So this goes on, and on and on, until the box is bare.
With complexion turning purple, you try hard not to swear.
You control your rising temper with all your strength and might,
A friend comes to the rescue, and offers you a light.
So when you're back in England, boys, and light your "Players, please,"
Remember "happy" Assam days and matches such as these!

ARTUS

In Retrospect

In time to come, this war will be
Recorded in books of history;
With trappings fine on glorious deeds
How Britons rose to Britain's needs.
Students will learn of our darkest hour
How we arose and showed our power
United, defending our homes and kin,
Pledged one and all, never to give in.
They will learn how the Allied might
At last put the enemy to flight—
They will point out and criticise all our mistakes,
Argue on why we should risk such great stakes.
They will declare that Might is Right
When used to prove that Right is Might!
But—will a record there be found
By curious students searching round
Of that lonesome, homesick, aching yearning
That has no place in historic learning?
They will not learn of Private Fear,
Of broken lives and a silent tear
Of those who did not want to die
For Freedom, Peace and Liberty.
But wished to live, and love—and laugh
And not be blown away, like chaff.
They will not know, no book will tell
That the price for victory was sheer Hell
For all who battled and all who fought
That peace was very dearly bought.
They will not know the mental strain
Of torrid heat and tropic rain,
Of dread disease, sweat, grime and dust
Endured—not for glory—but for "must."
Let it be shown at a future date
That the common man, and not the State
Suffers most pain and greatest loss
When nations start proving who is "Boss."
Let victory be shown for what it is worth;
Enabling men to act freely on earth.

Do away with such phrases as "Glory of War"
Lest future students should seek for more;
But rather, let it be understood
That out of this war came—little good.

JOHNNY ROB.

Christmas Day

'Twas Christmas Day in England, the snow lay on the ground,
The Sexton tolled the village bells—'twas such a joyful sound;
There is sound of joy and revelry, of greetings, fun and cheer,
When evening comes around, of course, there's still more fun, and beer!
The girls are always thinking of the lads across the sea
But just the same they're dancing with some guy from Tennessee.

'Tis Christmas Day in Assam, there isn't any snow,
Ye gods!—although it's Christmas Day the lads are feeling low.
There are no pretty girls around, there's no such thing as cheer—
We try to drown our sorrows with some hogwash labelled "Beer."
They say that Christmas is the same no matter where you roam,
Whoever said it must have spent the thunderin' lot at home!

ARTUS

Printed in Great Britain
by Amazon.co.uk, Ltd.,
Marston Gate.